Truths, Half Truths
and Little White Lies

About the Author

Nick Frost shot to fame as the gun-mad character Mike Watt in the award-winning sitcom *Spaced*; since then he has become one of the UK's most beloved actors. Frost has starred in a host of films, from the famed Cornetto Trilogy: *Shaun of the Dead*, *Hot Fuzz* and *The World's End* alongside Simon Pegg, to Hollywood hits *Cuban Fury*, *Paul* and *Snow White and the Huntsman*.

Truths, Half Truths and Little White Lies is Nick's first book.

Truths, Half Truths and Little White Lies

NICK FROST

HODDER

First published in Great Britain in 2015 by Hodder & Stoughton
An Hachette UK company

First published in paperback in 2016

1

A CIP catalogue record for this title is available from the British Library

Paperback ISBN 978 1 473 62088 9

Typeset in Sabon MT by Hewer Text UK Ltd, Edinburgh
Printed and bound by CPI Group (UK) Ltd, Croydon CR0 4YY

Hodder & Stoughton policy is to use papers that are natural, renewable
and recyclable products and made from wood grown in sustainable
forests. The logging and manufacturing processes are expected to
conform to the environmental regulations of the country of origin.

Hodder & Stoughton Ltd
Carmelite House
50 Victoria Embankment
London EC4Y 0DZ

www.hodder.co.uk

follow Nick Frost here:
Twitter @nickjfrost
Instagram @friedgold

To the many I lost who broke me.
And the one I found who fixed me.

For Mac . . .

Introduction

How does one capture the nuance of a human life in a book? Is it even possible? (Of course it is, you helmet, have you not read *Long Walk to Freedom*?) Sad as it sounds, I always thought if there was a book about loss and tragedy they'd probably ask me to write the foreword.

It has not been easy being me sometimes, but please don't imagine for a second this'll be all doom and gloom. How could it be? No life can really be all black, right? Even during the darkest, poorest, shitest, hardest times, what got me through that bleakness was laughter and time, lots of time. With enough of both of these things I reckon you could get over just about anything. Just about.

It was a difficult decision to write this though. Am I willing to lay out my total being in all its ugliness for the potential of selling 1,500 hardbacks? Do I just want to produce another 'celeb' autobiography, written by a ghost, telling you about the time I met David Attenborough? (He was lovely.) No, I didn't want to do that. If you're going to tell the story of a life, my life, tell it warts and all. That, to me, is a better reflection of a person. If the tale you tell is too saccharine sweet what can the reader take away from it? What do they learn about you? About a life? Fuck all. Write everything down. The shit, the death, fun, naughtiness, addiction, laughter, laughter, laughter, tears and lots of love and happiness. Surely this is a better reflection of what a person is and if someone can read the book and take something away from it then all the better.

These are themes that anyone can relate to. (Apart from all the foie gras, private jets and money fights obviously.) Who really cares about a story where a well-paid actor's feet hurt after forgetting to properly break in their new handmade shoes at a massive film premiere. It's bullshit.

Despite the job I currently do I would hope I'm just like everyone else reading this. Just like everyone else who will never read this.

So why now? I'm only forty-three, it's no age at all. I had lunch with two old people yesterday, friends of my eighty-year-old ex-father-in-law (gorgeous, gentle gentleman) and they laughed when I told them I was writing a memoir. I felt slightly embarrassed.

I think I'm writing this for my son. My boy. The best thing I ever did and the most important thing to ever happen to me. By thirty-nine I was an orphan. It's not that young compared to some but very young compared to many. I have a seventy-two-year-old friend, an actor I've worked with a few times, a good man, a gent. I asked him once what he was up to for the weekend. His reply:

'I'm off to Manchester to see Mum and Dad.'

It floored me and I couldn't help but blurt out, 'You got a fucking mum and dad!!!'

He laughed, fortunately.

That, I think, encapsulates the great randomness of life. You just don't know. Some of you may not even finish this book, you may be so engrossed one day by the narrative that stepping off the bus you . . . BANG!!! You never know.

Having had a relationship with my parents that one might describe as tempestuous and now having no parents at all, I often think of the stories they had that will never be told. The things I'll never know about them, about their time before each other, about their time before me, their courtship, their passions, their love. What did they like? What were they afraid of?

I know lots of things about them of course but there are holes in their story and I think that's why I wanted to write this book. I want my son to be able to read this at some point in the future and know what his dad was all about. The good and bad, because both are valid.

I'd also make a plea to you lot, you glorious 1,500; ask your questions now! Once they're gone, they're gone and those answers you crave can be lost for ever. I've kept a journal or a notebook for most of my life. Usually during the times when I was down, but I found writing a great way to escape and lick my wounds. It also makes remembering things pretty easy – that and music. Music helps. Some things are gone from my memory for ever sadly. I don't remember much about secondary school. There's also a bit of my late twenties missing. But mostly it's all up there, somewhere.

I've written chronologically but there are jumps in time and flights of angular fancy. Some of this is as it comes to me, randomness of thought, brain tics. Those of you who know me well, please forgive me if I've got it wrong or my timing's off. Bear with me, be gentle and please save your questions to the end. Let's do this.

Part One

I was born in a hospital in Hornchurch, near the sleepy village of Romford in Essex. The first house I remember was 111 Lindsey Road, Becontree Heath, Dagenham. There was a flat before this in a place called Harold Hill but I was too young to remember it. My parents, John and Tricia, told a story that when I was two and a half I climbed up on the railings of the balcony of the flat, some thirty feet above the concrete below, and stood there gurgling until my mum found me. She had to lie on the floor and crawl towards me, fearing that if I saw her I'd get excited and fall. I turned round at one point and laughed, she sprang up and grabbed me as I fell backwards. This book would've been a lot simpler to write if I'd have fallen then. Definitely shorter.

No, Dagenham is where my first memories begin to bubble up. There were always lots of people in that little terraced house on Lindsey Road. It was the mid-to-late seventies, which meant floor-to-ceiling brown and orange. I lived just with my mum and dad, with the occasional stay from one of my half-siblings. Dagenham felt like a community to me; we were always in and out of each other's houses. Kids playing outside, wandering off, knock down ginger, even the old bag of burning dogshit trick on one old bastard's doorstep once. Naughty.

When it was hot the whole street would gather outside to play cricket. I got run over once by a man on a bike as I reached to take a beautiful catch on the boundary. When I say boundary I mean the patch of dirt outside 105. It hurt like hell, as he seemed to run right over the middle of my body. That's the kind of place Dagenham was. You'd be playing cricket in the street and a big man on a child's bike could run you over.

Our neighbours on that street were lovely. Auntie Joan was on our left (not a real auntie). She had a very fat chocolate Labrador, and her house – always dark and mega hot – smelt like boiling tripe (it was the East End in the seventies after all). On the other side were Auntie Elsie and Uncle Harry (again, no relation). Elsie was old and looked like the actress Yootha Joyce. Harry was small and meek and always wore a tank top. After we moved away they stayed in our lives a long time. They were good to Mum and Dad.

During a rainstorm in 1974, Mum and Dad were dashing back to our house from Elsie and Harry's when Dad (who was holding me over his shoulder) lost a slipper, slipped, and flew into the sky. He landed on top of me on my face from a height of about five feet. Dad, of course, was distraught. They said my head swelled to the size of a pumpkin. What kind of pumpkin I guess I'll never know – this is why you should ask these questions now.

Dagenham was also the place where I hospitalised my dad for the first time while doing DIY. I was five and Dad had stupidly given me a large claw hammer to drive a nail into a piece of timber. His last words to me were, 'When I nod my head hit it.' He nods his head and I bludgeon him across his pumpkin with the hammer. When Dad regains consciousness he is in an ambulance on his way to King George Hospital. That was the last time we ever did any DIY together. I think this episode severely dented my own DIY career.

Shortly after this a second terrible tragedy strikes my family. While cleaning out his cage my budgie, Bobbi, escapes, flying out of the window and away into the filthy air over Dagenham. Two weeks later while whacking a bush with an unstrung badminton racket I find Bobbie's headless corpse. It is my first brush with death and one I struggle to get over my whole life.

Dagenham was also the place I had my first cigarette. It was Christmas Day, 1980. I was nine. After pestering Mum and Dad for ages, they finally crack. They falsely believe that by giving me a cigarette (a Piccadilly filter) it will turn me off smoking for ever; they were so wrong. I smoke it in silence, they watch me smoke it in silence, and I put it out in a style I'd seen them do, a kind of tamp down, fold-over thing. A beat, a moment, I turn and ask for another. Dubious parenting. If they were alive today my parents would be horrified I'm telling you this.

There's no doubt I'm Tricia Frost's son though, defiant and stubborn as a bloody mule. My mum was so beautiful, even at the end when she was nearly sixty but looked eighty she still had something. She was always well turned out. Lots of gold jewellery and a ton of Elnett hairspray. She used the same hair dye for years and years (Clairol light ash blonde) with perfect white smile (dentures) and perfectly manicured nails. She had a wheezy but infectious laugh and she was small (five foot two) like her sisters. Hobbits all.

As I got older, I started to become more like my dad, more of his traits, thank god. He was gentle. If the Bee Gees were in one telepod, and eighties Noel Edmonds in the other (the Noel Edmonds when he looked nice and not like a wrestling promoter), Dad would pop out of the third telepod. Back then he was a happy man, always quick to laugh or tell some corny

7

joke. Dad was a pun man. He'd do that thing where he'd stop proceedings by saying something like 'Hey, guys . . .' and then drop some awful gag. Groans all round. He'd laugh and his eyes would crease up making him look like one of the Mr Men.

I still have Mum's temper, that fiery red fog that descends; she left me with that and after reading this book you'd be forgiven for thinking she'd also left me her penchant for excess. This, for me, is a work in progress, a chance to not make the same mistakes.

When I was nine or ten I was getting bullied, not at school but on the bus. The journey there was usually cool; coming home was a different matter. Two brothers who lived round the corner, right little meatheads, they were. They'd wait at the bus stop for me, I can see them now, smiling, nudging each other as they see me. They'd kick me in the back of the legs and pull my bag. I hated it and it went on for months. I became a recluse, not wanting to go to school or to walk home.

Mum probed and prodded as to what was wrong but the stupid code of silence kids must live by forbade it. Snitches get stitches. I wish they didn't get stitches. I wish they got Snickers. Snitches get Snickers – there'd be a lot less bullying, more diabetes sure, but a lot less bullying. Looking back now and having a son myself, I'd have to say no matter what the fallout, tell someone! Do not suffer in silence. Tell someone.

The brothers always seemed to be there and because they lived round the corner they usually ended up following me home. One day they grabbed me just as I reached my front gate. Big mistake: Mum was looking out of the window. They aimed a knee for my young balls but instead thudded me in the thighs, then grabbed my jacket, pulled at my ears, laughed at me.

The front door opens and my small yet fearsome, big-armed mother comes thundering out. Before the meatbags know what's happening they're grabbed by her merciless hands and slapped dizzy. They squeal and beep as she kicks them down the road. What a woman. She grabs me and shoves me towards the house.

Sitting in the front room she looks cross and sad. She cuddles me to make me feel better. Watching those boys get theirs was a wonderful feeling. Mum goes into the kitchen to make tea. Looking through the window I see a big woman careening towards the front door. She knocks on it so hard it rattles in its frame. This will not be good. Mum tells me to get it. I stand and traipse over. I open the door.

'Is your fucking mother in?'

'Hang on. I'll get her.' I close the door gently and walk to the kitchen.

'Mum, it's for you.'

'Who is it?'

'I don't know.'

Mum walks through the sitting room wiping her hands with a tea-towel and opens the front door. She is immediately set upon by the big lumpy woman who is the mother of the two bullies. She punches Mum in the mouth as soon as the door opens.

After you've endured years of physical abuse at the hands of a very big man I suspect the weak right hook from a flabby Dagenham Madre feels little more than being hit in the mouth by an egg-heavy she-moth. (More on Mum's life before she met Dad later.) Mum shakes off the initial shock of the sneak attack and sets about systematically dismantling the woman bit by bit, ruining her hair, then her face, and finally her coat.

It was a hell of a thing to watch. It ended after Mum kicked her opponent deep in the vagina. She lay in a heap on the front lawn, her dinner ladies wobbling. Mum pants, knackered but victorious.

The woman gets up, angry still but not because of the justice my mum meted out to her disappointing bully-kids but because her coat has been ripped to shreds. During the scrap all the buttons have pinged off her coat and the pockets flap low and loose like elephants' ears.

'You ruined my farkin' coat, you cunt!' the lady screams at her.

Mum sets off towards her. Fearing another hefty boot to the baby-machine the lady stumbles backwards.

'Give me the coat! Give me the coat!' Mum gestures to the tattered garment. Big Arms is suspicious at first, Mum pulls at the sleeve, and the woman cautiously lets it slip off. Together they search the front garden and pick up the coat buttons.

'Give me two days and I'll have the coat mended.' Mum's words confused me. What was all that about? Some kind of secret fighting credo between working-class women?

'Fuck me up but don't touch my coat, it's my good one I wear to the towel market on Sunday.' Two days later that coat was good as new.

After Mum shut the front door I got it in the ear. She was cross I hadn't pre-warned her about the impending fury. I understand her anger now. After the fighting chemicals ebb away, Mum's upset. She cries and we have a cuddle, it cheers us both up a bit.

* * *

As well as Dagenham and Essex where lovely Uncle Brian and Auntie Francis live with my cousin Paul, my life extends to the south as far as Kent, home of cousins Caroline and Simon and their folks Uncle John and lovely Auntie Rosemary. My scope also extends west two hundred miles to where my mother was born. To Wales. To Pembrokeshire and the town of Haverfordwest to be more precise. This, even now, I consider my second home.

My gran and grandpa, Eileen and Arthur, live in a solid stone house called Millbrook. It's at the end of a long lane set in a dense forest. As far as idyllic locations for a child to be brought up, this was it. It was perfect. Every Saturday my mum and her sisters, Marion, Sandra, Betty, Melanie and Linda, would congregate at my gran's house. On top of the sisters and my mum's brother Emmy, all my cousins were in attendance too, me, Mathy, Simeon, Ceri, Naomi, Siobhan, Anoushka and Marcello. And then there were the friends, boyfriends and husbands too. The weekends at Gran's were fantastic.

I have the nicest memories of Millbrook. Everything seemed perfect. Apart from the bees. My gran's house had the biggest bees' nest in the roof space. Every summer me and the cousins could probably expect to be stung upwards of thirty times each. The bees would hang around waiting for us in a little bottleneck round the back near the kitchen. Striking our faces and soft necks.

The house in the forest and its small stream running through the garden meant this place was a haven for dens and general pre-teen hijinks. We were master denmakers. We'd leave the house early in the morning, *Star Wars* figures in tow, and spend the whole day out walking through the forests and splashing in the rivers. At some point we colonise a small island we name Rickmelbon and the Nettle Cutters Club is born.

At one point we decide to build a long, high zip line from a tree up on a ridge down into the raspberry patch. It takes us ages securing the rope and pulling it tight. Eventually we're ready to go. We draw straws – no we don't, we bully Simeon into doing it. He's pretty high. Twenty or so feet. He's nervous. We're nervous. The wind drops and he's off. And down. The rope untethers and he drops like a sack of shit into the soft earth below. He survives.

I think being at my gran's house as a young boy surrounded by my extended family, having my foul-tempered grandfather swiping at me with his stick for being half English, was the happiest time for me. I've been happy since then obviously but when I think about that place and the long endless summers it's only ever good. It's innocent, and it's fun, baking gets done, baby chickens hatch, berries are eaten off bushes, fish get caught and dogs get patted. The older I get the more things change, things always change, but back then it was perfect.

By the time my grandad came swinging into my memory he was already pretty old. I always remember he looked how men looked in pictures from the forties. Baggy trousers, white shirt, sleeves rolled up, braces. This was his uniform. His hair was wartime too. Classic short back and sides, maybe even a little Brylcreem. Grampie walked with a cane and would use it to attack us grandchildren at any moment. We'd play a game of roulette where we'd creep towards him as he slept – our aim was to twang his braces. He was never really asleep. As soon as we got within range he'd explode awake and scythe us down with his stick. It was all bluster. Sometimes we'd bundle him en masse and shower his scratchy unshaven chops with kisses.

We'd laugh as he feigned disgust. He smelt like whisky but nice whisky.

My gran was a white-haired joy straight out of central casting. She was compact and sturdy, a no-nonsense lady who loved to laugh. She smelt amazing and I loved running in from the car on those days I got to spend with her and burying myself into her smell. She mostly wore a kind of cleaning dress with deep, apron-like pockets in the front, the pouch always full of treats and tasty tidbits. To finish off her ensemble she wore wellies with the tops turned down. The only exception to this look was when Gran either went into Haverfordwest to shop or when she went up to Tre-wyn to play bingo – then she'd get dolled up. I loved staying at her house with my cousins, being looked after by Uncle Emmy while Gran and Mum and the rest of the sisters went out for the night. He'd tell us ghost stories and frighten the hell out of us. I'd lie in that massive soft, hot bed, in that creaky, windy house, breathing hard until fear eventually led to sleep.

Gran was quick to use her big rough hands to mete out country justice. In a good way of course. Those hands were so strong, she loved laughing and giving you a pinch or a little dig. Mum and Gran's hands looked exactly the same. I loved holding those hardworking, hard-slapping meat gloves.

Mum and the other Hobbit women of Dyfed had a weird connection with the occult, the supernatural if you will. This shit's hard for a kid to be around. One night back in Dagenham my mum is woken by a tremendously bright light; she tries to wake up my dad and failing to do so she sits up in bed only to come face to face with Jesus Christ himself. Not a spirit or a malevolent poltergeist but Jesus. She said he was talking to her but she couldn't hear what he was saying, he was just moving his lips. She turns to try and wake Dad who's lifeless, but when she turns back the baby Jesus is gone.

Looking back now as an atheist it's clearly an alcohol-induced hallucination or an ultra-lucid dream. She wasn't a massive drinker back then, that came later, but as her seven-year-old son and raised a Catholic I had to believe what she said. Why would I disbelieve it? My mum was completely convinced. She fled the house that night and sought sanctuary with our family priest Father Dodd. She stayed there for almost a week, drinking whisky, smoking cigarettes and trying to get to grips with what she had seen.

It changed Mum, she became slightly more devout after this (when it suited her of course). It was weird going into her bedroom while she was away and looking at the chair Jesus had sat on. It was a white high-backed thing with a purple cushion, very uncomfortable, classic Jesus. I stood and looked at that chair, touched it. I remember sniffing the seat cushion a bit, hoping that he'd left the scent of flowers behind. It didn't smell like flowers, it'd been too near Dad's arse and his dirty socks for too long for even Christ's sweet bum scent to permeate. Still, it felt creepy. I'm not sure why it would be creepy. Surely Jesus is anti-creepy?

My Auntie Linda, a small fiery woman with a jet-black bob, tells a story that used to chill me when I was younger. She went to work as a chambermaid in a big hotel in London and stayed with an old friend of hers who had a two-year-old son. Upon arriving she found all the rooms of the house empty, all the furniture from the flat crammed into one room.

The baby had his cot in the empty room next door. The mum, Linda's friend, hardly went into that room after the baby was put down for the night. At one point during their conversation that evening my aunt's friend described to her a thing that had been rampaging in their house at night. As Linda told it to me it always sounded like a classic poltergeist.

Linda told me that just then they heard a noise, a rhythmic thumping. They edged into the baby's room and saw the child standing in the cot watching a rubber ball bounce from wall to ceiling back to wall and so on. Like Steve McQueen with the baseball in *The Great Escape*. When the baby saw them he laughed and the ball stopped. Telekinesis. It went on for a few years. The older the baby got the less it happened.

Then there's Auntie Melanie (Melons). All the cousins are sure she's either (a) a witch, (b) some kind of night dweller, or (c) has a Dorian Gray thing going on, because she's fifty something and is still pretty fit in a kind of Kate Bush way. She always has been, and she doesn't seem to age as she gets older. Maybe it has something to do with never being awake during the hours of daylight.

She lives in a house on an estate on the outskirts of Haverfordwest and she too has always been surrounded by supernatural happenings. When I was seventeen/eighteen I spent a lot of time in that house and it was there where I've been nearest to things unmentionable.

I'd lie on the couch at night trying to sleep, my ears thumping, hair on the back of my neck standing to attention. There were things in that room with me. I'd hear the noise of our empty coffee mugs being gently pulled across the table. Porcelain sliding on glass. Stopping. Then sliding back. I'd bury myself under the blanket, I was so afraid.

What didn't help was that Melons's daughter, my beautiful cousin Siobhan, was a keen sleepwalker. Sometimes if I crept up the stairs to wee between phantasms I'd be met by a small girl with long blonde hair, wearing a Victorian-style nightie pointing at me. Terrifying.

* * *

When I was about ten my half-brother Marc came from Wales to live with us in Dagenham for a while. He was eight years older than me. I loved it having my big brother there. Debbie (my half-sister) would also come and stay for extended periods back then. Never Ian though; Ian was/is my other half-brother who died while I was writing this book. I'm so gutted. It was a phone call I knew would always come but it still punched me in the balls when it finally arrived. He was a man who struggled with grief and anger and alcohol and depression for most of his adult life. Taken away by a booze-related illness, exactly the same as my mum. I miss you, mate. I'm sorry I couldn't make it better.

I think Ian was too cross with Mum, believing, quite wrongly, that she'd abandoned him/them, Marc, Debbie and him. She'd really had no choice if she wanted to live. I wasn't sure at the time what the 'half' bit meant. As far as I was concerned these people came out of my mum. They were my blood.

My dad tried to be a father to my half-siblings. As much as he could anyway. I always felt he was very sensitive to his place in the food chain of their family. He was good like that. I think Marc and Debs quickly warmed to Dad. It took Ian longer to come round; that said, it was never tense or moody. There were never furious rows, just the odd stand-off from time to time.

When Debbie lived with us in Redbridge there definitely was the odd argument. She was moody and Dad wanted to stick up for Mum and let Debs know that she couldn't just do what she liked in his house etc. I guess similar conversations go on with step-kids every day. She was difficult though – boys, drinking, weed, boys, boys with motorbikes, thrush. Teen girl shit.

They loved my dad though. He was kind and funny and fair and adored their mum. What's not to like. When Dad died Ian made the journey from Haverfordwest with my cousins up to east London to attend his funeral and cried like a baby. He loved my old man.

* * *

It was 1980 when we started our fractious relationship with Barking rugby club. I say our, I mean Mum and Dad's. I think it was because of Marc staying with us and wanting to play for a local team while he was living in London that Barking RUFC became a big feature in my life. The coach journeys to away matches, the old clubhouse full of stolen trophies pinned, nailed, screwed on the wall, proud relics of battle.

Playing for Barking Youth was a treat, it was the camaraderie and physical contact young me needed. I don't mind saying I was pretty good. My brother Marc loved it there too, and because he was much older than me he seemed exciting and dangerous. Sometimes the door knocked at three or four o'clock on a Sunday morning and Mum would get her dressing gown on, cursing as she descended the stairs.

Opening the front door she'd be picked up by fifteen drunken rugby boys and bundled inside. It was Marc and his hammered teammates. My mum loved boys and men, she was a real man's woman. She'd never be cross but that wouldn't stop her from at least feigning anger. Slaps were dealt out but the charm and enthusiasm of the drunken lads meant she was easily swayed.

Mum, without fail, would always cook. She was like Martin Scorsese's mother in *Goodfellas* but Welsh. A 4 a.m. feast of sausage, egg and chips or bacon sandwiches was not unusual. She loved the fact that they all called her Mum. I'd stand in the corner and watch these boys. Once we woke up to find a bus stop in our front garden they'd cemented in overnight as a prank. Stuff like this happened all the time. I loved my big brother. He was courageous, generous and honourable.

In the mid eighties there was a new style of crime on the tubes and trains called 'Steaming'. Gangs of youths, ten or so strong, would get on a train at one stop, steam through the carriage taking everything they could, before getting off at the next stop and legging it or getting on another train to do it all over again. Devilishly simple, impossible to predict and difficult to combat.

Marc was sitting on the train eyeing up a woman when a gang of steamers boarded the carriage ransacking the place. When a youth grabbed this chick's bag and headed off, apparently Marc uttered the words 'This one's mine' to the woman and set off after them. He managed to get hold of her bag and began rampaging into the shocked gang like a drunken man-rilla. Sadly he ran out of steam pretty quickly and they fucked him up. Using his skills as a prop forward he lay in a ball clinging onto that bag until the attack was over. Bleeding and bruised, he gave the girl her bag back. I suspect, knowing Marc, he may have even given the lady a wink as well. He got hurt, not too badly, something broken, some stitches, but that was Marc all over. Gosh I miss him.

When Marc left us he spent a few years travelling the world on the lucrative sheep shearing circuit. If I remember rightly the 'circuit' was Australia, New Zealand, the States and somewhere in Scandinavia. Marc told me a story once. In the off-season from shearing, by all accounts a thing he was brilliant at, he took a job working in an abattoir, something he was really cheery about. The picture he paints of the place was horrendous, but he didn't seem to mind. I think the après-murder more than made up for the killings.

Lots of like-minded lunatics holed up at night in some dark, alcohol-fuelled Scandinavian abattoir bar. It sounded like one of the circles of hell, but with music. One day an old bull was brought in to be euthanased. After the grizzly act Marc thought it would be hilarious to de-cock the retired stud. Later that night after work when the lunatics were smashing it up in the bar, Marc waited until a number of people had gone off to the toilet. He hid the bull dick down his trousers and went to the loo. His friends made room as he edged into the trough. I imagine there was some casual chatting before Marc reached into his pants and unravelled a giant twenty-pound beef stick. It crashed into the steel trough splashing piss everywhere. People gasp, momentarily believing this titanic wang might just be his. There is screaming which ebbs into howls of laughter, which become tears. The way he told it, that beef willy was paraded around the place like a returning war hero. They propped it up at the bar and all night bought it drinks. I imagine it sitting there, fat and slumped over slightly, tired and triumphant like Hemingway himself.

At Barking RUFC one of the highlights for me was the food we got in the clubhouse after a game. Pie and mash with beans, or sausages, shepherd's pie, hearty grub suitable for the returning warriors all served through a mysteriously low serving hatch. Sometimes I'd sneak into the kitchen, the sweaty, steamy room on the other side of that low hatch, and watch the big-armed kitchen dollies sling out post-game delights. If I was lucky they'd wrap up a fantastically hot sausage in a napkin and give it to me to eat, and I'd rush outside and eat it under the bridge round the back of the club.

I was too young to fully understand what was happening in that clubhouse but I remember witnessing a fair amount of lunacy. It was always good natured and I enjoyed watching adults get silly. My dad loved it; he never really had many male friends that I can remember so I think he enjoyed the bullshit and camaraderie with the other blokes. I think that was part of my mum's problem: she lost control of him when he hung out there, he became one of the boys. Dad wasn't like that generally – he was a homebody; they enjoyed each other's company. They were together most of the time. But Mum was high maintenance. Dad was Mum's. That sounds mean but this isn't my intention.

On Saturday nights the clubhouse would be rammed and raucous. I don't think it really mattered whether we won or lost. If the first and third teams played at home the second and fourth teams would play away. At some point in the evening the battle coaches would return and the club heaved. Most of the time people would end up naked, steaming, frequently spraying Ralgex or some other heat-based embrocation on each other's balls and anuses. (That was just the women.) I've been fortunate enough to spend some time in the Sergeants Mess in the military hospital at Headley Court, Surrey over the years and it reminded me of the clubhouse at Barking.

Even during the chaos and the mayhem there were still rules and regulations to be adhered to. Failure to do so resulted in more and more drinking. A lot of this revolved around toasting and the wearing of correct clothing at all times, asking to go to the toilet. Not picking up on minuscule signs the others were secretly showing you resulted in drinking and balls being plucked or shaved or sprayed with a napalm-like substance intended to be used only in the event of a human being's spinal muscles going on strike.

Pints of beer would be flung everywhere, on the floor and all over each other. People would then fling themselves down the length of the clubroom, often leaving giant torso- or head-shaped holes in the plasterboard at the other end of the room. As a child this was amazing. I could do literally anything I wanted and a drunk man with no trousers on, balls the colour of a baboon's summer-rectum, would throw a pint on me, ruffle my hair, and tell me I was a good boy. Amazing. Maybe it was here that the seed of my love and terrible fear of mass lunacy was planted.

Round about this time, due to Dad and the office furniture company he worked for doing well, he got a new car. It was a really big deal – we'd never had a new car before. I seem to remember some of our neighbours coming out and cooing while the kids sat in the driver's seat making high-pitched engine noises. It was a brand-new Jaguar XJS V12, metallic mint green with a plush cream leather interior that smelled like wealth. He was a man going places.

He once drove that car on the motorway with me in it at 142 miles per hour. I whooped and egged him on. (I loved and still love the speed and roar of a very fast car, something my son has picked up, enjoying it when I stick my M5 into second gear and rev hard.) Dad had been cut up by an urchin. He looked at me, eyebrows waggling.

'Shall we take him?' I nodded excitedly. There's only one way to deal with an urchin on the burn-up. We hammered past him doing close to one hundred and fifty. I was later to beat his speed record by 13 miles an hour – on a closed circuit I might add! Eat that, dead Dad's speed record!

* * *

After an afternoon, an evening and a night at the rugby club, Mum and Dad had the first massive fight I can remember. It started simmering and boiling in the car and exploded when we got home. I could not escape it, I couldn't go around it and I couldn't go over or under it. I stood there in the corner eating a banana while a foulness in a black cloak, an ebony-wrapped tornado, raged all around me.

At its height, Dad, so frustrated by my mum's drunken belligerence, punched his fist through a door, breaking it badly (both fist and door). This is where I must have picked up *my* annoying and very painful habit of breaking my own hands. I've broken three or four hands stupidly over the years. That sounds weird – I only have two hands but I've broken them both several times. It's a way to unload a terrible need to hurt someone other than yourself while only hurting yourself. The last time I did it – and hopefully the last time I ever do it – was during the shoot for *Paul* in New Mexico.

I once had a big fight with Chris, my baby's momma, soon to be ex-wife, a good loyal woman and the best mother you could ever wish to meet. It erupted from a misunderstanding and a lack of emotional flexibility on both sides. I decided to take my frustration out on the thick, unyielding stone walls of our rented casa. I swing a giant right around, and immediately I connect with the wall I hear the sound of a man striking an oven-ready chicken with a heavy lump hammer, an explosion, the sound of bones snapping inside a fatty shroud of meat.

Pulling the hand away the first thing I note is my little finger's hanging off, hanging free, halfway down my palm like an unused Swingball. I automatically grab it and crunch it back into the position it should be in. It lolls free again preferring its new home midway down my paw. This is really bad. I pull it once more and an ice cold sweat begins to leak into my eyes. I rush slightly. Chris goes to bed. I set the dislocated finger back in position, I can feel the fractures clack together, before finally the snapped pieces marry and the finger stays put. Thank god. I pray that perhaps it's only dislocated. Tomorrow we start shooting. It really couldn't have come at a worse time.

I take a roll of thick gaffer tape and secure the finger with roll upon roll of sticky fabric. Perfect. Perhaps I can attend my 9 a.m. tennis lesson after all. I never make that lesson. I wake up in the spare room at 3 a.m. heaving with pain. My hand is the size and colour of a well-used griddle pan; the tape is buried in the fat, swollen meat of what used to be my hand. What a fucking idiot. If you're ever so angry you want to punch something, punch the air or a man of feathers, don't punch walls. If you watch the film *Paul* carefully you can see the character I play, Clive Gollings, is left-handed.

While Dad struggled to free his arm, Mum saw her chance to finish him off. She picked up a giant crystal ashtray, the type which was de rigueur in the late seventies, square, heartless and angled to fuck, and smashed it over his head. I think he's dead, at least he looks dead. He's actually slumped unconscious, hanging out of the door. At some point an ambulance is called. Not by me. I feel neighbours may have intervened, Elsie and Harry maybe. I sat, wide-eyed with fright, banana in hand, feeling terribly guilty. Why was I guilty?

I remember Dad telling a joke when he got home about the tetanus injection he'd had at the hospital. The nurse says to Dad:

'This shouldn't hurt, it's only a little prick', to which he responds:

'It may only be a little prick to you, love, but it's all I've got'. He booms his lovely, wheezy laugh out, grimacing as he feels a twinge of pain from his fucked-up hand. That was the kind of person my dad was. Even at his lowest ebb he always had a shitty joke or pun to hand. What a trouper.

So Dad loved his puns and his lame wordplay. I was always more into the physical comedy. I'll give you an example from back then. One Christmas when we lived in Redbridge, we were sitting chatting and laughing round the table after one of Mum's big beautiful Christmas dinners (she was a great cook). Mandy, my neighbour, and her family were there and I started flirting outrageously in a boyish kind of way. It peaked when I picked up a jar of pickled beetroot and pretended to drink from it. The jar had no lid. Me, the white tablecloth and our fine mint-green carpet were doused in litres of bright red juice and balls of earth fruit.

* * *

I still love a beer but I can't hide from the fact that alcohol, more specifically alcoholism, seemed to tear at and ravage my family like a coyote with a hen carcass. I see more and more of its casualties the older I get.

As a child, though, I'm completely unaware that this isn't normal. The flip between someone who likes a drink and someone who has a terrible problem is often difficult to pinpoint, even for them. As a young boy I didn't notice it happening. I didn't see it, such was the sophistication of its cloaking device

I had an inkling things weren't perfect. I'd even summon up the courage every now and again to say something to Mum, but I was immediately cut down and told off. It was none of my business, she used to say. But it *was* my business. I understood my place in the family hierarchy pretty early on though, so I'd shut the fuck up.

The way I describe my parents in this book, particularly later on, you'd be forgiven for thinking it was a terribly dysfunctional, co-dependent relationship. Which it was. At least at the end. To get to that point though where Mum looks after Dad after his collapse and Dad looks after Mum for the ten years it took her to finally drink herself to death, that takes groundwork. Years and years of groundwork and the laying of foundations of trust and a shit load of love. Mum and Dad were completely in love for as long as I could remember which made what came later all the harder to stomach. They were so romantic. Dad was a flowers-and-notes kind of guy which was great because Mum was a flowers-and-notes kind of gal.

With them holed up in a pub most of the weekend – something Dad grew to hate but due to his loyalty to Mum would never challenge – it meant I was allowed to rent any VHS film I wanted to watch at home. For a young, gore-hungry boy such as myself this usually meant *The Hills Have Eyes* (the original), *The Shining, I Spit On Your Grave, Poltergeist, The Howling, American Werewolf in London, Alien, The Living Dead at the Manchester Morgue,* etc. I remember me and my big sister Debbie giggling loudly one afternoon watching the credits to Dario Argento's *Suspiria.* We howled when we saw the soundtrack was by a band called Goblin.

I became numb to the images I saw, they were gore-filled and exciting. I liked it. I imagined everyone would feel the same. I showed *The Exorcist* to a mate of mine once, we were both eleven or so; he ran off thirty-five minutes in, muttering something about hearing his mum calling. Poor lad hardly slept a wink for a week. The screaming. We didn't play much together again after that. Shame.

* * *

When I first became aware of my mum she was a bookkeeper of sorts, but I never remember her keeping any books. Before that she worked in an electrical shop called Stanwoods, that's where she met Dad; he was some kind of manager and I guess with smiles and laughter and flirting they fell in love.

Dad had been married before to a lady who I think had suffered a terrible breakdown of some kind. Nowadays, the things that blighted that poor woman would have a name. From what my dad told me it sounded like a form of extreme OCD. Back then, sadly, such a malady was nameless. It was just something that ended a marriage. Dad had two daughters from his first marriage. They're my half-sisters. He bloody loved those girls.

She had a problem with my dad's new relationship with the woman I'd eventually pop out of. I completely get it. When Mum got pregnant it was too much for her to cope with. Shit happened and it got ugly. Soon after this she took her kids – Dad's kids, their kids – and moved to New Zealand. I understand it was what she needed to do. I'm not sure my dad did though, not then anyway. Over the years he suffered from not being with his girls. Having a child now myself I can only imagine what that feels like. I don't hold any kind of grudge against her in any way, shape or form. But it was a sadness he kept to himself. I've met her many times since and she is absolutely lovely, a warm caring mother and grandmother. Being under a terrific amount of pressure and losing love and face and dignity can make people, good people, any people, stumble.

* * *

After keeping books – again, no idea what this means – Mum worked at The Napier, a pub in Ilford. I remember getting a bus to the pub after school and sitting on a crate underneath the bar waiting for her to finish. I'd eat crisps and drink bottles of Coke through a flimsy paper straw which would collapse if over-sucked. I remember watching her flirt with the old regulars; she was the classic brassy barmaid, perfectly adapted to cope with pervy pissheads, she was quick, funny and tough. The punters loved her.

At the time I was attending St Peter and St Pauls Junior School in Ilford. It was a nice school but I do remember some turmoil. I didn't like it. The first week was a real nightmare. Poor Mum. I was a real mummy's boy and she doted on me something crazy. Mum had to drag me into school. When it was time for her to leave I kicked up the biggest fuss. It was like I was possessed. There was a red cage that wrapped around the staircase in the school so kids couldn't commit suicide I guess. I hung on to that cage like a demented ape for an hour a day for the first week screaming, while Mum and assorted teachers tried to prise me off, convincing me to stay. I did not want her to go. My little boy's a bit like that now. Still I'm stronger than him so

I'm ready for the fight. I think I'll bring a small lever and work on his fingers one by one until he's finally off and in school. I imagine me and Chris will need a deep coffee after this.

I don't know why I always hated going to school as much as I did – maybe the rules, being told what to do. I mean I came to like aspects of it, but generally school could've sucked my dong.

I think the beginnings of my current life as an actor started here. Getting off school by pretending to be dangerously ill takes skill, courage and commitment.

I had a lovely little technique where I'd take the thermometer Mum was using to check my temperature and rub it hard with my tongue, and blow hot air on the mercury-filled bulb. Anything to get it over the golden number, 101 degrees F.

The sickness gig was very to and fro with Mum, she'd threaten to call the doctor out, I'd say I was fine, and that it was just a bug etc. She always came round to my way of thinking. I was good, often interrupting a conversation with a round of coughing and dry heaves. I'd lie on the sofa pretending to be ill. It was a Bifa-worthy performance. Utterly compelling.

My enjoyment of *Jamie's Magic Torch* however was one day rudely interrupted by a brusque knock on the front door.

As a fake sickman there are times when you need to deeply immerse yourself in a role. Factors need to be considered. What do I have? What is the timeline for said viral infection? How sick am I? Last time we spoke how sick was I? Have I become dramatically worse? Am I feeling slightly better? What's the longest possible time I can eke this out for? Getting sick on a Wednesday means I will not be back at school till the following Monday. Come Friday at 4 p.m., I'd be feeling much better. The answers to the above questions give you the level of illness you need to pitch. It's pretty simple really. Stay in character. Commit.

This was a Wednesday and as such I was in the grip of a nasty Asian ape flu that had been going round.

In response to the door knocking I pulled my blankets up and moaned, as if deep in a Bronte-esque, soaked-by-rain-on-a-dark-heath-fever-induced daymare. I moaned, brilliant touch.

'MUM!!! DOOR!!!'

I could hear Mum talking to someone, I strained to hear snippets of a conversation: 'Thanks for coming . . . He's in here.'

I shut my eyes, and moan, shivering, so cold, so sick. The only way a human would be as sick as I was pretending to be was if he/she had eaten a rotten monkey-brain omelette in the central market in Liberia, West Africa. I hadn't.

My arms contorted in spasm and I woke with a start. Too much. Too big. Hammy performance. I opened my eyes to see our GP standing there. Tit bags. She actually called the doctor. I'm ruined.

The doctor, a big man, towers over me. Tough it out. Commit. You're one of the best poorly child actors in Europe.

'Has this child been to Liberia in the last ten days?'

'No.'

Maybe I'd pitched my performance just right after all.

The doctor takes my blood pressure and temperature, he listens to my chest with his stethoscope. I can see my smug mum behind him, smiling. She's called my bluff, what a dick.

Doctor's brow furrows, I drop out of character for a second, he sees this. He tuts and shakes his head. Mum and I lock eyes briefly. I pretend to get suddenly very cold.

The doctor slowly pulls his bookish, half-moon glasses from his noble Hippocratic face. (He didn't wear glasses.) He fixes my mum with a hard stare and barks out these words, 'Mrs Frost, would you be so kind as to call an ambulance please?'

I suddenly feel a lot better. Is this part of Mum's bluff? No, she is rooted and white as a sheet. This is actually happening. I'm actually sick. The doctor has diagnosed a potentially dangerous heart murmur; my dream of being a deep sea diver hunting for booty now lies in tatters. I was in hospital for three weeks. I never pretended to be sick again.

As the school 'postman' I went to church every day and afterwards I would pick up the letters and take them to the office (in hindsight I'm not sure why the school couldn't have just got the letters sent directly to the school and not via the church).

This was before Thatcher took away our milk. We drank a lot of milk in little bottles with blue straws, played a lot of crab-football. At the age of six or so we were called into the music room and all given an instrument to learn. I was so happy when they decided to give me a shiny trumpet like Miles Davis. So happy.

After several weeks of struggling with this shiny knot of brass the Head of Music called me and my mum into his office. He talked to Mum as if I wasn't there. He told her my lips were too big and I would never make the grade for a trumpeter. What. The. Fuck. Had this dick never heard of Satchmo? He took the trumpet out of my hands – *pulled* it out of my hands – and as I grasped at the thin air that used to contain a trumpet he stuck a trombone into my hands. *He gave me a trombone.* Apart from the tuba, it ranks as the fattest sounding of all instruments. If a tuba wasn't available and someone needed to soundtrack a mega-fatty struggling down the street with a big bucket of chicken, the trombone would be the instrument they'd use.

My stubborn streak – cheers Mum – surfaced at school one lunchtime. For whatever reason, although I suspect I may have been showing off a bit, I decide to get three portions of jam roly poly and custard, all piled high in one bowl. My friends laugh as I prod at the jammy suet. The bell rings and I make to leave. I'm stopped at the door by the lunch monitor.

'You're not leaving that.'

'But I don't want it.'

'Then why did you get so much?'

'Dunno.'

'You're going to sit down and finish it.'

'But I can't eat any more.'

'I don't care. Sit down please.'

I was giving some major attitude in front of my homies. Fuck this dude. I sat down. The teacher plopped the pile of stodge in front of me.

'When you finish this bowl you can leave.'

'I'm not eating it.'

'We'll see.'

'We will see. I'm not eating it.'

'You will.'

'I won't.'

And I didn't. I sat there from one o'clock until half-past four, when my mum was forced to come and get me. She was not happy. She was fine with me, but she wasn't happy with them forcing a little boy to miss a whole afternoon of lessons to try and prove a point. It was great having a woman like Mum on my side.

Paul Eaton was my best friend at the time; notable others include Sean Creagan and a kid called Peter who dipped toast into tea – it used to make me heave. I had my first kiss with a lovely Irish girl called Patricia Dugan, she had a shiny black wedge like Pam Ayres's. Rachel Cosgrave was the fittest girl in school; she had two different-coloured eyes – one blue, one green. It was amazing. I'd never seen anything like it. (Except for Dave Bowie.)

Around about this time Pope John Paul the Second got shot. Being a Catholic school it was a really big deal. We were asked/made to write 'get well soon' letters. Being a young funnyman I decided to include a joke. Poor bloke got shot for Christsakes, I thought he'd need a laugh. Off they went, my letter one of among thousands of well wishes from young Catholics all over the world.

A month later a letter plopped through our letterbox. The envelope was like nothing I'd never seen before. White, padded, rich smelling. Embossed on the front of the letter was the cross keys of the seal of Vatican City. WTF. My hands trembled as I opened the letter carefully. It was from the effin Pope! Actually from his personal secretary to be fair but close enough. It said the Pope was happy I had written to him and my joke had made him laugh! Holy (literally) shit.

My other best friend was a fiery loonie called Vincent Heggarty. He had an older brother called Brendan, who much later would become a really good friend and help me make my important choice to escape the UK to live in Israel.

That though was ten years away. At this point I was just his little brother's mate and he'd spend his time shooting us with an air rifle loaded with phlegm and tin-foil wrapped needles. Disgusting and painful.

They lived in Seven Kings near Ilford. One night when I stayed over in Vincent's hot, packed, Irish house all hell broke loose. We heard it floating up through the floorboards;

someone had died. I think this was the first time I was exposed to grief, Irish grief at that. Drinking, singing, crying, laughing, anger. This really affected me as a little boy, I cried my eyes out, although I wasn't sure why.

There are only fragments of memories about that school and my time there. Dad started working with Dennis Bennett, his old school friend, at Comida Contracts, a company that designed and manufactured high-end office furniture. He began when the company was tiny, first as a driver and then as a trainee upholsterer. He gradually worked his way up, eventually becoming managing director, hence the Jaguar XJS V12 (metallic mint paint, cream leather interior).

We got to the point in our lives back then, through Dad's hard work, hard work that bordered on the workaholic, where we had the chance to move away from the mean streets of Dagenham. Mum and Dad found a lovely double-fronted, three-bedroom house with a massive garden in Redbridge, Essex – 27 Babbacombe Gardens.

I was nervous, all my friends were going on to Canon Palmer, a secondary school in Ilford, and I was going to a place called Beal High School in Redbridge. I never saw anyone from my old school again more or less. That chapter closed and I was forced to move forward.

The new house was a two-minute walk away from the new school, which was nice. The place in Dagenham had been two buses and a long walk away from school; 27 Babbacombe was a real palace compared to our box-like and very terraced Dagenham house. For fun recently I looked it up on Zoopla. Two things struck me: one, I didn't remember it looking like that at all. My brain has completely made up a view of that place that the Zoopla image doesn't match, and two, it was pretty bloomin' cheap. (Relatively.) I seem to remember it was some kind of mansion. But no, it can be picked up for £400k.

The neighbours on our right were Dave and Jane. Jane was a stone-cold MILF, although the term MILF was a long way from being invented at this point. I reckon she was in her late twenties/early thirties. Lots of low-slung, tight jeans, flat, hard tummy and bellybuttons, long fronds of loose blonde hair, no bra, bending over to pick up a well-chewed dog toy – this was too much for a young boy to take. I remember Dave liked knives and Rottweilers, a frightening mix that should've guaranteed I kept my young horny eyes well away from his wife. It didn't, my burgeoning sexuality – I was twelve for godsakes! – and real need to see what a woman looked like was to get me into terrible trouble while perving on Jane as she sunbathed topless in the garden.

I'd cleverly worked out that if I stood on the toilet, and angled a CD (acting as a mirror) I could see her knockers. I'm ashamed writing this, ashamed and proud at the level of invention my perverted determination drove me to.

I thought this discovery was amazing, she was my first fantasy and I needed to confide this naughtiness to someone. Sadly I made the mistake of telling a big-mouthed friend who, literally the moment I finished telling him, ran up to Jane, who had conveniently wandered round the corner, and told her. (She worked as a dinner lady at lunchtimes at the school.) 'Miss, Nick perves on your bangers when you sunbathe.'

I couldn't believe it. This was the first time I experienced what has become known as a Heat Flash. I was/am to experience it many times after this. It begins in my feet, moving north, it flashes up my body at three times the speed of sound, leaving me momentarily deaf. The deafness is replaced by the sound of my blood pumping through my ears and then slowly, gradually, normal service resumes.

I imagine it to be a similar physical sensation to standing slightly too near a car bomb as it goes off or driving a heavily armoured vehicle over an IED. Once I've recovered enough to move, I set off at pace, running for home. I fly through the front door screaming to Mum that I wasn't very well and I get into bed. It's one o'clock in the afternoon and one of the hottest days of the year. I lie there wishing I were dead. (This is a perfect example of Karma in action and totally serves me right for being a horrible little pervert.)

Then there was a knock at the front door. I'd been half expecting it, the blood pressure whistles loudly in my ears, I knew what was happening, who it was, it was Jane. I hear her talking to my mum and then I hear the front door closing, someone coming upstairs. There was a tap on my door.

'Hello,' I croaked, pretending to be dangerously ill. Jane comes in and we fuck violently (we don't). Actually she was absolutely lovely about it. She very quietly, calmly and peace-fully told me that what I had done was wrong. And that was that. She went off and it was never mentioned again.

Next door to Jane and Dave lived the Ellicotts. They were a nice family with four strapping sons. Dad was a copper and their mum was a lovely, lovely Irish lady called Peggy, with a need to constantly feed people until their stomachs split. The house was very messy and the kitchen was packed to the rafters with bumper packs of food, cases of soup, cereal, eleven thou-sand slices of packet ham, fifty litres of margarine, a ton of Quavers on a pallet, chocolate, peanuts, chocolate peanuts, and the world's biggest private collection of tinned fruit. I guess having four sons means you need a lot of food. I have one son and I'm constantly amazed by how much he eats.

Every year the Ellicotts had a New Year's Eve party. It was always fun and crazy and was the chance to stay up late and steal cans of lager. It was at one such do that we all sat and watched Michael Jackson's *Thriller* video directed by the great John Landis. It was absolutely amazing. I'd never seen anything like it.

The Ellicotts's 1987 New Year's Eve bash provided the setting for a moment of young weirdness for me.

Sexy neighbour Jane had got over my earlier sexual misdemeanour, and asked if I wanted to go upstairs and smoke a joint with her. Course I did, the fact Mr Ellicott was the police didn't bother me much at all to be honest. Jane and I stuffed our bodies halfway out of a tiny window and hung out of it puffing, it was nice. There came a sharp knock at the door, I suffer a low-level panic, I frantically whisper at Jane to not open it, she tells me it will be fine. I trust her. Jane opens the door, her face softening.

'Who is it?'

'It's fine . . .' I relax. Jane continues . . .

'It's only your mum.'

WHARRRRRRRRRTTTTTTT!!!!

It was very odd, Mum was pissed, and I was frankly too high to care – in fact I even recall at one point relishing showing my mum how to smoke a joint properly. Weird scenes inside the Goldmine.

The next morning was awkward. I came down to find Mum washing up. I cleared my throat.

'Hello.' I was casual.

'Hello.' Mum was casual.

We didn't make eye contact. I grabbed my stuff and left for the day. Do you know that feeling when you end up French kissing an uncle while camping? It felt a bit like that.

* * *

On our left, at number 29 Babbacombe, lived Chris, Alan, Ian, Mandy and Martin. They become pretty important. My mum and Chris soon become best friends. Me and Chris's son Ian who was four years older than me also became good mates. Ian loved *Cagney and Lacey* and Status Quo and we spent a lot of time playing golf at Hainault municipal golf course. I kind of idolised him a little bit.

Mandy was Chris's daughter; she was my first proper love I think. Mandy was three years older than me, not much in the big scale of things granted, but when you're twelve it was a love forbidden.

Me and Mandy would play a game where we'd stand on the corner of the street kissing to see how many people would honk their horns at us. It never went much further than kissing but then it didn't have to, it was enough. I really liked her. She had other, older boyfriends; I didn't mind, I knew our thing was transient and just for giggles.

Mandy's year in school had their own common room, I was a few years below and being in that room flirting outrageously with the fittest girl in her year was taken by some as a major slight.

There was a guy in her class, the older brother of a mate of mine, who really fancied Mandy. Seeing her cuddling and kissing cute old me drove him crazy. He made the mistake of confronting me in front of everyone, an OK Corral kind of thing. He told me I didn't belong, that I should 'get lost'. He then made his final mistake, trying to knee me in the Goolie Bag. (As an aside he actually got my inner thighs.) This I couldn't take. Everyone was looking while he towered over me smiling like a cunt. My ears rang, my fist clenched itself up. (You'd be forgiven for thinking this was the plot point in *BTTF* where McFly clumps Biff.) I stand and begin moving a solid, powerful right towards his fucking head, I sit into it moving my body round so the arm whips around quicker, it pludges into his face, his neck whips back, and the world speeds up again. He slumps to the floor. Nunight.

This is the first time I ever did anything like this. I felt good slugging that pompous jerk-off. I felt good, for about a second. I've always been someone who overthinks things, works shit out and imagines the consequences of actions, my actions. Fighting left me cold. What if I hit him and he falls and hits his head and dies? He didn't die. There was a collective gasp. Is Mandy looking at me with a newfound pride and attraction or does she have the beginnings of slight conjunctivitis? I don't hang around to find out. My plan didn't include what might happen if he gets up with fight still in him, so I run. There is no come back. He never bullies me again and nor does anyone else. I guess a secondary school is a bit like a prison in so much as once people know you're happy to sling a fist or two they tend to stay away from you.

These people, our neighbours, were the closest friends we had. Up the street a little way lived my new best friend, at least for the first couple of years of school; he was a peculiar fellow called Brett Colley. He had perhaps the best and biggest train set I ever saw. It took up his whole room leaving a tiny space in one corner for his little bed. His brother Ricky was a much bigger boy who could ride really fast on his bike. His mum was like Dog Chapman's lovely wife Beth and I seem to remember his dad was a Fred Dibnah-style man, always stuck down in his vast shed/workshop taking apart and putting together old cars and engines. There was lots of that back then. Essex seemed to be a real hotbed of taking apart and putting together old cars. Me and my later crew had our own workshop in Peter Ashton's shed, we'd spend a lot of time sanding and filling old car panels and hanging them back on whatever shitty banger Pete was working on at the time.

I begged my dad to buy me a shitty banger and after weeks of me hassling him he did just that. It was a powder-blue Escort MKII. It was beautiful and fucked and I loved it. I think I was fourteen at the time. My intention was to work on it until I passed my test and then I'd have a car straight away.

It sat outside the back of the house in the alley for several months. I didn't do much to it. I think once I hit the engine with a hammer, maybe I sanded a wing. A few weeks later I try to jack the thing up. The car creaks and slumps and finally emits a loud cracking sound. The jack rips through the floor pan and lodges itself deep into the underbelly of the car. Try as I might, I could not get it out. Like the sword in the stone I was not worthy. I soon lost interest in that car and it was eventually pushed into a river and set alight. Don't judge me, I'm from Essex.

I often wondered what happened to Brett. He got a lot of stick but I liked him. He'd always have an angle and was a pretty savvy businessman, buying boxes of Mars bars at trade and selling to the other kids well above market place. I bet he's some kind of tech billionaire now.

Beal High School also had an ice cream van, a kind of mobile tuck shop if you will, that'd come in at lunchtimes for all the eager fatties. Brett worked out a deal where he would essentially do litter patrol at the end of lunch and get free sweets from the ice cream man. Brett was the only kid I knew that had all of the NatWest Piggies. He looked like a thirteen-year-old Freddie Mercury complete with partially formed bumfluff moustache.

I remember playing hide and seek in his house once; it was dark and we had our school uniforms on so I imagine it was winter. I found a place on top of a cupboard where I curled up and waited. While I was lying down wanting to piss – this is a sad side effect hide and seek has on me – I noticed the bulb-less light socket hanging from the ceiling and an odd plan of action made itself known to me. The voice in my mind said this . . .

'Stick your finger into the light socket to see if it's on or off.' I had to know and sticking my finger into the socket was the only way I could think to find out, so I did it. The whole room popped and for a moment the darkness became bright like a supernova. I woke up on the floor, muffled voices filtering into my consciousness; I'd been flung across the room, what a fucking idiot. I was absolutely compelled to stick my finger into that live socket, perhaps this is a valuable insight into my powerful lack of impulse control.

Brett also went on the school canal trips, and was the main reason really that I wanted to go. From my first year at secondary school until the fifth year when I left we went on the annual canal trip. It was a week over the Easter holidays with the groovy gang from the school's canal club travelling different routes around the highways and byways of Britain's majestic canal network. We were the uncoolest people in the world, but it was fab and I friggin loved it, especially the feeling of responsibility.

It was run by science teacher Mr Fisher, a big, bearded man who always creeped me out a bit. He had large hairless hands with big pores and was always a bit too touchy feely; because of him I now have a distrust of men with hairless big-pored hands.

In the run-up to the trips we'd attend a class after school a couple of times a week for about a month, teaching us the technicalities of narrow boats, how locks worked, safety on board and general waterway etiquette. Usually four boats would be hired, a twelve berth, a couple of tens and an eight. After a safety briefing from the hire company we were off. We were allowed to steer, operate the locks, and we all took turns cooking and cleaning as we pottered down the canals at 4 miles per hour (bliss).

On the canal trips there was always some kind of drama going on, lots of falling in love with people, drunkenness, little arguments, people falling in. One year a kid called Amit and a teacher called Mr Green had a major beef, fuck knows why. Amit could be annoying and a little bit hyper but he was essentially a good bloke. Green really had it in for him, I think at one point he pushed Amit over into some nettles. Nettles for fucksakes! I even seem to remember him holding Amit down in a muddy field and struggling with his conscience whether or not to punch Amit in the chops.

I remember the thrill of the Tardebigge flight and the terror of the mighty Pontcysyllte aqueduct, an iron trough two hundred feet in the sky with no safety rail. I remember smoking and laughing a lot with Peter Ashton, eating eggy bread, walking miles at night with a torch trying to find a phonebox! Finding a fucking phonebox. (I'm glad I straddle this era between phonebox and mobile.) I fell into the canal twice. I fell in love more than that.

The most memorable thing to happen to me though was on my last trip. I was fifteen and the trip fell on my sixteenth birthday. As it was my birthday they made a real fuss of me. It was day two of a seven-day trip. That night we were moored up in the Gas Street Station in Birmingham – a place I'll never forget. We had a small party on Mr Green's boat and I drank too much whisky. Too much for a sixteen-year-old anyway.

I begin to get a whisky rage on, the first inkling I may have Celtic Twilight in me. In a fit of rage and teen despair I smash a bottle and attempt to punch a bridge. It hurts and I trudge back to Green's boat; someone suggests I should stay and not stumble back to my own boat up the dark towpath. I find myself in the female teachers' cabin. I'm drunk on the floor on top of a thin mattress in a sleeping bag. I hear the words, 'Why don't you come in here, you'll be more comfortable.' Then something about it being cold.

How did this begin? What sparked it? When had it become this? What led up to it? Was there flirting? I don't remember guffing on her so maybe not. I was sixteen and she was at least thirty-seven. At school we called her Lumpy Linda. We used to joke about the way she walked, a kind of bouncy half tumble, and how she always wore these long pointy shoes, shoes a Turkish soldier might wear, while guarding the shrine of Atatürk.

I allow myself to be pulled into her tight bunk and then, space being a premium, I end up on top of her. I'm hammered and confused. The vast expanse of her big white tummy spreads out beneath me, an icy field of wrong. My head swims. How did we get here? Things become vague. I remember snippets of things, sure, but nothing concrete. I think I'm losing my virginity to a woman called Lumpy Linda. This is not how I imagined it to be honest; that said, I'm not sure I *had* ever imagined it.

Almost the second it's finished, Lumpy Linda leans her head out of the bunk and projectile-vomits all over the tiny cabin. It's like I just lost my virginity to Mr Creosote. The fact I ever had sex with a woman again absolutely amazes me. With the noise of the – whatever it was – and the puking the whole boat comes thundering into the cabin to help out. They fuss around and help with the vomit, torches are shone in to illuminate the scene. Shouts of 'Back to bed everyone!' Am I naked? Am I in my trademark Tanga briefs? Mr Green's there too, what did he think with his stubby legs, gappy teeth and desert boots?

The next day, and in fact the rest of the whole week, was fucking awful. Everyone knows. She keeps trying to catch me alone at the locks to talk about what has happened. I'm totally unprepared for this, talking about feelings is not what the sixteen-year-old me wants to do, can do. I'm completely without the tools to cope with this.

After a while it slips from the front page to page eleven and then it's chip wrappers.

* * *

Between fourteen and sixteen I spend a lot of time down in Wales. It's a place where I feel like I'm treated like a grown-up a bit. From the age of eleven I'd been taking the train or a National Express coach on my own to Haverfordwest. I loved being down there. Things at home had taken a turn for the worse and Mum's drinking was getting out of hand. I'd use Wales as a place to escape to. Staying with Auntie Linda or at Auntie Melanie's house on that little council estate up near the

cemetery was a dream. It was in Melanie's house I first saw
Close Encounters of the Third Kind.

They all found me hilariously funny and I loved showing off,
making them all laugh. Despite the shit there was a lot of
laughter at home, at least early on. I was the funny so and so.
Impressions were my thing and mimicking voices. Dad was a
pun merchant and Mum was dry as a bone. Guffs got a lot of
airtime. Lotta guff comedy at home. I remember as a young
boy I'd ripped my underpants pretty badly. I decided to use this
tatty garment as a prop. I ran into the kitchen in my gran's
house and did a very loud fart which I then pretended had
blown my underpants to bits. My gran and four or five of my
aunties howled with laughter at six-year-old me dancing
around, arse scorched from a flaming pump. Maybe I should
try and resurrect 'pant explosion' in a film sometime.

At sixteen, though, because of the pressures of home I was a
miserable so and so. Many was the time I'd sit on the bus driving from Haverfordwest to Fishguard and back again with my
Walkman on listening to the Smiths and watching the rain
trickle down the fogged-up windows. It felt right to be there.
What a moody little twat I was.

I'd hang out in a pub on the square. Some people knew me,
most didn't. I liked that. I'd write in a little notebook and be
miserable, I thought it was attractive to be mysterious and
sullen. When I was there I was definitely from London, I made
a point of not hiding it. At the weekends I was allowed to go to
the club with my aunties. RJ's was a real shit hole. On a Sunday
as part of the entrance fee you got a free sausage and chips.
What a place.

One weekend I managed to persuade my London mates to
drive down to Haverfordwest to stay with my gran for the night,

then go clubbing. I wouldn't say it was a disaster but it was a long way to go for a night out. We smoked joints on the way down and when we got nearer I told a story about an evil dwarf that lived with my grandmother. I managed to lay it on pretty thick and put the willies up them.

We were silent while we drove through the pitch-black lane, and a sigh of relief washed over them as we saw the welcoming lights of my gran's house. Now, the story I told them was not actually completely untrue: my Uncle Emmy had suffered from a terrible bout of scarlet fever as a child. It stunted him mentally and physically. He never really grew up. Emmy was amazing. Me and all my cousins loved him so much. He was small and wrinkled like a prune with the spirit and heart of a child. I knew the weed had bent their minds and I wanted to use this.

My lovely gran welcomed us into the kitchen. The guys, stoned off their minds, huddled around her big Aga cooker in silence; it was the same Aga that years before I'd seen her use to hatch half a dozen hens' eggs.

Uncle Emmy was a creature of habit. I knew exactly where he'd be, sitting in his chair, the one behind the door, watching the big old TV Gran owned. Knowing this, I sent the boys into the front room to sit down. They opened the door and essentially hid Emmy from their view. Once settled, Emmy kicked the door closed so he could see the TV. He omitted one of his funny trademark noises, a kind of long, loud hum.

From inside the kitchen I heard the boys shriek. Poor things. That night didn't go so well. The club was cool although at some point we thought someone had spiked our drinks. I have a vague memory of one of us getting punched too, or threatened with a punching at the very least. At one point walking down the lane deep in the forest on the way home I decide I need to shit more than anyone in the world. So I do, by the light of someone's Zippo. Bleak.

In the morning the terrible truth is revealed to me. While crouching to plop I had not cleared my own jeans. I had shit into my jeans and all down my white AS Roma away shirt. Oh dear.

I always had a vague notion I'd end up living in Wales. It was a dream, that's all. For all the issues and faults I had with and in London with Mum and Dad, it was still my home. But it was difficult. Things were difficult. Mum continued drinking, Dad's business was failing, leaving school with and for nothing, no job, a sadness descends. Looking back now at the age of forty something, I'd pinpoint this time as the beginning of a lifelong battle with depression. A battle I didn't understand was being waged in me until years after.

* * *

Although no longer at school, the boys and me were still mates at this point. It was just before Mum and Dad lost everything, before I was cut loose by my friends and forgotten, ignored. I spent a lot of time with the fellas in a shit car driving around smoking hash. We did that a lot. Our range was fairly big, from Gants Hill and Barkingside all the way to Romford and Southend. We'd just drive around listening to pirate radio or Public Enemy, Shut Up and Dance, Jungle Brothers, Doug Lazy, Twin Hype, getting off our heads.

There was a place up in Epping Forest near High Beach where we'd go and park and smoke joints. It was a tiny lane deep in the forest in the middle of nowhere. Early one evening the four of us were sat in a mate's shit beige Escort estate. I was in the passenger seat. So and So always drove, bullied and guilted into driving, poor fella. We'd smoked so much shit that I couldn't see the driver, we'd created what the Dutch call a Grade 5 'hot box'. Down the lane we saw two headlights slowly bumping down the track. 'Old Bill!' I joke. We all panic and then laugh like drains. Some paranoia flashes over us.

'Don't fuck about.' Another peel of laughter that's immediately cut short when we realise a police car has pulled up beside us and the coppers are silently peering into the smoked-filled car full of red-eyed lemurs looking back at them.

I whisper loudly, 'Don't open the windows.' They mishear me and the windows are opened immediately. Forty cubic metres of bright blue smoke are emitted into the low atmosphere around the vehicle and for a moment it looks like the car has a foggy afro. The police move off slowly, eye-fucking us. A terrible panic breaks out among the lemurs. Everyone fires off an opinion at once, and eventually in about one millionth of a second a conclusion is unanimously reached . . . DRIVE!!!

Why the fuck did we do that? That was one of several ropy decisions we made that night. The car, now clear of smoke, moves off at pace (7 miles an hour). I look back, praying I don't see lights, praying they don't turn around, the 1.2-litre engine screams under the bonnet. I see lights. On our left we see a parking spot full of early-shift doggers. In front of us a small hill, beyond that, the safety of Epping Forest.

We are all shouting our opinions, I catch flashes of sentences, 'pull in', 'let's run', 'the woods are our new home now' and 'they'll never catch us' among other things. What the fuck were we thinking as we come hammering into the car park, skid to a halt, exit the vehicle and make off across the field and up towards the safety of the trees?

Realising we'd forgotten our carrier bag full of snacks we turn back. We grab our Frazzles and the giant Fruit and Nuts we'd need to survive and shunt it up the hill. No one ever stopped and thought for a second what we'd do once we got there. I actually remember hollering out, 'If we get to the safety of the forest they'll never find us!'

The whelp of the siren throws my life into slow motion, the trees in front of me bathed in the flashing of a shade of blue light that can only mean one thing. You're fucking nicked, my son! I look across at H, we both have the same weird, almost peaceful look which is somewhere between 'having witnessed a rapture' and a 'dynamic young veal in an abattoir'. I recall us both laughing, although neither of us seemed at all happy.

The police shout something, I know not what although if I had to hazard a guess I'd say it was probably something like: 'Stop, you little fuckheads!' I do the only thing available to me at that point and I open my Frazzles. After the twenty-metre shuffle up the hill I'm absolutely knackered and happy to stop. I hate running and eating crisps at the same time, it's pointless, like a pub-crawl. Just stay in one pub and drink a lot. Why combine drinking with cardio? We turn and slowly trudge down the hill. People who'd been fucking in their cars quickly speed away. We are restrained but it's fine as I've finished my crisps.

Lots of things, confusing things, happen in the next twenty minutes or so. We're searched, the car is searched, souls are searched and discussions are had. The word 'arrest' is bandied around, some wee plops up, but oddly it's all pretty jovial, the atmosphere, not the wee. I wish this story had a better ending but we are let go! We were all completely amazed. They took our big lump of hashish and our Liquid Gold and threw it into a patch of long grass. To stop us spending three hours looking for it they made us drive off first. The deafening silence was broken by an eruption of wheezy laughter. What a fucking lucky escape. Thank you, lenient policemuns.

I have hash at my house so I suggest we spin round and grab it. This is exactly what we do. We pull up. 'I'll be five minutes.'

I let myself in and immediately notice that the TV is off. This is a terrible sign. Something's happened, someone has died. This first time I feel the dread of a silent room is when I'm 10 and we're staying in my Auntie Marion's house, in Broadhaven. I used to be able to do a weird thing where I'd lie in bed at night and make the light switch move around the wall just by looking at it. I'd stare and it would tremble and then move. Sometimes I could get it up on the ceiling. I'd seen *Carrie* so I thought it was a form of telekinesis. I wasn't telekinetic in the slightest and, I won't lie, was partly disappointed by the fact.

In the early morning I could hear a commotion coming from Auntie Marion's kitchen. I inch down the stairs peering through the banisters and notice the telly is off. Deborah had died. She was my dad's oldest child and my half-sister from his first pop at marriage. She was a beautiful eighteen-year-old, a talented up and coming actress and singer who lived so far away I'd only ever met her twice. One night after a show she came home, lay on the couch and had a massive asthma attack. She never recovered. No matter, my dad's anguish was now mine. To this day I can't bear to be in a silent room. Something always needs to be on.

* * *

Back home, high and cocky from my brush with the law, I poke my head around the door to the lounge and Mum and Dad are sat in silence, telly off. How long had they been there? How long were they planning on being there? In the middle of the room, in the middle of our mint-green carpet, was a giant lump, my giant lump of hash. It looks exactly like a brown Rubik's cube but obviously a lot easier to solve. Trouble now breaks out. Not a row, just a kind of Category C rumble with a drug pro and con to-and-fro-type parent deal. To be fair they make a compelling argument but I'm high, the guys are waiting, and I'd like to be higher. My counter comes in the shape of a rat out.

I decide to point out to Dad that me and Mum have indeed smoked hash together. This should relieve some of the pressure. It does and they turn on one another, it enables me to brazenly grab my gear and fuck off. I jump back into the car, I've been six minutes thirty-five seconds: 'Sorry I was so long.' We drive off.

What an absolute little prick I was. Writing this makes me feel bad. Yes I was young and naughty but this feels like something and someone else. Makes me feel like a schemer. I think it was the beginning of a turn in me and drugs seemed to be the catalyst and the accelerant. Of course my life at home and the things going on were the driving force of this escape but still . . .

I go through a heavy drugs phase round about now, lots of hash, poppers and tons of LSD. These were the times when I started going to my first, and indeed *the* first, raves. Raindance at Jenkins Lane was my first. I was terrified and I loved it. Others followed, unused farm buildings, weird old dilapidated manor houses near Basildon, industrial units near Tilbury, sometimes wine bars in Loughton. It was exciting. I was a little Essex druggy tearaway, an urchin, a scoundrel if you will but a scoundrel with a good heart.

For me it was all about the music and getting high. Getting to a place where the sun would collapse into itself, there'd be a tremendous flash, and I'd wake up in a white room surrounded by all the other most fucked-up people in the world. An orbital way station for people on a chemical vacation. Psychonauts fleeing their earth land.

This time coincides of course with bad shit personally. It was my escape from my mum's alcoholism which was a huge problem for me. I hated it and I hated her and I hated myself for feeling that way. Around then Mum and Dad decided to separate. A lot of my friends' parents were splitting up so for once I didn't feel behind the curve on a current social trend. This is a perfect example of why I wish I'd asked more questions even though it would've made for a difficult conversation. I can't remember why they separated. My overwhelming hunch was drinking. It had to be, right? What else could it have been? I've thought maybe one of them strayed but it just doesn't feel right. Dad was deep into his workaholic phase. I wonder now if this was to get away from Mum and her drinking.

Don't get me wrong – it wasn't like she was arseholed from morning till night at this point, god no. That was unacceptable to Mum. She was a woman who believed it was unseemly for a 'lady' to smoke a cigarette walking down the street. Oh no, with her it was all about public perception and image. Me and Dad would often crack up listening to Mum answer the phone using her posh voice. This feels dangerous to me now, caring what the neighbours thought. This is why things became hidden. No, Mum was a fully functioning drunk then. A mother and a home maker. Still I wonder if Dad coming home late every night to a G-'n'-T-soaked, angry, emotional firebomb was the thing that made them split. It feels right but I'll never know.

This was a time of weekend visits from Dad while he lived in Uncle Brian's spare room. I didn't feel like I was being denied a father, in fact I probably saw him just as much to be fair. We went on what felt like functional trips to places like the newly opened Thames barrier and the *Cutty Sark*. We both hated it really. He wanted to be home and I didn't really want to be forced to lose a weekend on my hot BMX.

We had a big fight one Saturday when me and Dad went to buy rugby boots. He tried to fob me off with bad boots with moulded rubber studs. Oh no. All the forwards from my team that season were wearing Adidas Flanker and that's what I wanted. He was so cross. He slammed the cheap boots down and walked out of the shop without me. I was in trouble. He really screamed at me in the car.

After almost a year Mum and Dad had worked things out and Dad moved back home. What a strange episode. I guess their years and years of relationship groundwork and the fact they had me meant eventually they couldn't be apart. They were in love, right up to the end. I think you have to be to go through what they went through. Sometimes it's just easier to keep going forward together than to leave.

My dad had gone through a big change. He'd left the company that he'd helped to build from the ground up when he realised he was not getting everything he should've been. Yes we had a nice house, and a nice car and blahblahblah but it wasn't what the others had and in terms of a work – life balance there was none as he was always working.

Dad decided to start his own company. Clover! It was the happiest I remembered him. (Not completely true but you know what I mean.) He was moving on and forward, he was doing something that would make sure we had the big house in Essex and the horses and the tennis court and the Ferrari and endless summer barbecues where we laughed and stuffed ourselves with meats prepared over open flames. What a life. If anyone deserved that life he did. Dad had worked from the ground up and had taught himself everything there was to know about the design, manufacture, sale and distribution of high-end office furniture. He was a good man who had made a lot of friends in the business and people wanted him to succeed.

Being a sixteen-year-old boy-man I was shielded from certain aspects of our family life. Things that might worry a young brain. Things kids don't need to know about, don't really care about until Christmas gets cancelled and you end up all alone in a shit council estate . . . Oh.

The things I was shrouded from was how Dad got the money to start the company. Essentially everything was up for grabs. The house was remortgaged up to its balls to pay for this venture. In hindsight it's a massive risk and it's easy for me to sit here at the free laptop Apple gave me because I'm a 'celeb' and criticise a man, a good man, trying to do the best for his family. Could I do what he did? I doubt I'd have the bollocks to be honest.

My mum and dad turned our shed at the bottom of our garden in Redbridge into a workshop to make high-end office furniture. They worked so hard. Dad spent the first few weeks out on the road selling Clover. He spent so long drawing little designs for logos and beautiful sketches for amazing chairs. He was so talented, such an amazing draughtsman. Dad was also

a fantastic watercolourist. So technical, creating perfect buildings and landscapes. I have all those paintings. People went
crazy for his designs but that's all they were at that point, just
designs, pictures on a pad.

Once they had enough orders in, Mum and Dad set to work
making the chairs themselves. Let me just write that again . . .
They made the chairs themselves! All the individual pieces were
manufactured off site then delivered and put together by Mum
and Dad in the garage. Some nights they'd be down there until
two or three in the morning putting together handmade chairs.
After a couple of hours' sleep Dad would load up the van he
rented and deliver the things himself.

I think a business of this kind needs to expand quickly and
take people on, otherwise you get swamped and can't actually
fulfil your orders. This was exactly the case with Clover. They
got a big order from a major company to make chairs for a new
HQ. This was it. Fulfil this order and we were fucking laughing. We didn't and we weren't laughing.

As I said, I didn't know and still don't know all the whys and
wherefores, but we failed. The order was just too big. The bank
sent notices, the creditors circled and we were finished. When
the end comes it's horrible. Everything my dad had worked his
balls off for was taken. Assets and dignity stripped away. In the
garage the frames of chairs, the skeletal remains of a dream
wrapped in sheets of soft Italian leather, lay waiting to be
reclaimed by creditors. Behind closed doors voices are raised.
Tears. Fists are pounded into tables. In public there is silence.
Dad gazes into the garden. Deep sighs. Thousand-yard stares.
Mum busies herself around Dad, cajoling, geeing him up,
trying to ignite something in him. Everything is gone, and with
it my beautiful father's dignity. He never recovers.

We were out on the street. The bank takes our home away. How can a bank be allowed to turn a family out onto the street? It's criminal. The council refuse to rehouse us at first, so we live next door with Chris and Mandy and Ian and Martin. They do what real friends do and they step up.

From our lovely double-fronted house in Redbridge where so much had happened to us, we now lived next door in one tiny room that used to be Mandy's bedroom. Three of us lived there with our massive Alsatian Sheba. It was weird to think that only eighteen months before I'd been sat in that room on Mandy's bed sniffing her novelty rubbers trying to think of new inventive ways to kiss her. Apart from death, I can't think of many things worse than losing everything.

We were all so stressed and sad and angry. I spent a lot of time suffering at the end of a Rizla or hiding under the saggy tumtum of a laughing Buddha.

To be fair the atmosphere in their house was always nice. Tea was always being made, *Dallas* was usually on, and Mandy was there which was a bonus. One night I came in fairly early. Everyone was up and about except Mum. She'd gone to bed early with a bit of a headache. Despite all our shit, I loved, still love, my mum with all of my heart. I pop into the bedroom to say goodnight.

Literally as soon as I push the door open I hear a very inhuman and yet totally human noise, a scream, a hollow roar, the noise of a mother hearing her son has been murdered. It isn't right and my spine and brain twitch. It's dark and I don't know what's happening but noises like that never mean anything good. Never.

I flick on the light and find her fitting violently. Her arms tight and thrust into the sky like a boxer knocked out with the perfect punch. Arms thrust upwards, defending themselves from a nightmare. Their brains are malfunctioning. My mum's brain is malfunctioning and it's the oddest most frightening thing I've ever witnessed. She's having a stroke.

I watch for what seems to be an age, one of her eyes focuses on me, pleading for help. I don't move, I can't move, I'm stone. She emits a growl and it snaps me out of my terror. I crash through the door with the little slats and pick up the phone.

I'm making a strange noise, which gets people off the sofa. They peer at me. I literally cannot talk but my noises leave little doubt that something is very fucked up. Chris sees me and sees my panic and as an ex-nurse knows exactly what's happening. Chris always had a very cool head.

I have the phone in my hand and 999 answers. I can't speak. I groan and feel tears tumbling down my cheeks. I try and talk but someone takes over and once again life quickens. An ambulance turns up, groaning Mum is rushed into hospital. The stroke was bad, and the doctors suggest it was brought on by drink and stress. It could've been a lot worse, we could've easily lost her that night. After three days of touch and go, her prognosis finally improves. Her speech returns – this has its good and bad points. Eventually her facial paralysis disappears too. Mum was so fucking lucky.

After this point with the company folding and us losing everything I feel truly alone. It's a sobering feeling the moment you become your parents' parent. For some people it's not until they're in their fifties or sixties but I was sixteen and it was too much for me to bear. After Mum's stroke my lovely gentle dad had a massive nervous breakdown and he was never the same again. The man I knew, the workaholic, the joker, always laughing but often absent through hard work, had disappeared. I never saw that man again. There were glimpses every now and then, especially after Mum died, but it wasn't the same.

I'd only seen Dad cry once up to that point, when Deborah died. After the collapse of us I saw him cry every day. The fact that my dad had failed, failed in business, failed as a man, to support us, his family. It killed him inside. The truth is not this at all, he didn't fail me. What I saw was a brave man who gave everything he had to make things better. I watched a man get beaten down time and time again and get up, slowly some-times, but get up and trudge forward. He has always been my inspiration.

He was different when he came out the other side. Not neces-sarily a bad different but different. He was quieter, gentler, softer, he needed Mum now more than ever and she gave him what he needed. Mum was a good wife and a fucking strong woman despite her issues. She held him when he cried, soothed him when he was frightened, and when it was needed she bullied and cajoled him into action. What that action was is hard to say. Dad never really worked again. At first he'd just leave the house in the morning and would spend all day out, just walking. He'd take the dog and walk along the River Roding sometimes for seven hours a day.

He started fishing through the river and reeds for lost golf balls near a local course. He'd come back with carrier bags filled with hundreds of balls and sell them to a local driving range. This was what he did for a long while. He just couldn't take it any more. He couldn't find it in himself to get smashed up by the baying, hungry rat race again. His heart was broken and he was a fragile thing, and if all he could face was collect-ing golf balls then that was fine by me.

Eventually, after a couple of months, the council rehoused us in a place called the Ray Lodge Estate in South Woodford. The first time I went there my blood ran cold. The room that eventually became my bedroom had human shit smeared all over the walls. There was also a big red puddle in the middle of the floor which the council woman suggested nervously was 'just paint'.

It was the worst place in the world to me. Hard kids with dead, hard eyes bogged me down, smashed-up washing machines and fridges lay everywhere, needles and burnt-out gutted cars littered the underground car park. How the mighty fall. As a sixteen-year-old it was a bad time to try and fit in. I'd missed the window. If I'd have moved here when I was younger I'd have just become a part of it. I never became part of it. Thank fuck I had a big dog, a big Alsatian, the gorgeous and talented Sheba. No one fucks with you when you have a big dog. She was my furry flick-knife.

Once we moved into the mouth of heck – so dramatic – my 'mates' distanced themselves from me. After everything that had happened it hurt me so much. They'd play games with me, not answer their phones (house phones I might add, this was a long time before mobiles). They'd not call me back, they'd say they'd come round and they never did and I don't know why. What had I done to deserve this? This was one of many cata-lysts that led to a descent that seemed to be unstoppable.

I was alone in a terrible place with an alcoholic mum and a father broken by failure. I think I probably wanted to be dead at this point. One day I'm very drunk at home in my room. I'd started stealing and squirrelling away Dad's pills, he had so many barbs and squeakers and downers he never noticed any missing. I liked the way they made me feel when I took a bunch with booze.

The drunker and higher I got the sadder I became. I took a handful of pills and washed it down with more booze. I write a goodbye to Mum and Dad apologising for what was about to happen and I try and attempt to lie on my bed. I don't make it. The *Close Encounters* soundtrack, a favourite album I find in a junk shop, blares out, my head fogs up and I collapse on the floor. Dead. I'll definitely miss everyone but I'm glad, to be honest.

I wake up the next morning. Balls. I'm still alive. My room has literally not been touched. My note has not been found, my *Close Encounters* album is still revolving on the record player. No one came in. No one lifted me onto my bed or called an ambulance. I feel like shit. I'm seventeen.

I leave school when Mum and Dad collapse. Partly because I hate school (apart from rugby) and partly through a sense of duty: we have no money. Nothing. We live off of Mum and Dad's benefits. I felt like I needed to contribute.

After a lot of interviews and looking in the papers for jobs I find myself employed. I start working at a shipping company in Ilford called Cowell Nicola. I have no experience but it doesn't seem to matter, they employ me and I like it. I really like working in that office.

I'm the youngest one there and they treat me good, the girls think I'm cute, and the blokes talk to me like I'm a football hooligan. At this point I was earning five thousand a year! It seems like fuck all now but back then it was loads, loads to me anyway. After I'd paid housekeeping to Mum and Dad I was free to spend the rest. Spending my money meant booze and petrol for our mate who drove, and McDonalds and raves and hard-house weekenders and hash and squares of paper with mystical symbols etched into them. If you ate the squares the wonders of the universe would be unveiled to you. Not bad for a fiver.

There were some great people at that company. Big Terry Musk, our office manager, heavy smoker, nice easy laugh. Kerry, who looked like a sexy poodle with her mound of heavily curled hair, heavy smoker. I fancied her a bit. Dave, a big brutish ex-hooligan, great at tennis. Dean, suave and heavily receding. Sue, busty, saucy and a real den mother, and Neil Driver, a Cooganesque section leader who made us all laugh a lot.

I liked the fact they treated me like a grown up, which I wasn't. The work was easy and they introduced me to the joys/regrets of afternoon drinking. Nipping out at lunch for a couple. A couple often turned into four or five. How could people work like this? Once a girl got so hammered at lunch we had to cover her in coats and hide her under our desks. That company felt like a little family, we'd do things together a lot after work, softball tournaments, tennis tournaments, parties, drinking in shit pubs in Barking. It was a good time for me, professionally anyway.

Home was somewhere I did not want to be. I'd work then I'd do drugs, mostly on my own. Mostly weed, sometimes other things if I needed to be really away. I needed to escape that place mentally if not physically. When I was there I was locked in my room listening to music, music was one of my escapes. I loved the Happy Mondays, loved the Stone Roses, Inspiral Carpets, Charlatans, Spacemen 3 and the illegal exciting world of pirate radio. I also began writing poems and painting. Could I have been any more of an angsty teen-twat cliché? My poor parents, my poor me.

At this point I fall for a girl who I knew from school called Lee Morris. She was so beautiful. She lived near work on her own and knew what I was going through; she was kind and let me stay with her sometimes. It felt intense and grown up, confusing. She lived in one room, a bedsit, she had a little TV and a black kitten that would flick cat-litter all over the floor at night. I have no idea why a seventeen-year-old lived on her own. If I did know the reason it's now gone. We sleep in the same bed but nothing ever really happens although I seem to remember trying a bit.

Lee was the first in a long line of girls who were way out of my league. I fell for them, hard, but they didn't feel the same way. They saw me more as a friend. Shit. Not good for a falling-in-lover like me. I feel the first delicious pain that only unrequited love can bring. I grow to oddly like that feeling. Sometimes you fall back to something you know and understand, even if it's something that hurts. You get used to it and at the end of the day it's better to feel something, even if it's pain, than feel nothing at all.

Eventually Lee and I stopped whatever it was that we were doing. We contacted each other recently on Twitter. She was happy and apparently makes amazing soup! All's well that ends well.

After a year or so at Cowell Nicola I began to think about moving up the ladder. I needed to be more than a Junior Freight Assistant. I think the truth was I actually wanted a bit more money. Cowell Nicola was a small company but well thought of and it looked good on my CV. I found a job – or was I headhunted? Maybe. That sounds good so let's say yes, I was headhunted, and began working at P&O Containers in Hainault on their Africa desk.

Again I meet good people. It was me, Iain Brymer, our team leader who we all love. Denise, a beautiful cockney firebrand who had a thing with Iain for a bit. Lydia, who's sexy and brassy as fuck, I'd literally never seen a girl like her before, she wore suspenders! This is my first brush with lingerie. Sometimes if you were lucky you'd get a cheeky little flash. Pervert. Me, not her. Last but by no means least the brother of my junior school mate, the one and only Brendan Heggarty.

We had such a laugh. I loved them all and I loved working there. I also got a pay rise, I was now earning a stunning £6,400 (p/a) which was frigging great!

Living with Mum and Dad in Ray Lodge, I took the train every day to Hainault, where the offices of P&O were. I loved going to work because it meant I could leave the confines of my council prison. I hated leaving the office at night as it meant I'd have to go back to Ray Lodge. Whenever I got close to that place my heart would beat a little faster, especially if I didn't have the dog.

It says something about the estate that I was relieved when I finally shut that heavy multi-locked PVC door behind me. Inside was a different type of nightmare but one I'd grown used to.

It wasn't all doom and gloom in that tiny five-room flat. For all the drama and alcohol there were times when we laughed and danced and forgot. The walls in that place were so thin I could hear when my dad ripped off a powerful guff. I'd laugh and then Dad, hearing me laugh, would join in. During this time the smell would waft up into my mum's sensitive nose and she would begin a series of very high-pitched dry heaves. This would send Dad and me into fits of hysterical laughter. Every time she heaved we would lie there on the other side of the gossamer-thin walls laughing our arses off. Mum would struggle to speak. Hearing her heave her way through the sentence 'John, you dirty bastard' was too much to bear. Sometimes I'd laugh so much I'd have to leap up and do a wee. I think it says something about my memories of that place that the best thing

I can muster is listening to my mum heaving to one of Dad's eggy farts.

I began hanging out with Iain Brymer more and more outside the office. He was my direct superior and a bloody good egg. I think he had problems with his mum too in their tiny flat in a tower block in Tilbury. Often I've found myself drawn to people, sometimes without even knowing it, who have similar issues to me.

Even though he was our boss, Bifta (Iain's nickname) often got into trouble for not wearing socks and his anti-establishment vibe meant he was a bit of a hero to me. He was a raver, a renegade and charming as all hell. Don't get me wrong, when we worked, we worked; even though we laughed a lot there was no fucking around. It was important to him and therefore to us that we had the best, politest, most efficient desk in the office and we did.

One day at lunch while Iain flicked through his copy of the *NME* (so fucking cool) he stopped us mid-sandwich and declared that we were getting tickets to see the Stone Roses at Spike Island. So this is exactly what we did.

We took a coach up to Spike Island, which was somewhere near Widnes. It was to be my first time in the Great North. Heck, I even made my own flares. Making flares is simple really, if you ever fancy it, essentially you cut sections out of the bottoms of your jeans and insert big triangles of another fabric, in this case yellow corduroy, simples. Apart from Bifta and Denise and I think Brendan, I have no idea who else came. It was a long coach trip up from Victoria with a real bunch of weirdos, us included. When we finally got there Widnes looked like a frightening shit hole.

The Stone Roses gig at Spike Island has now passed into legend, a defining moment for a bunch of floppy-haired revolutionaries demanding the freedom to party. The zenith of a cultural upheaval and a new Woodstock for what was called the second summer of love. Of course I remember next to nothing about it. Well, I remember bits, I'm not a complete morom. Microdots were ingested, things get wobbly, it was a very hot day I seem to remember, and at one point they play the noise of a freezing cold wind through the PA. I watch about twenty thousand people stand and put their coats on. I also see a man who had no feet, but hoofs, clip-clop by. This wasn't just me, everyone in the group saw him.

I do however remember the Stone Roses themselves; we were some way away from the stage so it looked like a flea circus to me but it felt amazing. Standing in that field on that island in the middle of the River Mersey surrounded by all the weird fuck-ups my subculture could muster belting out the words to 'I Am The Resurrection' was pretty fucking awe-inspiring. Those moments of complete synchronicity are rare and fleeting and pass so quickly. Embrace it when it happens.

On the drive home we listen to a man screaming about a baby being on the roof of the coach for two hours; it's weird and frightening and does nothing to aid sleep. I get off the coach in Victoria at dawn, wide-eyed, freezing cold and shattered. Being with Brendan and Bifta made me feel happier and I could almost forget about home and the fact my friends had abandoned me. I return home and cry.

* * *

I really should describe to you all the injuries my mum received while she was drinking. I've no idea why but I feel it's important for you to realise what I see growing up.

One evening during a holiday in Wales, Mum and Dad go out to a party. I'm there too but I don't remember much about the party but I do remember leaving. It was cold, icy and misty. Mum, drunk, took a tumble down some stairs. It was brutal. She lay there a while, silent, then she began laughing and, by this time, people were out helping her up. She was embarrassed and waved them off. We went home and went to bed.

The next morning I hear a moan coming from their room. I was frightened so I ran in and found Dad trying to help Mum up onto her feet. Both of her legs were black, she'd broken *both* of them in the fall and she didn't even realise. Poor thing.

I have a terrible phobia of porcelain dolls. I come in from school one day, aged about twelve, people were there, I think my half-sister Debbie among them. There was a kerfuffle of sorts, a tall box on the floor. Not bothered, I go into the front room and take my shoes off and switch the telly on. I turn to look into the kitchen and I see my mum staggering towards me, tottering, teetering, pissed up, arms outstretched, she's coming towards me holding a large, white-faced porcelain doll with curly blonde hair, Victorian dress, bonnet of lace. She's also covered in bright-red blood, it pumps from a deep wound in Mum's hand. The doll is crying tears of blood, its gaze and jagged smile fixed as Mum stumbles towards me.

On hearing I'd returned from school she panics and tries to hide the abomination. Leaning on the back of a chair, it over-balances and she tumbles backwards, slashing her hand on a sharp metal edge on the top of the radiator; she didn't even know. She had to have lots of stitches.

When we lived at Ray Lodge, Mum was in bed early one evening, pissed. Me and Dad had a perfunctory conversation.

'Where's Mum?'

'Upstairs.'

'Is she asleep?'

'Yeah.'

'It's six o'clock!'

'Yeah.'

'Right.'

'Do you want any tea?'

'No. I'm going to my room. You okay?'

'Yeah. You?'

'Yeah.'

I run upstairs and put my music on low, headphones plastered to my head. I'm hiding, hoping she doesn't wake up. When you're the child of an alcoholic parent more often than not you breathe a sigh of relief when you come in and they're asleep. You pray they don't wake up. Suddenly I hear a noise that sounds something like a forty-seven-year-old woman falling down a set of steep wooden steps. I fly out of my room to find a forty-seven-year-old woman, my mum, lying at the bottom of a set of steep wooden steps. Dad runs out of the kitchen and we stare at each other. She lies semi-conscious at the base of the stairs groaning. We wait for an ambulance and in the hospital later they tell us she has snapped the bottom inch off her coccyx.

One day Mum bought some false fingernails and couldn't work out how to secure them to her existing nails. Under the influence, she finds superglue and bonds them onto her fingers. A few hours later she comes into my bedroom – we still live in Babbacombe Gardens at this point – the same house where Mum would let me and all my friends sit up in my bedroom smoking at lunchtime. The door would kick open and a chorus of 'Hello, Mrs Frost' would ring out, she'd bring us all cake and sandwiches, mugs of hot sweet tea. Her rationale? She'd rather us be safe and warm at home where she could keep an eye on us than out on the street. Cool.

Anyhoo, she knocks and comes in, she is in pain and crying. The ends of her fingers have swollen around the plastic nails and the superglue means she cannot get them off. Pleading with me to help her, my thirteen-year-old self now has to perform a kind of light home surgery. I think about the task in hand and settle upon three different-sized needles and a slim steak knife. I sit Mum down and put her massive red hands on a soft pillow. I put two bags of frozen peas on her hands and leave her for a bit.

After a while we begin. I start with the smallest needle and I try and push it between the falsie and her existing nail. (As an aside my mum always had lovely hands and nails, and had no need to use false nails.) Anyway, after much shrieking and tears I get the needle down there. I waggle it about until the small needle moves freely, I then put the bigger needle under and do the same, then the biggest needle and finally the steak knife, which I use to prise the nail up and off. Mum's relief is palpable. I repeat this ten times in total. What a palaver. It does however give me a taste for home surgery. Something I still do to this very day. If any of you ever need a skin tag or in-grown toenail removed give me a bell.

Finally, the big one . . . Death. She died. I think for a long while I couldn't shake the feeling that she killed herself. I was so cross. I was so cross for years and years. Being angry at a dead parent is such a destructive thing it will eat you up and eventually end you too.

I'd hate for you to read this and just imagine my mum being some horrible drunk monster. I'd also like to point out that for everything she did, everything that happened to her, and us, she was the only mum I had and I loved her and still love her with all of my heart. She was a good woman who had a very hard life and in the end just couldn't go on.

Before you judge a person it's important to realise and understand what may have happened in their life to make them become what they eventually become.

My mum was one of many from a very poor family. The older girls were expected to look after the younger ones – I think sometimes at the expense of their own liberty and education. Mum told me it was a hard life. Gran and Grampie were strict but they knew nothing else and that's what they had, in that cold house up on Hazel Grove.

When she was still just a girl my mum left home and married a man who was older than her. I think she must've thought she was being saved from her life as it was. She was wrong. Isolated high up in the hilltop farm in the tiny Pembrokeshire village of Maenclochog, she was trapped and isolated. That's when her punishment began. She quickly had three children, Marc, Ian and Debbie. My half-siblings. My mum was strong and opinionated and feisty, cheeky, mouthy, she didn't, wouldn't, couldn't ever back down. These traits are sadly a red rag to a bull when you're living with a violent alcoholic. He beat the shit out of that girl time and time again. Along the way my mum lost all her teeth. He'd knocked them all out. *He knocked them all out!* This is the reason my blood boils when I hear about a man hitting a woman.

One day when Mum was in her twenties the police parked outside the house. They waited for him to leave, came in, told her to pack a bag and they took her away, frightened that her husband would kill her. The police put Mum on a train to London. So after years of physical and mental abuse she had escaped. But at what cost?

She'd been forced to abandon the children she loved. She had to take what she could carry and go. Having a child myself I can only imagine how heartbreaking that must have been. It must be a million times harder for a mother. It was one of the things that changed her for ever. I don't think she really ever got over it. How could she? How could anyone? That's why drunk Mum was so overly protective, so overly affectionate. I hated it.

She clung on to me so tightly and in the end she lost me too. I found it hard to forgive myself for a long time. I couldn't help it though, that drinking of hers. I couldn't watch her kill herself and there was nothing I could do to help her. I couldn't, wouldn't, watch her die. Maybe a better person would've tried harder?

I was on the *Shaun of the Dead* DVD tour in Los Angeles in 2005 when my mum died. It was the night I'd met Tarantino for the first time. Edgar, Simon, QT, our beautiful friend Greg Nicotero and me. I think a few others popped in along the way too and it would get most raucous.

We met in a little Thai place on Sunset, opposite El Compadre, for me the best Mexican restaurant in West Hollywood. Steer clear – or not – of their giant strawberry margaritas. The weather was terrible – torrential rain, Angelinos are shit drivers in the rain. I heard that there were six hundred crashes on the highway that night.

I call my mum and dad that morning, Mum is drunk. She sounds hammered, slurring, stammering – fuck, I was angry with her. Short, curt, I wanted to wrap her quickly and talk to Dad. I was angry with him too for letting this happen. As I tried to sign off from her she said the last words I'd ever hear her speak.

'You'd love it here, Nins. It's snowing in the kitchen.'

'You what?'

'It's snowing in the kitchen.'

Lunacy. I was cross.

'What are you talking about? Put Dad on.'

Dad came on the phone.

'Is Mum okay?'

'Yeah, she's all right.'

'Is she pissed?'

'No.'

'Right, I only ask because she just told me it was snowing in the kitchen.'

There's a pause.

'Oh, right, okay.'

'I got to go, Dad. Love you.'

'I love you too.'

And that was the last time I ever spoke to my lovely, troubled, anguished, beautiful, passionate, funny, angry mum. I had a phone call from Dad while we were at dinner; I was relieved in a way because it meant I could excuse myself from Edgar and QT's baffling conversation about obscure Japanese cinema. I feared they'd unmask me as a fraud and I'd be banished from the table. Don't get me wrong, I like films, I really like films, but they LOVE cinema. They are true cinephiles. I can hold my own with any movie geek or film buff but they are something else. It's baffling to listen to, like mathematicians talking about triangles. I excuse myself and take the call. Dad's voice trembles.

'Mum's sick.'

I feel my heart beating in my mouth.

'How sick?'

'She's really sick, Nins.' Nins is what they called me.

I paused. There's a long silence. I take this information with a pinch of salt. Her drinking had put her in hospital many times. A couple of years before, I was told to prepare for the worst, an artery had ruptured in her throat after a coughing fit and they couldn't stop it bleeding. Doctors believed that she would bleed out right there and then. She didn't. They saved her. I think my parents went to hospital a lot without me knowing, without wanting to worry me.

With all this in mind I tell Dad I love him, tell him to keep me informed, I hang up and go back to the table. It takes me a while to shake off the call. Simon notices, of course, and quietly asks what's wrong. I tell him but he's been through it all with me before so he does his best to tell me it'll be cool. I relax, the night I was about to have with the boys and QT would do its best to erase the call pretty good.

Being there on Universal's dime doing press for the DVD's release meant we had a driver for the night. It's a lovely thing having a driver. It doesn't happen that often but when it does it's a real treat. It means you can really tie one on and not worry about cabs or distance or time. This is exactly what happened.

We finished dinner and nipped next door to a 'British' pub for a few pints; it was packed and people went crazy for QT and, by association, the *Shaun of the Dead* guys too. It was crazy, we decide to bail, and someone suggests we head to a strip club that QT knows. We bundle into the SUV and head to East LA.

After a while cruising through the city the car pulls into the parking lot of a rough-looking shit hole. Nervously we step from our fancy, chauffeur-driven car and are immediately eye-fucked to death by a gang of fearsome-looking Cholos hanging around a low rider. (This cliché may or may not have actually happened.)

The tension eases slightly when QT jumps out. The Latino community love QT. The owner bustles out and we are greeted like family. Hugs, hands shaken, slaps on the back etc.

This does nothing to calm me. I feel fucking queasy. I've always had a great trouble detector, often leaving a pub or club moments before it kicks off. My 'danger – you may be killed by men' alarm is screaming, I can't silence its buzzing. I stop sweating and my hands and feet become ice cold, my body is preparing itself for battle. If I think the alarm was loud outside it was nothing compared to when we went inside. My danger alarm explodes.

There are close to four hundred of what I guess I'd have to call, reluctantly and not wanting to play to an obvious cultural stereotype, Gang Bangers. They have face tats, hair nets, and gang signs are being flicked all over the place. Latino machismo is literally being squirted all over me.

We are stuffed, stuffed, into this large, low-ceilinged, red-walled strip club. In the middle of the place was a raised runway packed with attractively chubby Mexican strippers. Along the back wall runs a very long bar packed with one-eyed lunatics. It is, without doubt, one of the top five roughest places I've ever been in.

It's about to get a lot rougher as the owner decides to shut the club early and turf out four hundred drunk, dangerous, very horny vatos, so we can have this deep-red hell all to ourselves! For a moment I'm slightly concerned we might get shot. I glance across at Edgar who looks pale and weak. Simon and I hold hands secretly for comfort.

We relax now it's just us and realise just how big the place is. Friends of friends have joined and all in all there are probably twenty of us. It's a good gang of blokes and we have a great laugh.

At one point QT sticks a big roll of dollar bills into my paw and assures me I'm going to need it. He smiles and waggles his brows suggestively. I smile. It begins. I spend two hours stuffing George Washingtons into the knickers of sexy brown girls. Much tequila is drunk, we laugh like idiots. My dinnertime phone call ebbs away from my memory with every dollar bill I twang into a G.

The MC brings us to attention, a show is about to begin. We gather around the stage and he announces the next girl, she is small, chubby and sexy. Music kicks in, it's a song I know, I've heard it before, it's a track on the *From Dusk till Dawn* soundtrack. If you've ever seen *From Dusk till Dawn* you'll know there's a scene where our heroes, now unwittingly trapped in the Titty Twister, sit up at the runway watching Salma Hayek do a horny snake dance. The thrilling denouement sees the sexy Vampire Queen Hayek sticking her foot into QT's mouth and pouring whisky down her leg straight into his gob. It's a sexy scene. It's also a scene that is now getting a twenty-five-cent re-creation right in front of me. I exchange looks with Simon and Edgar. We all laugh so hard.

At the height of the dance the chubby girl in the yellow bikini sticks her foot in QT's mouth and instead of pouring whisky down her hairy leg she opens a can of Tecate beer. It was amazing. I felt honoured to have witnessed this. I'm happy and for the first time actually begin to like the Hollywood thing. I like QT a lot. He's always been really good to me.

We leave this beautiful hell as the sun is beginning to rise. By the time I get back to The Standard I'm glowing and hammered. I get into my room, collapse on my bed and sleep.

I'm asleep a couple of hours before the high-pitched vibrations of my silenced phone wake me up. It's Dad with an update no doubt.

'Hello?' Nothing.

'Dad?' Silence. I get *the feeling* ringing in my ears. An orange flash that begins at my feet and moves north at the speed of light.

'Dad?' He breaks the silence.

'Mum died, Nins.'

'When?'

'Just now.'

It's my turn to be silent. I listen to the sound of my world collapsing in on itself.

After Debbie died I had counselling for a while although it didn't last long. I was smarter than the therapist and he offered me nothing new by way of personal insight. Although he did ask me what I'd like to happen, what I'd like to happen to Mum, to Dad, to me, to us. At the time, Mum was really sick and I loved Dad so much, it was hard seeing him having to care for this old woman. He was a remarkably selfless person. I thought about the therapist's question and I answered honestly. I told him that I wished my mum were dead. It was an answer that has haunted me ever since I heard Dad tell me that she was dead. I didn't mean it.

'I'll have to call you back, Dad. I love you.'

'I love you.'

My hands shake. My ears ring. I let out a noise. It is primal, it is guttural, I heave grief all over the floor, all over the toilet.

I can't believe it. I stand blinking, naked in the middle of that room, trying to talk, jabbering, jabbering, turning around in a circle, my computer is misfiring badly. I need someone, I need

Simon, I have to call Simon. I dial his room. Please be awake. He answers. He's groggy.

'Hello?'

I can't talk. I know exactly what's going to happen when I hear my boy's voice. I knew it would send me over the edge. I make a noise, the noise sounds like a gorilla punching me in the solar plexus. He knows. There's a level of instant knowing at the sound of a person who's lost someone close, really close, one of the big seven, Brother, Sister, Mother, Father, Husband, Wife, Child.

I drop the phone and slump to the floor. Simon couldn't have been more than two minutes but it was a fucking long, lonely two minutes.

I'd already lost two half-sisters and a half-brother at this point so I thought I was getting good at this grief thing. I was so fucking wrong.

Grief, like strong LSD, comes in waves. There are moans, weeping, tears, laughter, silence, random thought processes I have no way of controlling. I have no control. Simon grabs the situation by the balls and phone calls are made. Arrangements. Flights changed. Meetings are cancelled. The *Shaun of the Dead* press tour is over. My sense of responsibility and work ethic means I'm sad it's over but I can't go on. I can't do it. Nothing matters to me anymore except being with my dad.

Simon and me are on a BA flight that night. Sitting at the gate people ask us for photos. It's hard to say no to a fan especially if it's a kid, we had photos. I'd hate to see those pictures.

We board the 747 and sit upstairs in Business Class. While waiting for the doors to close a funny thing happens. A man, young, English, early thirties maybe, is also sitting up in Business Class, and he's what cockneys might call a Proper

Cunt. My backstory for him – I create a backstory for almost everyone I meet – was this: he's the young up-and-coming director of promos, ad campaigns, that sort of thing. He's arrogant and thinks he's entitled because he has a bit of money. That said, there's no way he paid for his own ticket. No way. People up in First and Business hardly ever do.

He's with an American girl, tall and very beautiful, catwalk model beautiful. A fit girl like this will always multiply the arrogance of a proper arsehole. He'll always feel like he needs to be edgier, more outspoken, more opinionated than anyone else because deep down he knows that she may jump ship at any second.

They were both being very loud, complaining noisily. They'd been denied an upgrade and now he finds his shitty, wide, tons of legroom seat has a tiny smudge of melted chocolate on it, he wants – no, demands – to be moved. The attendant sighs, she doesn't need this shit. Model girl still wants an upgrade but there are no seats. The flight is still full! The attendant, calm, professional, quietly spoken offers to put a blanket on his seat. It is literally all she can do unless he wants a downgrade? Model is starting to blame Dickhead for this terribly unfair business. He needs to save face and fast. He stands. This is going to be good. I forget my woes for a moment and look at Simon who gives me a 'this is going to be good' look. Dickhead looks around, takes a breath and declares . . .

'Fuck this. We're getting off.'

Wow. Big move. Big statement. She'll love that, I bet she has a wide-on. The Model agrees. After a lot of 'look at me'-style kerfuffle, they leave accompanied by some light applause.

We are now forced to sit at the gate for a further forty minutes waiting for their bags to be offloaded. Finally the doors are

closed; we push back and take off. I'm going home. I'm frightened. The ding noise dings and the seatbelt signs go off. We are
now free to walk about the cabin.

Two minutes later the lovely stewardess who had been
through so much shit with that pair of pricks swings by and
reveals two passports! One British, one American. What she is
showing us are their passports that he'd shoved down the side
of the seat! In the rush to get off the plane they'd left their fucking documents on board! Karma right there! BOOM! My mum
died, fuck you, you Chocolate-Seat Helmets.

* * *

I digress. This is all to come. For now I was still in fucking Ray
Lodge. Only one thing helps me escape my fucking pain and I
start to hit that shit very hard indeed.

I really liked my P&O teammate Brendan Heggarty. It's
amazing how a few years make all the difference in terms of
friendship. When I was his younger brother's friend, Brendan
hated us because we were little jerks. Ten years later, it all
changes. I was still a lowly freight rookie while Bren was a man
going places in the shipping world. But during our time at
P&O he never once fires a phlegm-centred foil ball at me. Not
once! On the contrary, I think he was the person who helped
save me from myself.

Working was my escape from a totally shit home life. I hated
my life, I felt so alone, so lonely. I didn't know what to do. I
found it all too much watching my mum kill herself. Watching
my dad, a shell of a man, broken, quiet, absent. My friends
absent, no girlfriend, me having to live in a shit estate.

'Oh boo hoo! Poor me.'

I think it broke me though. I was seventeen or eighteen years old. I didn't realise what depression was for another twenty years or so.

One afternoon in the office Brendan pulled me aside, suggested we go and have a beer after work. It's what geezers do when they need to put the world to rights. I met him in the Valentine in Gants Hill, a place I used to frequent when I was fifteen or so. We all hung out in pubs back then, playing the endless game of cat and mouse to see who could get served.

I think Brendan saw in me something he might've had in himself. After a while and several beers later he talks to me about his time abroad, talks to me about his travelling adventures. He tells me about a place he went to that helped him sort his shit out.

Like the French Foreign legion, this socialist commune accepts people from all religions, all colours, all creeds, no questions asked. All you need to do is work. He's talking about a kibbutz. My mind starts to race. I could go. I could leave and start again, be someone else. Leave this fear and paranoia here in England.

If it hadn't been for Bren's intervention I think I might have died. Everything was killing me.

The problem was I had next to no money. Fortunately for me, back then in the early nineties we didn't have the instant connectivity there is now, banks didn't talk to each other as much, this was perfect for what I needed. I found a place that had four or five different banks pretty close together. I started at 11.59 p.m. and stopped at 12.01 a.m., going from one cash-point to the next drawing out all the money I could. I managed to get almost £700. Minted. Let's roll.

I found a company called Project 67 in Edgware Road that could get me to Israel and place me on a kibbutz.

I don't remember what my mum and dad's reaction was to me leaving. I think they were shocked but they didn't try and stop me. If this is what I wanted then they'd support my decision. We had a little farewell BBQ at Uncle Brian's house where I was presented with a shiny new backpack.

Mum kept a stiff upper lip until we got to the airport where she crumbled slightly. Poor thing. Dad's wounds were beginning to scab over so he was on good form, cuddling Mum and cracking shit puns. We had a three-way cuddle and that was that. I was gone. When you share joy and tenderness and sadness at the prospect of a long time away from people you love it's easy to forget for a moment the reason you're leaving.

Part Two

I had NO idea what I was getting into. No idea whatsoever. That said, I was happy to be away. I immediately felt lighter, my soul felt lighter. I liked being on my own. Anything that happened to me now was completely my own doing and completely my own responsibility. I had no one else to blame but me and I liked it.

The El Al plane landed late at night in Tel Aviv's Ben Gurion International Airport. Wow. My mind was completely blown. What a place. It reminded me of Mos Eisley spaceport. It was the hottest, most alien place I'd ever been. I couldn't believe you could reach somewhere like this by simply flying east in a plane for four hours.

It was amazing, frightening and utterly beguiling. The noise of mopeds, alien languages being coughed up into the air. Crowded mouthfuls of brown and broken teeth. Hundreds of cigarettes being smoked by men in long white robes. And then there were the soldiers, which of course meant guns. Lots and lots of guns.

A few of us who'd come through with the same operator bumble together, terrified, shuffling around, not knowing what to do at all. We wait alone for ages, we're approached by men who raise their eyebrows and finger our shirts. Some of the blonde girls have their hair sniffed. Not me though, no one tries

to sniff my hair. Not then! By and by, Project 67 (the tour operator) vehicles turn up, names are shouted out according to
kibbutz. Goodbyes and good lucks are uttered and one by one
they disappear. It feels like waiting to be picked for football. In
the end the van that was coming for me and three or four others
didn't materialise.

The rep sticks me and the leftovers in a hot, loud taxi. It
takes us to a youth hostel behind Ben Yehuda Street. I'm led
with the others through a maze of hot, humid alleys into a
tiny lift in an art deco building. I generally don't like staying
over at other people's houses, I hated it as a child and even
today if there's a chance I can have my own bed, I'll absolutely
take it.

Now, however, I have no choice. I stand in the reception of
my first ever youth hostel. I actually feel homesick, I want my
mum, it's an unfamiliar feeling for me. To want my mum.
Maybe it's not weird for me. I think I always wanted my mum
really. Just not the Special Brew version.

All around reception are seasoned, battered-looking travellers, all dust and beaded goatees, they sense the freshness of
my meat. They know something I don't, they have the look. I'd
get it eventually but it would take a while. To be fair they may
have also been looking at my brand-new Berghaus rucksack
(65L), a gift from Uncle Brian and Auntie Francis. God, I must
have looked so young. I *was* so young.

I got checked in for one night – the next morning I'd go to
the Project 67 office and be assigned a new kibbutz placement.
For tonight though I'd be free to kick up my heels in Tel Aviv!

I'm assigned a space in a dorm. Four hard, metal, functional
bunk beds in a very dark room. Wet towels hang from a spider
web of twine strung across the room. Bags litter the floor. I see

the shape of people sleeping under thin sheets. It's so hot, and so smelly. I find a bed with a free mattress and haul my bag up. My bunk was the top one, there's someone's stuff on the bed beneath mine but they're not there. I don't unpack. I grab my secret bum bag, the kind you hide under all your clothes and reveal to would-be robbers the moment you have to haul your new shirt up to pay for anything, and meet the others in reception.

I buy a cold can of beer. It is called Goldstar, she is a stranger to me at first but would soon become my friend and part-time lover. She is so cold and so wet and delicious I devour her right there in the lobby. I don't care who sees or hears my groans. I must imbibe her.

I think there were four or five of us in our little team of refugees, other forgotten souls like me, left over from the selection process. I don't remember anything about them. Soz. Not names, not the girl:boy ratio. I'm not even sure what we did, not really. I vaguely remember walking around, eating a fucking great falafel and drinking beers. Then at one point we're all on the beach. It felt so strange and different to me. Who knew that by taking one flight everything I had on my shoulders would be gone. It was that easy. (Of course it wasn't, but sitting on that warm night beach, flirting and drinking beer felt a world away from Ray Lodge.)

We go back to the hostel, a small group of tipsy, noisy kids on holiday. I stumble into my assigned cell. Beds that had previously been filled with human-shaped lumps were now empty and empty beds now full of breathing, snoring human-shaped lumps.

Being a Bigmun there are universal truths you must quickly accept – limitations, one might say. Climbing silently up a flimsy bunk bed while a bit pissed without it shaking to fuck is one of those things. And volleyball.

Sure I made a bit of noise, and you can't just climb into a bed and lie completely motionless, there's always a period of adjustment and re-adjustment. It's how it is. Maybe the bolts were a bit loose? The bed did look very old, worn. It did wobble, though, I'll give you that. It wobbled. In hindsight I accept that now.

The motion of my ascent settles by and by. I lie there knowing what was coming next, knowing what I have to do, I don't want to but I'm compelled like a Wolf or Chihuahua and it begins, I roll and turn a while trying to get comfortable. I come around for the third or fourth comfort roll and I notice an old man standing five inches from my face.

He has long white hair in a loose plait and a white beard. He is shirtless although he wears a fetching denim gilet. I then note that in his left hand is a shiny ten-inch hunting knife. I say ten inches – it could've been eight. We regard each other in silence for an age.

'Hello.' I babble, he stares, unflinching, then speaks.

'I was in Vietnam.'

'Oh, an American!' Why did I decide to play it so chipper, it was an odd choice. His cold blue eyes blink for the first time and he heads back down to his place.

Fuck it's hot! Don't move. You'll be killed. When I was little I'd wake up and run to get into bed with Mum and Dad. It was always a massive mistake but I never learnt my lesson. Once in the bed they'd fall asleep leaving me wide awake, sandwiched between the two of them unable to move. This was me now. Don't move, for fucksakes don't move. I lie there most of the night terrified John Rambo might push that long piece of cold, forged steel up through the series one boxset-thin mattress and into my ribs and soft, fragile organs within.

At some point I nod off, when I wake up it's morning and I'm still terrified so I lift silently into the air and still horizontal I levitate off the bunk and gently land on the floor, silent like an autumn leaf. There's not a wobble in sight. The bunk beneath mine is empty, the bed is made with a coin-bouncing, military precision. My nightmare has gone. He was so lucky.

Later that morning I appear at the Project 67 office in Tel Aviv. Apologies are made, as are phone calls, and I'm shown a list of kibbutzim with available places for volunteers. Some of the others have places already in mind: a couple want to go down near Eilat for the beach and constant sun, some near Jerusalem for the history, Haifa for the . . . container port? I chose one at random. I say random – I really fancied living high up in the mountains, all the other would-be volunteers wanted the relentless organ-frying heat of the Sinai Desert. That was not for me so I chose a kibbutz called Bar-Am, high in the mountains in the far north of the country about two hundred metres from the Lebanese border. I'd considered climate over safety. What a bell-end.

I was given enough shekels for the bus ride north, a set of instructions and a contact list. An hour later I was in the old Tel Aviv bus station, hung-over and famished. It was here I stumbled into my first piece of good falafel-fortune. I find one stand among many and it does great falafel, they have a unique selling point and it's this: as long as your pitta bread is intact you get free refills of the crispy falafel balls. What a joyous discovery! I find the secret is applying the minimum amount of tahini. It's not easy but it ensures you keep the bread intact for longer. I think I had three refills. It's enough. Three is more than enough for even the chubbiest of Rabbis.

It's almost time for my bus. I grab a cola-style drink and a bar of chocolate with cartoon basketballs depicted on the wrapper and get on the coach, which dreamily is air-conditioned, lovely! I settle down for the ride, I like bus journeys in foreign countries, it gives you a chance to see a lot relatively quickly. The journey takes about four hours. Sitting alone on that bus gave me a chance to think about where I was and why I was there.

Tel Aviv, apart from the art deco sections, which are beautiful, and the beach, again Copacabana-esque in its loveliness, was a bit of a hole. Don't get me wrong, I saw less than five per cent of the place but none of it looked finished to me. Maybe it wasn't? Bomb damage? The Intifada? First Gulf War? I guess these things all take their toll on a place.

Once out of Tel Aviv things brightened up a bit. The weather was great, on my left I could see the bright blue Med and I was heading north fast. I like moving, north, south, whatever, just keep moving. Between Tel Aviv and Haifa is a dense corridor of industry, a busy, heavily populated strip of land sandwiched between the sea and the desert. That's Israel all over.

We stop in Haifa and I have to change buses. I'm stood loafing around eating another falafel, of course. I watch a car, can't quite remember which type, but if I had to hazard a guess I'd say a white Peugeot 306, it hammers into the station at pace and an elderly, kindly-looking Palestinian man jumps out and leaves the engine running. A small amount of hell breaks loose, a light panic rises among the folk, soldiers begin hesitantly to remove their battle rifles from their shoulders and start shouting things in Hebrew. People swarm away from the car, sirens begin. This is a fucking car bomb.

I'm about to be torn apart, first by the concussive blump of the pressure wave and then by razor-sharp sections of the white Peugeot 306. The panic begins to reach a crescendo and the kindly Palestinian man comes running back out of a shop holding an armful of bread. He is immediately surrounded by twenty IDF soldiers pointing Galil assault rifles at him. It is now the Palestinian man's turn to panic. Poor fucker. He only ran in to get some bread, he's now one bad decision, one quick movement away from being killed. He's roughly pulled from the car and led away. The mood immediately lifts as people laugh at the crushed loaves on the pavement. I'm stunned. I stagger onto my bus and leave, heading north towards the mountains.

My bus stops, it'd been nice and quiet before now. The doors hiss open and the bus fills with essentially thirty or so catwalk models. Sexy sexy sexy women in army uniforms carrying a selection of sexy assault rifles. I was frightened and nervous and terribly horny. The hot girl warrior that sits next to me senses my horniness, she doesn't return my desperate attempt at a smile, she moves her Galil assault rifle around so it's now sitting between us. Bit rude.

The warm weather and the gentle bumping of the bus sends her to sleep pretty quickly. As we bump along the muzzle of her rifle comes to rest on my thigh (as a rule heavy assault rifles don't really come to rest, they dig in and this one was really digging in).

I'd never seen a gun until two days ago and now there are probably sixty on this bus alone, one of which is leaving a red circle on my chubby white thigh. I decide to push it off a bit. As soon as my paw brushes the unrelenting iron of her Jewish kill-broom her eyes spring open and her finger skips off the trigger guard and onto the trigger. How did she know?

'The, the, your, um, your gun is digging into my leg, miss.'

She huffs loudly, she's starting to fall for me, I can tell. The rifle's pulled and repositioned away from me. Please don't go off. I fidget nervously. I press my head against the vibrating window and doze off.

When I wake up the bus is quiet and almost empty. The war models got off at a kibbutz called Sasa. I wish I could go there. The next stop is me.

I'm always a bit sad arriving somewhere after a long journey when it's dark. I want to see what a place looks like. That said, I like the surprise of seeing it the next morning but I guess I'm impatient like that. Night is falling rapidly and the bus belches me out. The doors hiss and it rumbles away leaving me stood on my own, surrounded by sticky warmth and a cacophony of the loudest night sounds imaginable. It's the first time I've ever heard cicadas and it's fucking loud and beautiful.

In the failing light I shuffle downhill towards a brightly lit guard hut. Seeing me, the soldiers inside trudge out, rifles slung low, they clearly don't see me as much of a threat. What they're guarding is a massive gate, thick steel, bright yellow. Fences run off left and right to who knows where. The ten-foot-high perimeter is topped in acres of razor wire. It looks like a category A prison, a place where only the hardest fuckheads need apply, but it wasn't that, it was simply a farm.

When I see the rifles I slow, then stop, there's a slight standoff while I'm worked out. After speaking Hebrew to one another they wave me forward. More Hebrew is spoken. I show them my passport and the letter from Project 67. There's head nodding. This is good. The soldier inside does something to a lever or a button and an orange light starts spinning on the gate. The giant portal slowly pulls back. I wonder briefly if they have a T-Rex. I'd like to say I remember a giant siren making an ERR URR-ERR URR noise as the gate withdraws but that would be false.

I'm given directions to a work office, a small room under the dining hall in the main building of the kibbutz. Even in the tightening twilight I could see the place was covered in trees. It was dark and warm, the whole place smells like pine and forests. I'm not in Kansas anymore.

The release and relief from my responsibilities mean the tiredness has caught up with me. The bright lights hurt my eyes, and people stare. I was lost and new and gleaming white and everyone could see it. I was relieved to be there, proud at what I'd done but feeling very alone. A sudden dawning of what I'd done shuddered over me.

I knock on the door. Someone shouts something from inside and I enter. A woman who looks like Nana Mouskouri sits behind a table that's stacked high with paper. She stares at me through her thick, black-framed glasses. She is the embodiment of the seventies. It was 1991.

'*Ken!*' (Hebrew for yes.) I shuffle in, my rucksack banging the frame of the wooden door. She smokes and tuts and refuses to look at me. She gestures at a chair. I struggle to sit. I give her my letter. She reads it and finally she regards me. Softening slightly.

This is Vicki. Over the next couple of months I get to know her and really like her. She was a hard woman, blunt, direct, no fucking around. She wasn't everyone's cup of tea and didn't suffer fools gladly but I was always really cheeky and she liked it.

Vicki was the leader of the volunteers, our mother away from home. She drew up the work schedules, gave us what we needed, at times told us off. She was an avid smoker. She also had a little dog that followed her everywhere, a mean and nasty little dick. I'm getting ahead of myself but the little dog was later badly injured after being hit by a car. I think it must've severed his spine, he followed Vicki down to her office one Tuesday as normal but the little thing was dragging his back legs behind it. Limp, dead. It didn't seem to dampen his spirits anyway. He was still a mean son of a bitch. I asked Vicki what was going to happen to him. 'I have to put him down.' I laughed, disbelieving her. She didn't laugh. She meant it. Two hours later there's the noise of a single shot from a high-powered 9mm handgun. We never see him again.

This was a way down the line though. For now she looked at me like a sweaty human shit sitting behind her desk, which is exactly what I was.

Kibbutzniks have a wariness of volunteers, the travellers so necessary to them at the busy harvest time but generally overlooked as just a bunch of sex-crazed alcoholics who needed to be avoided at all costs. In hindsight they were actually spot on. It takes a lot of hard work and time to gain the trust of the Israelis.

The details of what happened after this point are a little hazy. I have a memory of other Israelis getting involved and me being led up to the dining room. It was massive, more than capable of fitting all six hundred residents in comfortably, which it did every Friday during Shabbat meal and various high days and holidays.

I sit alone watching other people eat supper, I enjoy the pleasant murmur of a conversation I can't understand. Vicki returns with a housing list and I'm assigned a bed in a four-man room, she offers me dinner, and I accept. I wish I hadn't the moment I see the horrors on offer. I have never seen so much veg and salad and unknown grains and pulses in my life. I never realised that food came in so many colours. For me food had always been brown and beige and a crossover between brown and beige, a colour I'd come to know as Broige. Also some yellow. The bread was nice though and the butter was diamond white in colour, I should say that ice-white butter takes some getting used to for an English like me, for the first few weeks it feels like I'm eating dripping.

I eat, I try and eat, I pack up my tray and then I'm led down to where I'd be living. It was a nice gentle stroll down-hill to the two, two-storey blocks that housed the animals, us. They were squat white-ish buildings with an area of tattered lawn in the middle. People sit around swigging from bottles, laughing, a fire blazes. I see a young man with a guitar and I panic slightly, fuck it. I steady my ship. A new start means it was a time to accept new things, new people. Just let it go, Nick, please, please just let it go, it's just a guitar for fucksakes.

I'm introduced to people. New people. Something I'm not really very good at.

'Hello,' someone says.

'Also hello.' It's standard basic human interaction. I'm terrible at it and it frightens me. I smile a bit, I seem like an oaf, I'm embarrassed and shy.

'Where you from?'

'London.'

'Cool. See you later.'

'Okay. Goodbye.'

The blocks are tatty, paint peels and there's broken glass on the floor, a million fag butts, a dented kettle lies dying in one of the hallways. There's very loud music, chatting, laughter. I buzz a bit, the first inkling that I could grow to love it here.

My new room's upstairs, first on the left. The door's blue and covered in stickers, they do a bad job of hiding the odd boot and fist hole. There are three other boys in that room and by god I can't for the life of me remember who they were. Please forgive me. In that tiny room were four beds, four tiny metal-framed beds with pancake-thin mattresses. The bed in the bottom left of the room is free. I unroll my new sleeping bag and stick it on the bed.

I get shown around, the shower room has many cracked tiles. The toilets are thick with limescale, like a Mother Shipton's cave of chuds if you will. The place is dirty, cobwebs every-where, vast cathedrals for our arachnid overlords. Other rooms are visited, cheery 'Hellos' are waved. People come and look. It was always a thing when someone new turned up. I was led to the common room. Wow, what chaos. What a shit box. I love it. It was two rooms knocked into one; the walls were covered in graffiti, there was a kettle, a toaster and a big old TV bolted into a large wooden box on the wall.

About thirty people were lying on the floor on cushions watching MTV and drinking heavily. Some girls made toast and passed it around the room. I did a lot of awkward, what I like to call Edgar Wright-style waves. It's basically mouthing the word 'Haloo' silently and waving at the same time.

The deal on the kibbutz is this: you're there to work! That's it. You work for six days a week, six or seven hours a day, and in return they feed you, clothe you, give you alcohol and ciga-rettes and anything else you need/want, you even get paid a little bit, almost £30 a month! Sweet. They didn't necessarily care what you did, except fighting and drugs – fighting and drugs were out. Anything else as long as you worked hard seemed to be fair game.

In the summer you started early to avoid the crushing heat of the day. It meant you finished early too. Your working day was 6 a.m. until 12.30 p.m. and then the rest of the day was your own. Simples.

In the winter it was cold and dark in the morning so you'd start a bit later which meant you'd finish later. Some jobs, like picking cotton or working in the vast fishponds, were about an hour's drive away in the superheated Bekaa Valley. You'd start at 4 a.m. and be finished by 11.00 a.m. Lovely.

That first morning though my little travel alarm goes off and I groggily get up and follow the others. My first ever job was to work in the apple-packing factory. If kibbutz jobs were the army, apple packing was definitely the infantry. A boring, easy, tedious, meat and potatoes kibbutz job.

The factory was pretty big, exciting, it was the first factory I'd ever been in. The main section was a cavernous warehouse with a brick room on one side and offices up to the left, in the centre was a giant machine. The apple packer. I was instructed to sit at a low stool on one side of a long conveyer belt. Above was a machine that channelled empty apple boxes down to us ready to be filled. We all sit waiting.

A round and chunky Israeli man with tight permed hair bustles to the front of the conveyor and utters the words I will hear many times, 'Guyth come to thee pleath.' This is Eli Azer and he has a lithp. He's one of the good guys, quick to laugh, and heavy handed with the volunteers he liked. I was to receive over six hundred dead arms from him in the next few months.

Later I'd do impressions of Eli Azer to make the other volunteers laugh. Boom! Dead arm! When the phone rang in the office a loud bell would ring across the whole factory, it was always for Eli Azer. A voice on an intercom would cut the radio and the factory-wide PA squeaked to life, 'Eli Azer, Eli Azer, *telefon mer ve shtayim*.' Essentially it means 'Eli Azer, telephone line 102.'

I discovered I could do a pretty good impression of the voice from the office, so sometimes I'd sneak off the work line, use the phone as an intercom and say the words, which would then blare out across the factory. We would laugh so hard watching Eli Azer trot to the phone to find no one there. Eventually they caught on and I was rumbled. Even Eli Azer found it funny in a kind of 'now you're going to get a really fucking dead arm' kind of way.

That was to come. For now he kept his distance from me. I was an unknown. He, like all the Israelis, had to ascertain what my work ethic was. Am I there to work or am I just going to drink and fuck about? I guess it's also some kind of defence mechanism; being raised and living on a kibbutz means that people leave, volunteers by their very definition are bound to be transient. Don't get close to us. You'll be hurt when we go.

We gather round and watch Eli Azer pull apples from a hopper; he packs them with a speed I never could've imagined from sausage fingers like his. What a talent. There I was thinking you'd just stick them in a punnet. Each different size and type of apple had a different technique. A technique designed to fit exactly the right amount into each punnet. Clever. Easy. Boring.

After the lesson a buzzer sounds and the machine creaks into life. The apples tumble down onto the conveyor, you pack them, face them up real pretty then you do it again and again and again. Once you'd done two boxes, you'd drop your little packing plinth down and roll them onto another conveyor that led to a workstation we called Wrapping and Stacking. This was where the cool kids in the factory worked. Jobs on the kibbutz were very hierarchical. The longer you'd been there, the harder you worked, the better job you got.

Later in my kibbutz experience I myself would become a Wrapper and a Stacker. I'd intercept the apples as they thundered down the roller thing and sling the boxes, with great accuracy and just the right amount of power, onto a pallet until they were seven or so feet high. Four cardboard corners would be secured around the stack and then you'd use a really annoying ratchet machine to bind the whole wobbly lot together. It was a good fucking job. If you worked strong and fast you could move thirty tons of apples a day. It was a point of pride to see how many tons you could shift. After doing this job for a couple of weeks you got giant, well-defined forearms and shoulders. Furious wanking also helped.

Whatever jobs you did – except if you worked down in the fields – you'd work for a couple of hours before breakfast, and it took some getting used to. When I wake up I usually need to eat immediately. A hooter would sound and we'd hammer up the hill towards the dining room to feed. Breakfast was rushed and primal; as a volunteer I was hungry most of the time. We'd spend a lot of time talking about the food we missed and what we'd love to eat right now – weirdly it was usually roast dinners or McDonalds with the odd Full English thrown in for good measure.

I was a fussy little sod back then when it came to food. Crisps aside, I essentially didn't eat any vegetables. It was like this until I was thirty or so when my taste buds changed and I couldn't get enough of the things. At this point though I'm a strict carnivore, crisps aside, so being in Israel surrounded by nothing but crisp, fresh salads was an absolute fucking nightmare. I eventually found things that worked for me and stuck to them.

Breakfast was all about the eggs on toast, soft boiled eggs, mashed up in a bowl with mayo and plenty of black pepper. The problem with breakfast eggs on kibbutz though is they never seemed to be fully cooked. I love yolk and I think yolk with cracked, black pepper to be one of the greatest flavour combinations known to man, but I hate food which is gluey or snot-like or shrouded in jelly. I was in Japan once with the lovely Joe Cornish and had to eat a lot of McDonalds as everything came shrouded in gluey phlegm. (A slight over-exaggeration but you know what I mean.)

Sometimes at breakfast I'd open nine eggs just to find one usable egg. Let me tell you a 9:1 usable egg ratio is a really poor egg ratio. All those wasted embryos! The food was generally bad, not bad per se but bad for me. That said, the longer you were there the more scams and angles you could find.

If you knew where to look in the kitchen, what pots or pans to peer into, you could find the delicately poached chicken breasts they cooked specifically for the elderly Holocaust survivors. This insensitive scam, though delicious and meaty, was essentially a bit naughty. It was fine when it was just me on the sniff but when the other meat-craving volunteers caught on the gig was up. We were warned off and rightly so. Imagine surviving the horrors of Auschwitz only to have some fucking Herbert half-inch the only food left you can stomach.

Still, you could supplement meagre rations a few ways, toast and ketchup being one of them. I still to this day love toast and ketchup. Another was to befriend the guards in the guard

TRUTHS, HALF TRUTHS AND LITTLE WHITE LIES

house. They always had tons of food. On a Friday night after the disco (more on the disco later) I discovered that the soldiers would cook chips. Wonderful handcut, proper chips. The Israelis would fry half an onion in the oil first before putting the potatoes in. It gave the chips a unique oniony flavour that was delicious and quite unforgettable.

If you were nice/pissed enough and hilarious they'd give you a big bowl of those lovely, oniony bastards. A few times they'd even drop me back to the block in their battle jeep afterwards. I'd usually try and ponce fags en route too. Naughty.

After breakfast we'd amble back and pack more apples until the coffee break at about ten-thirty. Coffee break was fun, we'd gather in the break room and the Israelis would bring out nice biscuits for dunking. It was a chance to chat about packing apples and have a laugh with our Hebrew overlords. After break I'd have another couple of easy hours' work and that was that, the work was done.

Essentially every day, every week, on the kibbutz was the same. It was like being in a prison for alkies. Any deviation was to be mistrusted and embraced. Apple packing was the first job most people did. Generally you did one job for weeks, if you showed a natural flair for one thing chances are your gang boss would want to keep you there.

Before apples could be packed they had to be picked and that meant working in the orchards which were lovely. This was one of the kibbutz's main jobs in the summer. They'd need all the volunteers they could get to bring in the harvest. I liked working in the orchard, it was hot, the sun was always shining and you could eat all the apples you wanted.

You also got these lovely buckets made of canvas that you'd strap on with a harness (I love a job with equipment). Once the basket was full you'd shout the Hebrew word for basket, '*SAL!*' Someone would turn up, take your basket, give you a new one and on you'd go. It was great, you'd chat, talk about food, who you fancied, who was fucking whom, music, family, anything, sometimes silence would reign and you'd enjoy that, it was sweet.

The volunteers, like me, were fuck-ups from all nations. Adventurers, drifters, gap-year kids or people just heading through. Swedes, Danes, South Africans, Kiwis, Australians and loads of Brits make for a heady mix of ideas, cultures and boozing styles. As a guy on kibbutz the holy grail was a new group of Swedish girls arriving. What a treat, so blonde and shiny, hair glinting like freshly cut gold.

Water and coffee were very important things in the orchards, if either was left back in kibbutz it'd cause a real stink. Someone would have to go back. We'd take our midmorning break sitting in the shade of the apple trees, they'd bring ice creams, what a wonderful treat. Sometimes while picking you'd hear a volunteer shriek loudly. It'd be one of two things, either chameleons, which took great pleasure in grabbing on to the hands that reached into leafy canopies looking for apples, or little furry grey tarantulas that would nestle under the stones and logs at the base of the tree. Terrifying. Sometimes if you were lucky you'd see volunteers stumbling backwards screaming with a chameleon attached to their arm. Big funs.

The kibbutz had acres of orchards; one of my favourites was right on the border with Lebanon; actually most of the kibbutz was on the border with Lebanon, but this orchard was *right* on the border. We'd heard a rumour that if you threw something at the security fence (a fence that runs the entire length of Northern Israel, Lebanon, Syria and Jordan) tanks would come! Working in the closest orchard our curiosity got the better of us. After much hysterical debate, one of us did it. A big apple was found and we – notice I'm saying we – flung the fucker over the kibbutz fence and into the security fence beyond. The first time we did it we absolutely shit ourselves panicking, we lay trembling under the trees, I needed the toilet so badly. After some silence and nothing happening, we first heard and then watched two tanks rumble up to where we'd tossed the apple. Holy Balls. This was the coolest thing ever. After the first time it got less stressful and slightly less fun but we endured. I thought it important for the defence of Israel that the tank crews be well drilled.

I've always thought that if I didn't do what I do now I'd want to work on the land or as a water sheriff. The kibbutz was generally perfect for this, plenty of chances to be outside.

So when I looked at my work rota for the week and saw I'd been assigned to work in their plastic factory it was a real blow. The only upside, it was air-conditioned. Lovely, lovely, cold, really expensive air. The plastic factory had two basic jobs you could do. One was done dressed in a white clean-room hygiene suit. You looked like the Oompa Loompas that send Mike TV across the studio in *Willy Chocolate and the Wonka Factory*.

It wasn't a fun job, the stuffy Israelis in that factory meant chatter was not encouraged and the day always seemed to go on and fucking on. The plastic factory, Elcam, made one thing and one thing only, the little plastic valves they'd put in your arm if you were unfortunate enough to ever need a drip. Essentially it's a small plastic chamber with a needle at one end and two wheels the other end so one could direct or restrict the flow of intravenous medicines. (Where did that come from?) And that was it. For six hours we'd turn a tiny valve onto a tiny screw. For six hours. Not much talking, just screwing. A few clever people brought Walkmans (if you're not sure what they are, Google it) but generally we'd work in silence, save for the odd inevitable giggle outbreak.

The other job in the plastic factory was worse, much worse. The shift would run from midnight until 6 a.m. and it was a job for just one person. Tonight it was just me. Me and my mind, which can be difficult at the best of times, to be honest. Joining me tonight is a giant machine that does something and the soothing *ping* of their onsite reactor. The reactor was used to irradiate and sterilise the product. The *ping* was an indication that everything was okay. Why the *ping* couldn't just happen when shit gets fucked up I'll never know. If I was lucky someone would let me use a cassette player so I could try and blank out the *pings* and *beeps* of the factory with a well-worn tape of house mixes.

Being in that place alone at night made me nervous, especially if the gap between the *pings* suddenly lengthened, even by a fraction of a second. My imagination being what it is, I'd often see myself in the centre of a Three Mile Island-style melt-down, immolated in an atomic power throb. STOP THINKING!!! Near enough every five minutes I'd spin around convinced there was someone sneaking up behind me. It's the same feeling I get snorkelling in the Med.

The job was this: you'd sit on a stool peering through the window of the giant machine, every two seconds the machine would hiss, a hydraulic head would spin round and you'd have to put a tiny, threaded, plastic head onto one of the valves. The machine would hiss again, take away your valve and replace it with a new one. That was it. That's what you did all night, for six hours.

I think I've always been able to shut parts of my brain down and thus nullify certain brands of monotony. Which was very useful for this type of work. On the right of the machine was a small white counter, it told you how many valves you'd done in a minute. It helped with my boredom. I spent hours trying to break my own record.

I must admit I've always kind of loved every job I've done no matter how shit it was. Whatever, I've always given it my all, a trait I inherited from watching my dad over the years. However, there were two exceptions to this:

1) Working in a warehouse that dealt with car parts. Hated it. Itchy shirt. Lasted two shifts.

2) Barman in Tony Roma's (St Martins Lane). Hated the manager and told him to fuck himself after four hours.

I've always felt life is too short to stay in shit jobs. Fortunately my dad was very supportive of this view. He'd say, 'There's always a job somewhere if you look hard enough.' I still believe that to be true.

The plastic factory has a small kitchen, little Plancha grill, hob, kettle, tea, coffee, milk etc. However, in the fridge was a veritable Aladdin's cave of delights. Cheese! Fucking cheese! Amazing. Some kind of ham, turkey, chicken, eggs and meat, delicious meat! Steak to be more accurate, beautiful thin minute steaks. Part of the deal of this shit shift was you could take, prepare and eat whatever you wanted. I'd usually make a big omelette with lots of cheese and ham, or I'd have a rare steak with a fried egg on top and mill of fresh black pepper.

Those breaks were actually pretty nice, sitting alone, silent, save for the comforting *ping* of the atomic reactor, enjoying a cheese-heavy omelette. After my shift ends and before leaving I grab a bag and stick some cheese and ham in it. I wrap it up and stuff it down the front of my boilersuit for later.

I'm not sure when it starts or how but I think I know why, the dangling twin carrots of boredom and hunger. I become a cat burglar. I never burgled houses for money or jewellery, no, the only thing I'd ever steal, the only thing I wanted at the time was food and my quarry was the fridge inside that plastic factory.

The old disco on the kibbutz was under the gymnasium and the walk home led me past Elcam. One night I am walking home pretty drunk when I see the factory looming up before me. An idea crackles into existence. I was fucking hungry after all that drinking. That was the thing about kibbutz, there was no food anywhere after hours unless you'd squirrelled shit away or bought Cup-a-Soups from the shop. Eating after disco usually meant all of us crammed into the common room eating round after round of cheap ketchup and toast.

But tonight would be different. In my state I decide to see if the door is locked. It isn't. The factory is silent, no night shift during the Sabbath! The door to the kitchen is also unlocked. The fridge is full and I begin my raid. I make lots of sandwiches; rifling through a drawer, I find a carrier bag and stuff it full of cheese and Jewish turkey-ham, there was so much they'd never notice. I make my exit and casually trudge back to the common room and plomp the sandwiches down onto the counter. It's gone in moments and there is much happiness and rejoicing! I feel like Robin Hood but with sandwiches.

Over the next weeks I raid the factory twice more in this manner, filling up with sandwiches and cold cuts. It was a dream, as a group we were in clover. We had all the sandwiches we'd ever need. One drunken night I set off on a raid. I try the door to find it locked. Locked? WTF? Questions reverb around my mind. Why, why was it locked, why now? I would not, could not, let this deter me. I had customers that were relying on me, that needed the good shit I could get.

I knew of another door in another part of the factory and thought I'd give it a go. Bingo. It was open. Suckers! I found a set of dark stairs that took me up to the plastic factory and completed my raid. Would this be my last? Were they catching on to me? Did they keep count? Take stock? No? They might? They might now? I should stop. I can't stop. I won't stop. I need it. I need cheese and curious white ham-style turkey meat. NEED IT. I need that buzz of burglary, and the curious white ham-style turkey meat. Nothing's gonna stop me. NOTHING!

HAHAHAHAHAHAHAHAHAHAHAHAHHAAHHAH! Meat.

Next time I try the door, it's locked again, no fluke, those fuckers know. The downstairs door is still open though, what chumps. I sprint silently up the stairs taking two steps at a time, through the dark corridor to the break room. I turn the handle to the kitchen door. It's locked! This is a problem. I panic briefly then shut it down. Think. Turn back, end this now. I can't. At this point I question whether this is about the cold cuts or the thrill of the crime. Go home, you've had a good run. In the kitchen door near the bottom is a panel probably twenty-four inches square. In the panel are slats of frosted glass. I have an idea. I gently tug upwards at one of the slats, joy of joys, it gives, it simply slides out, I lay it gently on the floor and get to work on the others. That done, I crawl through the new hole, fill up with booty, re-slat the hole and I'm gone. Textbook meat theft.

This could be my life's greatest work. In fact, I'd say apart from my son and my accent in *Hot Fuzz* (which was flawless and for which I received no recognition), this series of robberies was the greatest thing I've ever done.

The last one I do ends in stalemate. I get to the door and the slats have been removed, replaced by a square of plywood nailed over the hole. Who was the genius that'd bested me? I considered mule kicking the plywood away and doing a crude snatch and grab. I didn't, I couldn't, it wasn't my way, and it wasn't elegant or clever enough, not for me. I learnt a valuable lesson that day about the business of cold-cut theft: know when to walk away. This was my time. My career as a thief of cold meats and cheeses was over. The Case of the White Ham was closed. Or so I thought . . .

The next day there's a message on the notice board. An unscheduled volunteer meeting had been called that afternoon, after work. Balls. My creeping fear is confirmed. It is a meeting about the theft of food from the plastic factory. They didn't know who had done it but whoever it was should stop immediately. I'm sure Vicki's gaze lingered over me for a second. Paranoia. It was over. For days after, lots of us suffer come-downs, cold turkey, cold ham, cold cheese. It was okay. We were okay. For a time, I'd been someone, I'd been a champion of the people, a hero to some, villain to others. Now? Well now I was just like every other civilian craving a sandwich. I still have the memory though, the memory of those heists, and it still tastes so fucking sweet.

After assignments like apple picking, apple packing and plastics came the more specialised jobs, jobs you got if either the Israelis liked you or you'd been in the country a while. Working in the fishponds and in the cotton fields were both great jobs. Each offered a great deal of kudos. I should probably offer up a note on kibbutz fashion here. There wasn't any and therein lay the fashion. Newbies wore their own clothes to work, jeans, shorts, Ts, tops, dresses, and skirts, whatever. Oh,

I have a theory on why English holidaymakers always stand out so much while abroad. We always buy brand-new clothes! We look ridiculous. Anyway, on kibbutz everyone gets issued with work boots so usually they got worn; however, trainers were also acceptable.

The longer you were on kibbutz, the more you wanted to look like an Israeli; this transformation happened pretty quickly for me, I bought in. I loved it from the off. There was a big box with old secondhand work clothes in Vicki's office that we were allowed to rummage around in. I found some absolute gems. Ideally you'd want to wear a T-shirt with Hebrew writing on it, something from a factory, something denoting heavy industry, a happy apple in a hat, perhaps a giant tractor tyre smiling? This would be combined with blue canvas work pants tucked into work boots (military style) and a blue canvas work jacket. I looked like a poster boy for Chairman Mao's dig for victory campaign. The clothes always had to be worn with a healthy covering of earth or dust. Instead of wearing a belt, I had an old shoelace that I'd cleverly knotted between two belt loops. I've never looked cooler or felt more comfortable. I'm not a fashionable person so to live somewhere where everyone essentially dresses the same was absolute bliss to me.

Looking like a farmer also set you apart from the newer volunteers. It was a badge of honour. The only time you changed out of this garb was during disco night when everyone would get dolled up. Which in itself was also kind of fun.

Although my hair was long and parted in the middle I made the decision one day to shave it all off. Bald. Number zero. It was a decision I quickly regretted. After being 'in-country' for months I'd got a lovely tan everywhere except for under my raver's bob. For weeks I had to suffer the embarrassment of walking around looking like I was wearing a grey swimming cap.

Working in the cotton fields was some of the hardest physical work I've ever done. Cotton was an hour's drive north-east. I loved that drive. Because of the travelling time (which was included in our workday, bonus!) we had to leave really early (4 a.m.). The cotton fields were down in the Bekaa Valley so it was much hotter than our mountaintop kibbutz. We'd usually finish by 11 a.m. and at that point the temperature was already into the low hundreds.

The drive from the kibbutz was beautiful. We hugged the Lebanese border until we were south of Kiryat Shmona (the Town of the Eight). There was a great bar there called Bar Hash. Buses from all the kibbutzim across the north would bring volunteers to party. The place was pretty spectacular. It seemed to be a vast amphitheatre, an open-air stadium for lunacy. Through the middle of the place ran a small river. The DJ booth was a VW Beetle covered in thousands of tiny mirrors. It was very, very cool.

Once I ordered chips at the bar and when they came I ripped open packets of salt and sprinkled them on top. The Israeli bartender looked at me weird.

'What?' I asked.

'Why are you putting sugar on top of the chips?'

Balls, it was sugar. Front it out. I leaned in and shouted over the music.

'It's what we do in England.' I winked and headed off to throw my sugarfries into a bin.

During the drive down to the fields most people would catch up on their sleep. I tried not to, I preferred to sit in silence and watch the stunning sunrises. Those dark blues and vivid oranges as the sun shimmered through the atmosphere over Syria were the nicest sunrises I think I've ever seen.

I spent two weeks working in cotton and I only did one job. Sadly that wasn't picking the cotton itself, wrong season. What I did was less fancy and a lot more gruelling. There were five of us and for six hours a day we walked behind a tractor pulling giant rocks out of the sun-baked earth and tossing them into a trailer. I loved that job. It was a big fucking field, by my reckoning I'd say a kilometre wide by three of four kilometres long, it really was the hardest work. I love any job where, when I finish, I'm shattered and gasping for a cold one. This job, like many on the kibbutz, guaranteed both. We had such a laugh, I felt like a prisoner on a chain gang plus you finished work at eleven o'clock! Brilliant. I'd heard by all accounts that harvesting was pretty nice too, they let trusted volunteers drive big fucking tractors. Foolish.

Fish was also totes sweet. A similar gig to cotton in terms of time, workday and location, fish was also kudos-heavy! It was a chance to hang with the Israelis, smoke dangerously strong cigarettes and drink thicker and blacker than thick, black coffee.

The kibbutz had several giant fishponds, each housed fish at different phases of their development. Once the inhabitants of a pond had reached maturity, they lifted up giant nets from the base of the lake and funnelled the delicious carp into a corner, up a conveyor and into the back of large water-filled trucks. My job was to stand in neck-deep water hauling the net in and helping the fish up the chute.

When the temperature is over 100 degrees, the best place to be is in neck-deep cold water, it was heaven. If there was a downside it would be the stink of fish, which was difficult to remove. You'd also find large, shield-like scales in the weirdest of places. Every now and again big, heavy carp would try and escape. These rogues, some weighing almost 30lb travelling upwards of 20 knots, smashing you in the chops can be really painful. The final downside and the worst one for me was their screaming. I can still hear it sometimes at night. Apart from that, it was ace.

There were three other jobs I did, two were amazing and very cool, very kudos-heavy. One was absolutely awful, where to start? Good first. The kibbutz had a small museum and art gallery. I thought at the time (and probably still do secretly) that I wanted to be a painter, an artist like my dad, he was such a talented watercolourist. I painted some childish pictures and became friendly with the tiny old man who curated the collection; they were shit paintings but he seemed to like them, seemed to like the fact I showed some interest in art. He supplied me with paper and acrylics and one day offered me a job. Sweet! No more hard labour for me, no more intense heat or 6 a.m. starts. Instead I was to be surrounded by cool cool culture. Jubbly.

I was essentially an odd-job man, which was great and I was eager to learn. Back then I was much better with my hands than I am now. I'm terrible now, I think I just can't be arsed.

My job was varied, anything from digging holes to fixing toilets, sometimes I'd help collate the collection, sometimes I'd whitewash wooden cubes ready to display the museum's many sculptures. If I was a good boy I'd get to help hang the new exhibitions. Sometimes Old Tiny – I call him this as he was old and very tiny, a bit like a Jewish Yoda – would bring in cookies and cakes for us to have with our coffee at break time. It was very nice. Nice work in a beautiful building in the middle of a forest.

Often, and this was my favourite part, Old Tiny would go out and leave me to my own devices. There was a little radio that wafted out classical music, the only music allowed to be played in the museum. I'd sneak into the storeroom and look through the hundreds of canvases they had there. I loved it so much. Sometimes I'd play a game where, turning up the radio, I stalked the silent, empty galleries holding a large claw hammer pretending I was Patrick Bateman. HELP ME.

My other favourite job was with Michel. Michel was the most laidback man I'd ever known. Sometimes speaking seemed like too much of a bother – instead he'd gesture and make noises. His eyes were mega droopy and he had a massive red Afro of loose bouncy curls, he also loved reggae. It's amazing now looking back that I never imagined he was a pothead. How did I not see it?

He was the kibbutz plumber and heating engineer. I was essentially his plumber's mate. We had a tiny van and we'd bomb about fixing radiators. It was sweet, after the summer and before autumn we overhauled the boilers ready for the winter. Any job where I get to use Swarfega at the end of a shift is all right with me. Eventually I'm trusted enough to drive the van and have my own tools.

I dressed like an Israeli. I spoke some Hebrew; I had my own van with tools. Finally my transformation was complete. I felt like I belonged. I was an Israeli heating engineer and plumber, I was happy. Home seemed like a million miles away.

The Girls' toilet and shower had a savage blockage at one point during a hot day at the end of the summer. The place had become like a Woodstock for bluebottles. I was tasked with crawling under the building, which frightened me anyway (the thought of snakes and big fucking spiders a constant fear in my mind, even now), finding the main sewage pipe, opening it and clearing the blockage. It really couldn't be easier.

I find the pipe in the intense heat and fiddle to get the elbow free, it pops off and I shine a torch inside. I see nothing. Michel finds a coat hanger, unfolds it and hands it to me. Suspicious. I stick the bent wire inside the pipe and I ram hard. There's a hiss, a rush of dead air grabs hold of my features like a Face-Hugger, a gurgle, the sound of a thick liquid now moving freely and in a moment I'm covered in a foul broth of shits, pisses, condoms and almost a thousand used tampons. Holy. Fucking. Christ. I lie there for about thirty seconds while this fluid glues itself to me. After a while it stops, I casually screw the elbow cap back on and shuffle out. Michel laughs at me. Hilarious. I'm hosed down while people point and laugh.

This was nothing compared to the hen house. Chickens was the worst job in my life. It was terrible. They knew no one wanted to work there so they'd wait outside the disco at 3 a.m. and snatch people as they came out. It's what the old navy would call a pressgang. We'd become crazed, senseless ship rats, leaping this way and that, over hedges, under vans, anything to avoid working with the chickens.

There were four houses, two hundred metres or so in length. Each housed chickens at different stages of development. The birds went from little chicks to fully grown hens in three short months. I'm no bird farmer but this seemed very quick to me. They weren't battery hens in the truest sense I guess – they weren't caged – but there were almost twenty thousand birds crammed inside.

We wore white coats, and white dust masks that would usually be soaked in cheap cologne. I was told the reason for the 3 a.m. start was so all the chickens would be asleep. It felt like clearing a ghetto, the irony was not lost.

We'd sneak into the hen house, the smelliest, hottest place in the world, to be confronted by a sea of white feathers. Thousands of hens sat in their own acrid shit fast asleep. The large double doors to the mega-coop would open. The lights would be put on but dimmed so as not to rouse suspicion among the hens. A low caging vehicle would then be driven into the house and it'd be game on.

We were usually pretty hammered coming straight from the disco, you had to be, and sometimes a collective insanity erupted. The noise of the machine and eight of us a-hootin' and a-hollerin' meant the chickens began to wake, but not all at once; the nearer you got, the more of them would rouse.

I used a technique that's known in the trade as the four-bird lift. If you had to breathe it was in deep hard gasps through the mouth. No matter how drunk you were the smell of all those hens crammed into a shit-filled shed in ninety-degree heat was too much to bear. I'd run in and grab the birds by the legs, four in each hand, they'd then be transported to the vehicle and stuck into a metal crate. Grim.

We mostly encountered little or no resistance. Mostly. Some of the bigger, bolder roosters would rally and slash at us with their razor-sharp talons. The defence of their hens, though noble, was ultimately futile.

Small running battles would break out all across the front which had formed across the width of the hen house. Every now and then you'd hear the word 'cunt' shrieked out as an angry cock slashed at our soft white hands with his ankle daggers. It would be a point of honour to pursue the male who had cut us and dispatch him into the vehicle.

Within four hours it would be over. The house would be clear. Sun rising, we'd stand, breathing heavily like Gomer Pyle, vodka wearing off, ashamed, confused, some considering veganism. The Israelis kindly let us keep all the dead and dying birds we found, they allowed us to eat them. Not raw – we'd BBQ them and serve it with a kind of simple chimichurri sauce we'd invented, we weren't barbarians.

All this work and high jinks soon led up to my first Christmas in Israel. It was actually really nice. We'd become a little family at this point. A rag tag bag of emotional refugees, fleeing who knows what. These were my friends and through my own choice the only family I had or wanted.

Arrangements were made for a proper Christmas dinner and a carol concert, not usually my kind of thing but fukkit, vodka. The Israelis screened films for us all day, they asked us what we'd like to see and the answer was simple. Bond, James Bond.

We all got up early and exchanged gifts. (Vodka.) Then, still in our jimmy jams, we made our way to the common room where we snuggled in to watch a Bond triple-bill. I loved this time in Israel, where you'd all just hop into bed and have a cuddle. It was fairly innocent in a kind of 'tops and fingers' sort of way.

The English girls spend half the day preparing a fantastic Christmas lunch. We have a tree and some decorations and the Christmas dinner itself is absolutely delicious.

Eventually I have to speak to Mum and Dad. It's Christmas. I can't remember the conversation but I remember crying a lot. Our lovely Welsh den mother Mary came and cuddled me. Lots of people came and cuddled me. Sorted me right out. It felt amazing. I'm not sure I'd ever felt so loved. (Not true but *I* know what I mean.) I think I was crying because I finally felt like there was enough distance between me now and me back there to afford myself a moment of Yuletide acceptance. I came out of my foxhole, Mum came out of hers and, with Dad refereeing, we played football in no-man's-land.

* * *

A little while after Christmas the weather turned bad. Until that point it'd been hot. Not chilly, not wet, not cloudy but hot. Then it started to rain. A lot. Which was nice, torrential and cooling, and it meant no flies, which was also nice. The flies were terrible. At times we were forced to shit in an old paint tin and cover it in syrup. It would then be left some way from the house so the flies would feast on that instead of the liquid in our eyeballs. It's an old Berber trick apparently.

The downside of the cooling rain was the hordes of giant black spiders it would drive into our living quarters. I remember watching ten stout men do battle with one of them in a shower block one night. It was horrible and it was weird. I watched the beast bristle and shimmer forward, the shirtless men panic and run here and there. To and fro the battle went. Why? It was a thing so heavy it made a *pudpud* sound when it walked. Eventually it fell. No one ever mentioned it again.

By mid January the rain stopped, and it started to snow. I never imagined, stupid young man, that it would snow here in Northern Israel but it did. It snowed loads and that meant one thing for hungry volunteers. Chips! Lovely, lovely chips. When it snowed on kibbutz they served chips. What an amazing rule. Chips, proper, handcut potatoes, deep fried in sun-hot golden oil. It was a very special thing. I still didn't have a great relationship with the food on kibbutz. Too many vegetables. I know chips is a vegetable but it was deep fried so fuck it.

At times – and when I say at times I mean most of the time – there was a shared lunacy among us, among the volunteers. Our life was so monotonous you'd be forced to focus on and cling to the smallest things.

Apart from six hours of hard labour a day you had the other eighteen to do what you wanted. Usually those precious hours of R and R revolved around drinking, heavy bastard drinking. I had left my junior drug fetish behind and had effortlessly slipped into the guise of a semi-professional alkie. Mum would be so proud.

At one point during chip season and the spider battles the DVF was formed. The Drunk Volunteer Force was an unofficial paramilitary (paralytic military) arm of the Israeli Defence Force. It meant that we drank a lot but unlike the other drinking that went on this was officially endorsed by us. Lovely.

The drinking club invented some fun called 'the Shotgun Challenge'. You take a can of beer, cut a small hole in the bottom of it, hold it to your lips, pull the tab and suck down the turbo-charged brew. Easy. It starts off as a bit of fun, something to do. But with the official formation of the DVF shit became real, we sat and wrote rules, we knocked it into shape.

An official table was constructed, essentially a cardboard league ladder where competition drinkers could be moved up and down according to official timings as the season progressed. I'll try and explain the rules as I remember them.

A shotgun was only official if it was witnessed by three or more members of the DVF. It could only be counted official if it was timed using the official DVF Alcometer, essentially my watch, a simple Casio. Once the hole was cut into the can it had to be scrutinised by two DVF officials. The size of the hole was important. There's a set of stringent measurements. The hole could be as small as you wanted but it couldn't be bigger than the rigid specs laid out in the DVF bible.

The officials, once satisfied that the regulations had been adhered to, gave the nod and the drinking could begin. Almost. The competitor would raise the beer gently to his or her mouth, being careful not to overflow the shotgun can's newly jagged aperture. As the official timer I would say the words that every official shotgunner heard.

'In your own time, when I hear the click.'

I'd stand, fingers ready on the buttons of the Alcometer, a collective hush hangs, all betting stops, a small cancer-ridden Vietnamese man screams 'Diddi Mao!' And this thing is fucking on. Once I hear the first hiss rush out of the can I'd press start.

An eruption of sound and immense noise, pushing, screaming, weeping, two or three other emotions. Generally the best technique and one that, like the Fosbury flop in high-jump, completely revolutionised the sport, was the 'Suck and Squeeze'. As the name suggests you'd open your throat – not everyone can do this – and suck the turbo-charged beer down while squeezing the golden piss out of the can.

The shotgun challenge was quick, fast and explosive. At the time there wasn't another spectator sport in the world as fast-paced and exciting as the Shotgun Challenge. We were it. The only game in town. Once the competitor was finished the can would leave his or her lips and the Alcometer was stopped. The can was immediately handed to me; failure to do this would result in instant disqualification. I'd then place the empty can on an officially endorsed flat surface, a step or something, and the precise measuring could begin. The can is swarmed by DVF officials scrutinising the vessel.

If any liquid could be spilled out of the can, even as a thin vapour, it was immediately classed null and void. If nothing dribbled out of the can it was a good shotgun and all eyes moved over to the official timer, moi. The time would be read out, cheers or commiseration would then follow. Your tab would be moved up or down the league table dependent on your time. What mindless larks. Everyone loved it.

Being a face around there and a world-class drinker I was close to the top of the table. It was a long hard season and your surge for glory had to be timed just right. I was competing against some real fucking animals, big strong boys all vying for the crown. Top of the league was a powerful Dane called Hans Jacob Jespersen. He tweeted me a few years back. He was doing great, a big shot in the Danish army. Towards the end of our time together he admitted that he dreamt only in English, which I found amazing as I dreamt entirely in Danish. I once asked Jacob what was the worst swear word in Danish he could think of. He pondered and told me he'd have to think about it.

Later that evening there was a soft knock on my door. It was Jacob.

'I've been thinking about what you said.'

'About what?' I'd forgotten.

'About the swearing thing.'

'Oh, go on then.'

He stumbled slightly, ashamed that he now had these awful sounds inside himself.

'I don't really . . .' He trailed off.

'Come on, cunt, out with it.'

'Okay, the worst insult I can think of in Danish is this . . .' Even I had reached a point where I wasn't sure if I wanted or needed to hear these mystical killing words. I tremble.

'Look, if you don't want to it's fine . . .'

'No, I need to.' After a moment he swallows and says it. The most insulting thing he could think of in Danish was . . .

'Long-haired communist fag,' he blurted.

I lay in bed, stunned.

'What did you fucking say?'

'I won't repeat it.' He nods shyly and leaves, shutting my door quietly behind him. I can hear him on the other side, breathing. After a moment he pads off and that was that.

Swearing aside he's a giant of a man and a damn fine shot-gunner. I liked him very much.

The last day of the championship was upon us; a long hazy season had almost drawn to a close, Jacob sat on top of the table. The final shotgun of the season was mine. And it was massive. All or nothing, death or glory. Something or another something. The lights go green; I hear the words, 'In your own time, when I hear the click.'

BOOM!

I power that motherfucker down. I care about nothing and no one at that moment. I'm deaf and I'm blind, sucking down that cold can of Maccabee like nothing else mattered.

My lips undocked from the can, I reeled backwards, eyes wide, grunting and held the can aloft, an official taking it off me. By the ripple of cheers erupting from the crowd I knew it was good, it felt good, it felt really good. People crowded the timer, confusion reigned. The can was officially stepped and to my absolute horror a tiny bubble of lagery foam bleeds from the hole. NOOOOO!!! The championship had gone. I knew then that it was gone. What was the time?

1.92 seconds. A new world record. A clear second faster than Jacob, but it didn't count. I didn't count. It was the shotgun heard around the world. My career as a shotgunner was over. It hit me hard.

Things in the DVF become darker. I'm becoming a kind of Colonel Kurtz-style character. I spend a lot of time wearing a multi-coloured towelling robe, sleeveless for comfort and convenience. I've also taken to carrying around a metallic blue kettle I call the 'Kettle of Doom'. Where it came from I shall not say. The kettle was our holy grail; our piece of the true cross, our Alma Mater, and wherever it went, alcoholic mayhem ensued. Inside the kettle was a vodka-laced punch and about a pound of rotting fruit, slowly fermenting. My own micro still. I never took the fruit out, and I never washed the thing once.

At volunteer parties the drink of choice was a terrible fruit punch. Fuck loads of it. We'd borrow a massive pot from the kitchen, fill it with bottles of weak squash, fruit would then be added and then the booze, vodka, shitty shitty vodka. It was our drink, it was cheap and plentiful. For special occasions and shots we'd have lemon vodka but there was another kind. Another altogether darker kind. The fathers of the DVF – me, Kiwi Shaun, Little Pete and Dave – one day stumbled upon a new pain. A pain so powerful it had to be purchased in a hard-ware store. It had a plain white label and always reminded me of the bottle of booze Belloq gives Marion in *Raiders*. On the plain white label written in Hebrew and English the legend said simply, *Alcohol*. That shit was 95% alcohol, not proof, alcohol. Bear in mind whisky and vodka are usually 40%. Now with hindsight being 20/20 I can only assume what we were drinking was turps or paint thinner. Agreed it seems like total lunacy but it really wasn't that bad when you mixed it with Coke or Sprite.

Do you know that feeling when you spill white spirit onto your hands when you're cleaning a paintbrush? It doesn't trickle off, it just kind of goes in. That's exactly what happened when you drank it. It's making me heave slightly to remember this. I never swallowed a mouthful of that shit, it just kind of went in. A triumph? A disaster? Heave.

If there was a party people would draw lots to see who'd go on the booze run. Usually it needed three of us, not always the same three, but three was the minimum number needed to carry all that booze back. Those going would have to ask permission to leave work five minutes early in order to catch the bus to the nearest town, Safed, the jewel in the crown of the Galilee region.

With the hour there and the hour back it gave you about two and a half hours to get what was needed before the last bus returned. It wasn't just booze, we'd have a long list of things people wanted, needed: good shampoo, chocolate, nail clippers, nail varnish, Pot Noodles, tights etc.

It was always a special treat to leave the kibbutz. Safed was pretty in a bullet-ridden kind of way, built up into the hills overlooking the Sea of Galilee. It's mentioned in the Bible apparently too, if you're into that kind of thing.

For the booze run itself it was important, no imperative, that you shopped as quickly as you could, booze booze booze then shampoo. Get it done fast, then kick back and eat.

Compared to that healthy muck they served on kibbutz, Safed with its numerous pizza places and falafel stands was heaven. One place stood out though, a pizza restaurant serving perhaps the greatest NYC-style cheese pizza I've ever tasted anywhere in the world and that includes New York.

I'm not sure if it was actually that good or just because we were all desperate for it but it was amazing. Crispy, cheesy, buttery. My tongue has a hard-on. Sometimes a couple of us would save up and take a day off, jump on the 10 a.m. bus and spend four or five hours eating slice after crisp buttery slice and downing litres of ice-cold Goldstar beer. It was absolute bliss.

The parties we had were fucking mental. So much so that all I really remember was wearing a toga, and that's it. Once during the festival of Purim I thought it would be fun to dress up in my friend Eli Azer's Israeli army uniform. I woke up at 6 a.m. outside somewhere after having the shit beaten out of me by two drunken soldiers. Eli Azer forgot to tell me he was a Military Policeman, generally disliked by the other regiments in the IDF. Unable to talk, I was too pissed to explain I wasn't an Israeli soldier.

Every Friday was the volunteers' disco. It was a big night. First you had to get Shabbat meal out of the way. The whole kibbutz would sit together in the main hall eating dinner. The volunteers were ghettoed up one end. The Israelis generally wanted to keep their distance, afraid they'd catch what we had. That was not always the case. If, like me, you'd been there a while you sometimes got invited to sit with a family to eat Shabbat meal. Not me, that never happened to me but I was told it was most pleasant.

Shabbat meal was generally a lot of fun, food and, foolishly, free wine on the tables, sweet, spine-vibrating Shabbat wine. Silly Israelis.

Friday after work I'd swim, play football for two hours and then sleep until about five o'clock. You'd wake up, shower and, for perhaps the only time that week, you'd wear clothes that you'd brought with you from home. There were exceptions, long-time volunteers could rifle through Vicki's box of old seventies clothes. Clothes would also be handed down from volunteer to volunteer. People left, clothes stayed.

It was a treat seeing the ladies get all dolled up. During the week they usually looked like part of a socialist land army, sexy in a Marxist kind of way. Friday night though ... Hello! Make-up, perfume, the lot. Sometimes even shoes!

Once dressed we'd do shots, not too many as you still had a big formal dinner to sit through and Shabbat meal was important, you had to behave. Public drunkenness on kibbutz was frowned upon. As a volunteer you had to behave. Up to a point. Friday was the only time volunteers got table-served by the Israelis. We loved that. Loved making it a bit difficult for them, especially if the Israeli serving us had been a ball/boob breaker during the week. The food was always good too, much better than the usual rations.

There was usually a candle lit, a prayer or prayers, a song, a poem. This bit tended to drag, we just wanted to eat and drink wine. Trying to be quiet would just make us worse. Giggles stifled. People coughing loudly. This high-pitched noise emitted by people trying not to laugh, Errrrrddddd! I'd do this thing where I'd let a long string of gob hang off my tongue and then at the last possible second I'd whip my tongue up and a chandelier of phlegm would arc up and plop onto my forehead. Big lolz from the boys. Admiring glances from the girls. Phlegm chandelier got me so much pussy.

As soon as prayers are over, eating erupts. The drinkers among us had a very important job to do. It took planning, clinical observation, patience and stamina. While hammering through the wine on our table me and the other DVF members would be constantly scanning the other tables around us. How much have they drunk? Are they drinking? When are they going? It had to be played just right though, the locals would frown upon blatant wine collection and hoarding.

The key to a great haul of free wine was simple. Sit near the old people. They never drank much if any and they'd fuck off early. Cool. You tried to stay at your table as long as possible, even while the room was being cleaned around you. Once most of the Israelis had gone you essentially had your pick of about three hundred bottles of shitty Shabbat wine. Time it right, get up and casually stroll out grabbing bottles and sticking them wherever you could. That wine would then either be drunk immediately pre-disco, or stored underground for when the lean time came. (Monday.)

Between the end of Shabbat meal and the disco opening there was a two-hour wait. It was a tricky period. If you went off too soon you'd be so hammered that you wouldn't make the disco, and it was the only chance to go out in the week. Not good. A couple of times going off too soon meant I even failed to make Shabbat meal, which was a terrible shame. I got so pissed that I fell asleep outside a small warehouse leading up to the dinner hall. I was shaken awake by a furious Vicki who sent me home and banned me from the disco that night. She'd received a couple of complaints from elderly members whom I'd apparently growled at, although that doesn't sound like something I'd do at all.

For an avid cockroach like myself Fridays were a good opportunity for more foraged treats. The Members Club near the dining hall would allow volunteers in to drink coffee and eat biscuits on the Sabbath. We'd rarely drink coffee; instead, while browsing the English novels on one of the shelves of the small library, I'd be stuffing biscuits or little cakes into my mouth, pockets and sometimes even turn-ups.

Ten minutes before the disco opened we'd trudge up the hill towards the bar. When I first arrived at the kibbutz the disco was in a giant room under the gymnasium. A month or so into my stay the disco was moved into an old bomb shelter under the Members Club. It was much nicer. I must point out that the word 'nicer' in this case was relative. It was a big concrete room that had a sound system and stank. We loved it. I had some of the best times at those discos.

The DVF would always post up at the bar for the first hour or so. It felt nice, normal, a bit like home. Sitting at the bar bullshitting with the Israelis, laughing with good mates, drinking tall, cold, draught Goldstar. Even better perhaps it was all free. Free. All free. Ha-ha. Free. The. Beer. Was. Free. And it never ran out. Never! (Well maybe once or twice but you get my point.)

After a while we'd spin our stools around and break ranks to flirt and chat and dance. Dancing was important. Everyone would dance like crazy. House of Pain's 'Jump Around' and 'The Sign' by Ace of Base were both favourites. It was totes bacchanalian.

I remember a lot of injuries and mishaps in that place. Beer spilled, skiddy floors, trips, slips. You soldiered on, alcohol-based injuries and not making work because you were pissed or injured or hung-over were not tolerated. My poor friend Theresa, a tall, broad, Irish lunatic of a woman, fell over one night and knocked her two front teeth out. She couldn't afford to get them fixed so she stayed like that for weeks. This horrified the Israelis.

When the disco was over, it was usually well past three in the morning. There were no sneaky afters or cheeky lock-ins. We'd leave and either I'd break into a factory for ham or stumble back to the common room to eat ketchup on toast and drink vodka, usually with a juice of some kind, although mixing it with water and drinking chocolate was not uncommon. Filth.

Saturday was never without a hangover. It was our day off so that was cool. I once woke up covered in a hundred partially digested cherries. I'd obviously fallen asleep eating cherries and had woken up, honked and gone back to sleep. It looked like a bloodbath. Waking up with the bed and walls covered in red liquid was absolutely terrifying. I believed my kidneys had been removed while I slept. Another time I woke up with my head plastered so close to the wall that I screamed and rolled off the bed thinking I had been struck blind.

It was all high jinks until the DVF discovered the pain of the 95% and things took a more sinister turn. It took us over. We had become a coven of drinkers. It was no longer a big group of us laughing and joking around, it was like we'd stumbled into the darkness. The alcoholic occult. We took the pomp and verve of the shotgun challenge and x'd it by a thousand and crammed it into a Ouija board. It was like *Jumanji* with crying.

Four of us would sit in one of our rooms. The door would be locked. Tea lights were lit. A small ornate table would be positioned in the centre of the room, on it the official ashtray would be placed.

We'd sit at the cardinal points on the compass, north, south, east and west. The four were usually me and the aforementioned Kiwi Shaun, Pete and Dave. These were my best friends. The term 'best friend' is perhaps a strange concept on a kibbutz. People you grew to love, who when their time was up would pack up and leave, move on, go home, go somewhere else. It's the way it was. I think I got good at being left. You had to really.

But these three were my best friends and I loved being with them. By now my time on kibbutz meant I'd been upgraded to sharing a two-bed with Shaun. We were really close. Many were the times I woke up from a boozy coma to see Shaun humping off on his lovely Danish girlfriend Margritte.

Shaun and I would also, from time to time, have the odd drunken altercation. It would start off as a competition to see who could slap the hardest, or some other lunacy, but it would soon become serious and more often than not we'd have to be separated. The next morning he and I were always thick as thieves again, eating a hangover breakfast and laughing like idiots. It'd confuse people but it was our way and we kind of liked it like that!

The other two players were Pete and Dave, friends from home who had travelled to kibbutz together from Scotland. They were alcoholic fuckheads and total degenerates. Just like me. I loved them and we laughed a lot.

Not one of us ever questioned why we were doing the 95% séance. What possessed us to dabble into the occult? We just did it. It just emerged into existence. It created itself. The first bottle – I say first, it was normally the only bottle – was usually, brought to the table under a veil of lace. A bell would sound and the shroud would be lifted. At this point the cardboard game wheel would be revealed. (Of course there was a game wheel, we were bored and clever.)

I think the wheel and therefore the game was called the 'Wheel of Destiny'; it'd be retrieved from its dusty sarcophagus and the fun would begin. The only other things allowed on the table were a small chalice (big shot glass) and a two-litre bottle of red death (Coke).

Let me tell you a little more about the Wheel of Destiny. It's important you know so you can avoid the mistakes we made. Avoid the regret, the tears, the confusion.

The wheel was divided into twelve sections, each home to a ratio. Either 80/20 or 60/40 or 20/80, 90/10, 70/30 and so on. The first number was the amount of 95% in the chalice, the second number the amount of red death. There were also some fun curveballs in there too: one said 'Don't Drink'. Why? Why would it say that? Another decreed 'Everyone Drinks'. That's better! Some had a small 's' in the corner. These were fun, the 's' stood for 'shake'. You essentially did a slammer inside your own headbox. You take the drink and shake your head until it felt like your eyes had come out and by that time the liquid had vaporised across the blood/brain barrier and gone into your mind.

I was going to call those nights fun, but I'm not sure fun would be correct. Sure we laughed a lot but it didn't feel like fun.

That shit was so strong, we'd drink about 250ml each in shot format with a mixer and it would be goodnight Tel Aviv. The night went like this: laughter, laughter, laughter, death. That's how it went. It turned us into babbling zombies, lunatics. We'd begin at 6 p.m. and by 7.15 p.m. we were absolutely ruined. Complete blackout. People would tell me I'd been mobile, shuffling, spitting but making no sense.

Places I woke up after drinking 95% (all true): up a tree, on a large flat rock, in an empty, pitch-black bomb shelter (it took me an hour to find my way out), lying on the border fence trouser-less being licked awake by a giant Rottweiler. These and other such shenanigans meant that eventually the use of 95%, much like chemical weapons in wartime, were banned by the DVF. It was too dark, too many people – good people – were hurt. Here endeth the lesson.

* * *

About a year or so into my first tour I decided that I'd had enough and I wanted to go home. God knows why. I seem to remember a little light pressure from people to stay, to become a member of the kibbutz. That meant either joining the army or getting married to an Israeli girl. The army wasn't interested in a drunken Catholic, albeit lapsed. And in terms of Israeli women, they were very hard to woo, you had to be in it for the long haul, the ones I knew on kibbutz anyway. No, I was strictly a Friday night Euro-banger at this juncture.

I packed my stuff, Vicki arranged for me to get a lift down to Tel Aviv and I went. The only thing I remember from the flight was the smoking. It was the last time I ever saw smoking on a plane. It's so weird to think, and I say this as a smoker sadly, that at one point in the not so distant past one could smoke in a plane, with kids there too, or on the tube, on buses, in restaurants for godsakes – as if the notion that a small, low wall separating the smoking from the non-smoking sections made a blind bit of difference to where the smoke would float!

* * *

In fourteen months on kibbutz and with the help of very little food, tons of exercise and ball-breaking labour I had gone from nineteen stone to eleven! This was a big shock to my parents who were waiting for me at the airport. I stood straight in front of my mum and she didn't recognise me. She craned her neck looking for her chubby little soldier. Eventually she realised this tanned, thin, shaven-headed kibbutznik standing before her was me.

'What have they done to you?' she sobbed.

She grabbed me and hugged me so hard. Dad got involved at one point too and I think we all had a little cry. It was really nice to see them.

I'd almost completely forgotten about 214 Ray Lodge Road. It was a real shock to be back there. I felt that big, wet, black blanket drape itself around my shoulders almost instantly. I say home. It was a house and my parents lived in it. I just couldn't be there.

After being away for so long and blooming, breathing, changing, growing, I'd half expected it to have happened to everyone here at home too. This was not the case. It was exactly the same. Nothing had changed. Nothing. I had to leave. I took my passport, the one with the stamp in it that said I couldn't come back to Israel. (I was arrested at the airport for overstaying my visa by eleven months and effectively deported.) I wasn't going to let this stop me. I tore my passport up, went to Petty France and reapplied for a new one. Cunning twat.

I have an odd relationship with passports. (I wonder if these words have ever been written before?) Years later Simon and I made an arrangement to spend five days writing in Helsinki. We wrote nothing by the way. I love the film by Jim Jarmusch, *Night on Earth*. The Helsinki vignette always fascinated me, it made me want to go there. So we did. The promise of snow was too much for me and Peggy to bear. We love snow. We were very excited.

Two days before we leave I try and find my passport. I can't. I look everywhere. It's gone. Lost. Balls. My personality is such that losing things is bad for me, it unsettles me, makes me feel disappointed with my brain. I don't want a glitch in my matrix. I turn my place upside down looking for that fucking document. After a while I call Simon, tell him regretfully we'd have to cancel. He was furious.

I think the problem was we'd built up such a picture of this winter wonderland over the previous couple of weeks that to have it snatched away like this was too much to bear. He was so cross. I hung up saying, 'Leave it with me.' I couldn't let my little soldier down. I remember I had an old passport in an envelope in a box in the shed. After rooting around I find the thing. It's musty, out of date, cancelled and also cut in half. Clean through. Two pieces. Oh. As I sit at my desk I feel like Donald Pleasance in *The Great Escape*, headlamp blazing, scalpel and a roll of clear Scotch tape in hand. It took me almost three hours but I'd surgically taped that thing back together. We were going to Helsinki!

This was pre 9/11 so security was pretty lax, but still I was shitting a brick. If I had a kilo of squidgy-black taped to my calf I couldn't have felt any guiltier. Cut a long story short, we got there, just. Being poor at the time, our cheap tickets meant we had to trans-ship via Amsterdam so this meant three sets of checkpoints; they looked at the passport, looked at me and waved me through. Fucking hell. So illegal. In Finland it didn't snow once. We drank about 700 Lapin Kultas, laughed a lot and had brandy for breakfast – it was cold, so well deserved and purely medicinal, we believed.

Once again I said goodbye to M and D, took a train to Gatwick and flew back to Israel. I'd spoken to Israeli friends on kibbutz and they were happy to have me back. There'd been a change of administration in the weeks since I'd been gone. Vicki had left her post and a lady called Yael Arnin had taken over. She was tiny, beautiful in a Dana Scully kind of way and most formidable. I loved her and thanks to my cheekiness we got on well. She was really good to me.

Even though I'd only been gone a month the turnover of the volunteers was such that I hardly knew any of them. No matter, they knew me, I was still a Master Sergeant in the DVF and that meant something. I get back to work, keep my head down, drink, flirt, laugh, make new friends and don't think about the future. I loved the day in day out of kibbutz life, same thing week after week. Four-forty a.m. alarm goes off, teeth brushed, work, lunch, swim, sleep, dinner, drink, sleep, four-forty a.m. alarm goes off.

Friday was Shabbat meal and the disco, this you know about. Wednesday we were allowed to use the shop. On Tuesday Yael opened her office. We'd get a hundred fags a week and five aerogrammes, which I never used; I'd stockpile mine and use them to trade for extra ciggies with some of the Danish girls, many of whom were avid letter writers.

I'd drop my dirty laundry off in the office and it'd be returned on Thursday all folded up in a little canvas bag, clean but essentially smelling of nothing. These were the routines I lived my life by and I liked it. I could do it with my eyes closed. I need routine. Even now, I'm shit if I don't have a routine, really bad.

My twentieth birthday was approaching and my mum called to ask me what I'd like. A few people had planned a trip to Tiberias and I really wanted to go. I told Mum about the plan and she assured me that she'd sort it. Great!

Money, generally, was never an issue on kibbutz because no one had any. You didn't need it. It was only when you wanted to venture outside that you ever needed to think about cash. On kibbutz, we had something called funny money, essentially coloured squares of paper assigned a value by the inclusion of a number on one side.

Tiberias is on the western shore of the Sea of Galilee, deep in the heart of Jesus country. I liked it there, great food, and amazing falafel. Outside the city's central bus station there was a long row of lovely falafel stands, colourful, beautiful; with giant bowls of salad, chopped vegetables, beans, pulses and the smell of chickpea patties frying in golden oil. Yumfuckingyum.

A couple of days before my birthday a parcel arrived from home, I eagerly tore into it. This is going to be good, weekend away here I come! Out of the package tumbled forty Benson and Hedges (Result!) and a fiver. Five pounds. Five. A fucking fiver. Sorry to sound ungrateful, I know they didn't have a pot to piss in but still. Why assure me? I didn't feel assured. I laugh a bit, confused, look back into the parcel, empty. Oh. Gutted. I laugh when I think about it now but I was definitely crestfallen.

I had unconsciously prepared for this kind of eventuality. I'd scrimped and saved up bits here and there and just had enough to get to Tiberias and back. The fiver actually came in handy for a few beers once I'd exchanged it so I was happy enough.

A bunch of us bussed it down to Safad and then hitched from there to Tiberias. We grabbed supplies of fresh pitta, cans of tuna, cheese, ham, vodka etc. and headed north around the top end of the Sea of Galilee. It was a long way and very hot but it was my birthday and we were in high spirits.

By the time we arrived at the campsite it was late afternoon. It wasn't strictly a campsite, it was a beach dotted with life-guard towers, and if you could find one that was hippie-free you could sleep on it. Which is exactly what we did. We laid out the sleeping bags and had a little picnic on the beach; we drank a little and swam in the Sea of Galilee. It was pretty magical. I felt free and happy. We stood in silence in the black, tideless water and watched the sun go down.

Later we lay around in our nest eating crisps and, taking long swigs of lemon vodka, we chatted and laughed. At one point I have a vague memory of one of the boys deciding it would be a good idea to piss all over us. The lemon vodka was beginning to darken the mood, I needed to be alone and so I wanderstumble off.

I sit on the beach, hearing europop drift across the sea from Tiberias, campfires up and down the beach fill the air with smoke, I hear the noise of a guitar, girls giggling, the soothing 'AchAch' of ancient Hebrew.

At some point I make the stupid decision to wade out into the Sea of Galilee. It starts off innocently enough as a little paddle, then I witness myself wading and then marching out further and further. There comes a point when I can barely touch the bottom. What a fucking stupid thing to do. So drunk I can hardly see, neck deep in the unknown.

Two things happen to me at this point, one is a realisation, the other is a physical incarnation of my deepest primal fear. The realisation is remembering how terrified I am by deep, unpredictable water. The sea hates a coward and in the sea I am most definitely a coward. I'm not a good swimmer and the notion of currents unseen, of tidal ebb and flow, makes me afraid – I'm just not good in the sea. It's a primal environment and far too much for my imagination to cope with.

On holibobs I'll happily wade and I'll even have a little snorkel in the warm, clear Med, lovely. But I'm not in the warm, clear Med. I'm here, on my own, three hundred feet from shore in the pitch-black Galilee. This is not a good place to be. I blink and instantly become sober enough to understand the predicament I'm in. Breathe.

My Jiminy Cricket is now sober too, he's really cross and shouts at me, 'Chop-chop, dickhead, back to shore!' That guy's always shouting at me.

I turn and begin my swim/doggie paddle/terrified bounce-run back to the beach when the second thing happens.

Under the water an unseen entity brushes against me. Something of enormous size and power. It is massive and it is silent. I don't or can't move and plips fall out of me. The top of the thing brushes against my chest, the base of the leviathan brushes against my shins, for a moment we have full body contact, it glides through me. I feel the scales on its flanks, big as saucers. It's so big and powerful that the current it creates when it pulses its tail and glides off picks me up and spins me further out to sea, away from the shore and to a place where I definitely cannot touch the bottom. I've never been so frightened.

I'm going to either drown or be eaten by a monster, they'll find nothing of me but my fat head on an Israeli lake-beach and it'll have a little crab living in the eye-socket. I don't want a little crab living in my eye-socket. Not yet. I'm treading water, panicky, terrified. Jiminy punches a button on a panel in my control centre. A flash of an idea. 'Swim, you fucking dick!'

I explode into action and doggie paddle back to shore. I beach, exhausted, gasping, frightened. I check myself all over and find I'm fine although the ring I wear, a ring my dad gave to me, is gone. It's a beautiful green-and-black signet ring with flecks of fiery red and it was now lost at the bottom of the Sea of Galilee. Maybe the ring falling off my finger was tariff enough for Neptune that day. I'm bummed but totally alive.

* * *

The second time on kibbutz was different from the first. Not worse necessarily. It's all about the people. Obviously different people give off different kinds of vibrations. Some are nice, with a pleasant frequency, you yearn to be in the company of that person. Some are high-pitched, twangy, jarring; it warns you subconsciously to stay away.

It's like dogs or bees or rats picking up the scent of cancer or landmines. People have no control over the vibes they give off. It can't be disguised by a shallow smile or a pat on the back, you just sense it, it's a gut instinct and it should *never* be ignored.

At that time and generally, volunteers were a tight-knit bunch. We knew each other, we loved and looked after one another. It's how it was, how we liked it. There was little or no trouble. When new volunteers showed up it was usually in small groups, ones, twos, the odd three. People generally made the effort to integrate and we embraced that and they were then part of the gang. Easy. There were no cliques and although you'd naturally get on with some people more than others, we all generally got along.

This changed one day and it affected us all. The vibes got dark. Four boys, mates who'd known each other a long time, pitched up. They were already a crew and had no need to make the effort to blend in. I have a very well-tuned aggro-sensor and it went off the moment they showed up.

Over the days and weeks there was a certain amount of natural cultural osmosis. They softened slightly, or at least appeared to soften, they made friends, sort of, but I never trusted them. Their vibes were rotten, they made me feel like a hen in a fox coop. The primal-fear alarm bleated every time they got close.

Before coming up to us in our mountain kibbutz they'd spent a couple of days in Tel Aviv. Apparently they had 'befriended' a kindly Israeli man who offered to let them crash at his place. In the morning before their hung-over host was awake they opened his closet and decided to take a shit in all his shoes. Who the fuck shits in a man's shoes?

I got on with everyone on kibbutz. I liked everyone and hopefully most people liked me. I worked hard, I was loyal, I was funny, and I liked making people laugh and generally people like laughing. All these likeable qualities had sadly put me firmly in their cross-hairs.

Out of the four, one was nice. He was good at heart and he knew that I knew it. I could see that he was using kibbutz as a way to start again perhaps, try new things, and meet new people, distance himself maybe. One of them was on the fence; on his own he was fine but with the others and a drink in him he changed. The other two were different. The one who was their self-proclaimed Boss was cunning, volatile and violent; he was a controlling bully trying to keep a crew together, a crew that perhaps had seen that maybe there was another way. A way that didn't include shitting in the shoes of a kindly stranger. The other was an ex-junkie, very paranoid; he could be controlled, manipulated, have his will moulded, have his mind fucked with by the Boss. To be honest, I didn't mind the junkie. He was all right. We got on and when we worked together he laughed a lot. The Boss had a problem with this. I sensed he knew his control was being diluted by volunteer life. Culture, art, music and laughter can do that really easily. His hold over them was loosening, and he hated that loss of control. The Boss was unpredictable and he frightened me.

One Friday night at the disco I'm having a slash, Bossman comes in and starts pissing next to me. He's happy and smiling, banter ensues although I'm always guarded. As I zip up and leave, this aside takes place.

'Oh, mate, meant to say, Junkie wants to see you.'

'Oh, right. What's that about?'

'Dunno, he was just looking for you.'

'Where is he?'

'Downstairs. You should go and find him, it seemed important.'

Lots of smiles and nods from Bossman. I leave and head downstairs. I find Junkie sitting in the corner on his own in a booth. I go over and sit down. He's different. Pissed, stony-faced. My alarm goes off. His opening gambit sends a red pulse up my feet and into my ears.

'Bossman told me you've been telling everyone that I'm a fucking queer, you fat cunt.'

Oh dear. He is nervous and jangly, his body jerks involuntarily, he looks down and my eyes follow. In his hand is a Stanley knife. I'm fucked. He's going to open me up, I have no doubt about that and I have no doubt I'm not his first.

What follows over the next twenty minutes, a twenty minutes that seems to go on and on, is some very quick, clear talking. An honesty and a truth he had not been expecting. He tenses and wants to cut me twice during this conversation. I can see the battle inside him. Eventually I talk him down. I see him soften, see his eyes change and I know I'm going to be okay. He retracts the slicer and sticks it back in his pocket. I get us a beer each, we clink and it's done. Inside I'm crying. I breathe a secret sigh of relief.

I look at Bossman and see that he's livid. His plan to get me wasn't meant to go down like this. It reinforces to me just how dangerous he is. I feel like someone has just tried to assassinate me. Junkie's failure to carve me up sets off a chain of events that'd lead to the senseless assault a couple of weeks later of a quiet Swedish boy. That boy did nothing to deserve being fucked up. I don't know what happened to kick it off, I don't think with people like that anything needs to happen. The bent perception of an insult is often the only thing needed to spark off a kicking.

The police come, an ambulance, but he refuses to press charges. It's too late though, the Israelis have seen enough and they're expelled. Two leave and two, Good Heart and Junkie, can stay. Over time they're assimilated, they become like us. I hope they stayed that way.

* * *

From time to time during my extended stay in the Middle East there was a little armed conflict. Obvs, I lived on the Lebanese border. Sometimes security got beefed up for one reason or another, more tanks and jeeps than usual would rush around. Sometimes shots would zip overhead, bright tracer rounds pinging off into the night. I'd been at a safety briefing once where I was told that if I received packages that smelled like almonds (Semtex, the plastic explosive, smells like almonds), I should stick it in a bucket and alert security. I was glad Mum never sent me that marzipan.

Sometimes on a Saturday I'd be sitting outside on the lawn, chilling, smoking, whatever and I'd watch jets and assault choppers, heavily laden with missiles, roar overhead, quick and very low. Thirty minutes later they'd head back, unladen and very high to avoid enemy surface-to-air missile batteries. I quickly got used to the sound of jets tearing overhead smashing the sound barrier. At first that noise sent the fear of god up me but, like most things, you get used to it. It was exciting to me.

One morning I had a special work detail in a new orchard working with a volunteer called Steve. He was sleazy as fuck and probably thirty-five, which is pretty old for a volunteer, and he emitted a Gary Glitter kind of vibe I couldn't ignore. Steve always had some kind of tummy bug or a boil or explosive diarrhoea. He had a thick sheen of sweat dripping off his heavily receding hairline, and his smoker's cough, and his need to hawk out ball after ball of smelly brown phlegm only added to his sexual allure.

They dropped us in a field, a shadeless brown rectangle fifteen minutes from home, and left us. To find out we were the only two people working in the orchard bothered me. Steve gave me the willies. Still it was hot, the sun was shining and the work was honest and hard so who was I to complain. We had our polystyrene cube filled with cold water and we had our tools. It was all we needed. Steve and I sat and smoked a ciggie and eventually began our day. We dug holes in the ground and popped saplings into the earth. Digging, planting, watering, so sweet. I would've rather been on my own of course but I wasn't so what the fuck. Crack on, big boy.

Later that morning a formation of attack helicopters roared overhead, whatevs. It wasn't unusual but I'd always stop what I was doing and look up, it was exciting. The choppers entered Lebanon and attacked a convoy of vehicles. In the vehicles were the leader of Hezbollah and his extended family. I didn't know this though. I was planting apple trees with Steve who was doing a series of really dribbly guffs. I heave. I hear pops and rumblings – it's not Steve, it's the sound of tanks and artillery on the move. This is normal, normal to me anyway.

Steve tells me the dysentery he contracted in Cambodia has returned. He limpjogs off and does a noisy shit. I heave again. I understand more than most that if you have to go you have to go. I get it. The problem I have now though is we're in a big field, there's no cover, no big tree or ditch to do it behind or in. There's nowhere to hide. I'm forced to watch sweaty Steve, throbbing boil on his neck, hanging off a young sapling grunting out jet after jet of broige liquid terror. I want to die. After five minutes or so I've seen enough, I have to turn around. I cannot watch another plip. I close my eyes but I could still hear it. I *can* still hear it.

From the security fence a very loud siren begins to wail. I'd never heard that siren before and it unnerves me. Steve joins me, rubbing soft earth into his hands to de-clag his slim, hairless fingers. They are stained brown, it could be tobacco, although it didn't taste much like tobacco.

While we look north into Southern Lebanon the siren continues. Probably just a drill. I see a small shape arcing high into the air – to quote my darling Jimi Hendrix it's 'a giant lipstick and pencil tube shaped thing'. It's silent and quick and beautiful. Clearly it has somewhere it needs to be. It's a missile. It passes overhead and drops beneath the horizon into Northern Israel. Thud. A concussive boom. An explosion. Then another.

All over the sky from the north I now see similarly shaped things heading our way. This is Hezbollah's response to the convoy attack. Steve and I instinctively lie down in the field. We have no other plan. The Israelis will come to get us, right? While we're lying there we have a cigarette, why not, nothing else to do. I don't feel afraid at this point. My fear comes later, much later, maybe twenty years later, to be honest.

This shit is too trippy to be afraid. It was more unbelievable than fearsome. After thirty minutes or so an army jeep roars into the field, angrily sounding its horn. Eyal, who is Yael's husband and the kibbutz's head of security, jumps out, he's a handsome bugger and definitely not to be messed with. He has a cheeky grin and likes to laugh so we get on well. He motions for us to run to him. I finish my fag and scarper.

We'd been the only two volunteers working on our own and we'd essentially been forgotten. When I get back to the kibbutz I'm cross, I also find out they've decided against serving lunch, I don't understand. I kick around the car park fuming, grumbling about being hungry. A rocket screams overhead. Eyal shouts at me to run and get down into the volunteers' bomb shelter. I kick my heels and walk at my own pace. What a helmet.

When I shuffle into view of the shelter the Israelis shout at me again! Twice in one day. How rude, I'm hungry! They're amazed at my stubborn moody shuffle as missiles rain down all over the north of Israel. I'm ushered into the shelter, I continue my grumble about lunch.

The bomb shelter deal was this: if it was an air raid we'd be put into the shelter. If it were an incursion by terrorists we'd have to go to our rooms and lock the door until an all-clear was given. The logic behind this was simple and stark. Terrorists could kill more of us at once if we were all in the same place. There was brief mention of a bag of grenades being stuffed into air vents.

The bomb shelter was a thick concrete square sunk thirty feet into the ground, dusty stairs led to the outer giant steel door lined with heavy rubber seals in case of chemical attack. That led to a small chamber on the left and a storeroom on the right, this led to another massively heavy blast door, through this the bomb shelter proper. Our home for the next two weeks.

On the walls around the shelter hung metal bunk beds, suspended from thick chains and stacked three high. There were probably thirty-two or so bunks in all. The rest slept on mattresses on the floor. It was fun at first, novel, but that soon wore off – fifty people in a damp dusty shelter getting bombed by Hezbollah gets old really fucking quickly.

Despite the bullshit and bravado we were afraid and nervous. Outside, rockets thudded into the holy earth, inside we'd hear the concussive thud and the sound of dust raining onto the crispy polythene outer shells of our sleeping bags. No one sleeps that night. The next three days were bad. The IDF move heavy artillery close to our position. It was no longer just Russian-made Katyusha rockets heading south, it was now also the relentless *thump thump thump* of the IDF's merciless response heading the other way.

Again sleep proves difficult. I lie awake listening to the boom and counter-boom of the exchange. I think someone got killed in the next kibbutz over. We were lucky. One or two degrees clicked either way on the rudimentary sighting mechanism and it could've been us. It could easily have been us.

The days pass, we rally, our spirits lift and fall. The nights are still shit and weird but during the day we are allowed to leave the shelter and go to our rooms or work inside the kibbutz a little bit. Sometimes the sirens would begin again and we'd be forced back underground.

There's a security meeting one afternoon to review the situation. If the Israelis were serious you could guess the situation

was serious. The Israelis were serious. They spoke about potentially evacuating us south to Tel Aviv. There was a murmur
from the volunteers, not one of us wanted to leave. We were all
really close and needed to see this through together. The
kibbutzniks never forget that. We were treated differently after
the war.

At night when all seemed quiet, me and some of the other
boys would creep up the dusty concrete stairs and sit outside
on the roof of the shelter smoking. One night we watched a
missile streak overhead, its engine burned hot and blue across
the night. We watch in silence, the engine flickers and the flame
dims. It falls from the sky some way across the horizon. A silent
flash. A thud and it's done. We finish our ciggies and decide to
go back inside.

This sustained bombardment is bad for my nerves, everyone's nerves. A decision's made, the Israelis move us south for
a couple of days, relieve the tension. Our work boss, Michel,
the laidback afro-cowboy, invited a few of his faves to ride in
the VW Caravelle with him. Sweet, I loved those Caravelles.
With Michel at least you could be guaranteed a nice bit of
reggae on the radio. What you need during a bombardment is
some 'Bam Bam' from Sister Nancy, it's good, it helped.

We leave at pace heading down the side of the Bekaa Valley
on a hairpin-heavy road onto the baking valley floor below.
The Bekaa Valley in the north of Israel is the northern limit of
the giant fissure, which eventually travels south and becomes
the Great Rift Valley. It's amazing.

Once we're down Michel pulls into a petrol station to fill up.
We all get out of the van and following the Israelis' lead smoke
ciggies right there on the forecourt. I love a lack of health and
safety. I smoke and casually drink a cold Kinley, it's a kind of

Fanta. Michel pays and leaves the shop. The moment he exits the air-raid sirens sound.

A forecourt packed with smokers filling up their cars empties in twenty seconds flat. Some people run towards the nearest shelter. Others speed away heading south. I panic slightly, we all panic slightly except Michel who pats his pockets looking for a lighter. Do we run to the shelter? Do we run into the vehicle and flee? I'm essentially standing on top of a concrete box filled with thousands of gallons of a highly flammable accelerant. I don't feel comfortable standing here.

Michel, who's the most unflappable man I ever met, is now stood looking at something in the middle distance. He casually flicks out a ciggie from his soft pack and lights it up in one smooth motion.

'Guys, come to see.' He points north as his lazy, semi-closed eyes scan the horizon, it's the most animated I've ever seen him.

'There!' He points at something, sure enough a long, sleek, black pencil, with a very basic computer and a nose packed with high-explosive, sharks over the lip of the valley. It skims the geography with no effort at all. It's beautiful and deadly and I can't take my eyes off it. It ghosts its way towards us before swerving left, jinking hard right and slamming into the road we'd just driven down ten minutes earlier.

I love it when you actually get to see the difference first-hand between the speed of light and the speed of sound. I'm fascinated and afraid. I see the missile pummel into the mountainside and a large section of earth silently slumps into the air and slides like water down the valley. A second or two later a giant bang. A supersonic shockwave hammers around the valley. Its noise amplified by the steep sides. It leads me to think about how it'd be great to be assassinated by a highly trained sniper with a Barrett .50 cal sitting 400 metres away, high in a clock tower or minaret. I think that's how I'd like to go. No pain, no awful illness. That giant cartridge would turn my soft computer into a sticky pink foam in a thousandth of a second, long before I ever heard the bang of the gun. You would literally be dead before you knew it. Cool! I digress. I've just watched this science right in front of me, live.

'We should go,' mutters Michel, and we go.

* * *

I'd been in Israel, give or take with my first bit and now, for twenty months. I have my own room now, it's real 'big-dog' shit, no more sharing for me. I'd taken all four single beds and I'd lashed them together with zipties to form a single mega-bed. That's real power. Colonel Kurtz was back. It was time for me to leave.

Easier said than done. I was in a rut and I liked it, it was what I knew. I was comfortable swaggering around like I owned the gaff. Something had to change and naturally the catalyst was a girl. I met her and fell for her and when she left my heart wasn't in it any more. Three weeks later I was gone.

I didn't actually like Rachel very much at the beginning. I was sitting with Dave in the common room and she swanned in and turned the TV over while we were watching it! That's not on. You don't do that. She drove me bonkers (a sure sign I liked her).

From the off I was always fighting a losing battle, but I didn't really care. I liked her. I knew she kind of liked me too but I probably understood from the get-go that long term it wouldn't work. I was so different then, confused and very jealous, wanting someone to cling to. She wasn't it. Not then, we were both really young. Rachel, originally from the depths of Virginia Water, was a free spirit. A traveller, and the most sociable person I knew. Everybody liked her. She also spoke fluent Hebrew.

We'd been hanging out together, having a laugh, not having a laugh, being together, not being together and definitely not having sex. It was a confusing time. One day Rachel invited me to spend a night with her down in Tiberias. I was excited and nervous. This had never happened to me before, a weekend away with a girl! I felt a bit grown up. It was Passover and she had to meet her grandmother who was an Israeli. I wasn't Jewish and could not be relied on to behave so I wasn't invited to meet Granny. Which was fine by me.

She'd meet her Bubbie, I'd hang around drinking and we'd hook up later and spend the night in one of the lifeguard towers. As ever, food was a big draw for me, I was happy to leave the culinary monotony of Bar-Am for a couple of nights. The thought of rich, crispy, buttery pizza plus the chance to hang out with this nice girl who liked me was a dreamy notion. I talked at length on the journey down about that pizza.

When we arrived in Tiberias I had my spirit crushed pretty fucking quickly, my dream lay in tatters. This had nothing to do with Rachel. This had everything to do with Passover and kosher law. It meant pizza places couldn't use leavened dough. Instead of thin, crispy, buttery NYC-style pizza it was kosher cheddar and tomato puree sprinkled on a stack of matzo crackers. This was a bad omen. I should've turned round and gone straight back to kibbutz. No woman was worth this.

She said shalom and we arranged to meet later. The year 1992 was a time before mobile phones, for me anyway. To think of a time before mobile phones now seems utterly ridiculous. Life was different then. You made an arrangement and you had to stick to it, there was no texting a raincheck an hour before. I found a bar, post up and ready myself for the wait.

I was a long way from having to meet her grandmother. During an earlier trip we'd tried to meet members of her family. It didn't go so well. We were in Jerusalem on a kibbutz trip, all the volunteers, including Rachel and me. It was great. She had family in Jerusalem so while the rest of us went on the piss she went off to visit them. We'd arranged to meet Rachel and her cousins in a bar called The Underground.

The Underground was like an Israeli version of the cantina in Mos Eisley. It was a place where one could do shots, have a shit falafel, eye up the birds, punch on, piss yourself and quaff litres of cold draught beer. I'd done all of these things by the time Rachel turned up with her handsome teetotal cousins. I was not good when they arrived. I was shirtless, jeans around my ankles soaked in my own wee-wee liquid. I lay semi-conscious over a large wooden barrel, dribbling. It's all about first impressions, isn't it?

I completely understand Rachel's decision to not allow me to meet Granny. It was probably wise. I wasn't ready, I'll be the first to admit. I'd never really had a girlfriend, sure there were crushes and teen fumblings but this felt like next level potential girlfriend shit.

A couple of hours later we hook up, and keeping my promise I was definitely not pissed. We got our shit together and headed south out of the city on foot in search of somewhere to stay. It was getting late and the more we walked the more we could tell our plan of sleeping on a lifeguard tower had a few flaws.

That winter there'd been a very heavy and prolonged snow-fall all over the north. Which was great, I loved snow because as we know on kibbutz snow means chips. It also meant that the melted snow had added almost fifteen feet of water into the Galilee, this meant no beaches and the lifeguard towers we were planning to sleep in were half covered with floodwater. I heard a story about a biblical zoo on the banks of the Galilee. It houses all the animals that lived in the Holy Land at the time of Christ. They had a few Nile crocodiles. Sadly in the spring their enclosures became deluged by almost fifteen feet of melt water, and simply swam out.

It took us an hour or so to realise our plan has gone to shit. We turned and headed back towards Tiberias. We're tired and end up squabbling a bit. It's close to 1 a.m. and we're not really talking. In the distance we see the lights of a car coming towards us.

All good slasher/hitcher films start the same way. A car pulls up fifty feet away. Stopping slowly. It's brightly lit from the front so we see a nice silhouette through the back window of the faceless driver. We look at each other, excited that we have a lift and run towards the Zodiac Killer – I mean our lift. He leans over and opens the passenger door. We crane to peer in. He's a heavily decorated soldier. We're saved! Rachel lifts the front seat up and I jump into the back, she sits up front and a conversation in Hebrew begins.

I now get my first look at the Zodiac and ironically he actually looks a bit like John Carroll Lynch. He's a major in the IDF, fancy! He also has an Uzi in his lap. No biggie. He speaks to me in broken English, he seems all right, he opens the glove box and slings me a bottle of vodka. Brilliant. Free vodka. I like this guy. We pull off and I take a big swig and pass it forward. He swigs too which is unorthodox but what the fuck. We drive in silence except for the odd Hebrew from time to time. More vodka is quaffed.

After about twenty minutes we turn down a pitch-black dirt track, he pulls up, turns the engine off and we sit in silence for a time. Some more Hebrew breaks out. The major is looking back at me smiling, talking Hebrew to Rachel. I happily smile back and nod and continue my assault on his bottle. To say I was totally oblivious to a growing weirdness would be a little inaccurate, I had sensed the beginning of a minor weirdness. Rachel suddenly jumps out of the car and ratchets the seat forward. She shrieks at me.

'Get out now!'

'Why? Free vodka.'

'Get the fuck out of the car.'

I bumble out of the back seat, grumbling. I was so sick of walking.

'What the fuck's going on?'

'Just walk, go, right now.'

I was starting to get the point. I half walked, half ran away from drunken Major Zodiac with his curly hair.

After some running we stopped and turned to see him still sat there, lights on. He was making a decision. Thinking things through. The car starts and slowly begins to reverse. Rachel relaxes enough to tell me what happened. When Zodiac was talking to her in Hebrew, even though he was looking back at me and smiling, he was propositioning her. Trying to convince her to fuck him, even suggesting I could stay on his couch while it went on, which was nice of him I guess. He was fairly insistent towards the end, forcing Rachel to leap out. Poor girl. What a blind idiot I'd been.

We trudged back into town. Our common enemy meant we were actually in a bit of a better mood. We walked round the city a bit and eventually found some stairs leading up to a large flat roof. We checked it out. It was clean and quiet so we made our bed up there. It was nice to finally be together. We snuggled in and fell asleep.

After a few hours we were awakened by the sound of a Muezzin calling the Muslim faithful to prayer. It was fucking loud. We'd inadvertently slept on top of a mosque. We were also now surrounded by thirty cats. It was nice, I like cats.

* * *

When Rachel left Israel I missed her so much. I felt hollow. I wanted to leave. I'd been there long enough. So I left, again. When I got home Mum and Dad told me of their plan to move to Wales. Back to the place it all began for her. I think it was the right thing to do. Mum and Dad were not well, they'd got the council to rehouse them in a little place called Letterston, it's a small village on the main road into Fishguard. This news meant I had eight weeks to get my shit together and find somewhere to live. Great.

I'd made a mate in Israel this last time out, a man called Pat. He was a lot older than me and kind of a serious person. I liked him though. He was Irish and loved the Craic. One day on kibbutz I noticed a big red scar under one of his arms, near the chest. Me being nosy I asked how he got it; at first he wouldn't tell me, he seemed sheepish and quickly covered it up. So I left it.

Weeks later, after a few bevvies, he starts to tell me a story about what he did back in Ireland. I'm made to promise not to tell anyone. I'm excited, my interest definitely piqued. He tells me he's an officer in the Anti-Terrorist police in Northern Ireland and the scar is a result of being shot in a firefight with the IRA. During a pause in the battle, Pat rolls over onto his back to grab a fresh magazine which is strapped to his chest and he's shot by a sniper in the only part of his body not protected by his armour. Right under the armpit. Holy fuck. Tough break. Poor him. That was that. He never mentioned it again except to say he'd come to Israel to convalesce. After that we became mates. I completely trusted him.

A couple of weeks after I got back from Israel I get a phone call from Pat. Amazing. He's in London and wonders if he can come and crash at mine for a couple of days. Absolutely you can. He turns up, we embrace, hugs, laughter. I introduce him to Mum and Dad, he's charming and funny, brings a bottle for Dad, something for Mum. Real textbook shit.

Pat stays, we have a laugh. I like and trust him. He's my mate. Most mornings he'd head off to use the phonebox on the corner, he needed to check in with his commanding officer. Cool. Our flat is so small that having a big Irish lump on the sofa is making the place feel even smaller.

Mum and Dad start to hassle me, rightly so. A few days has turned into two weeks! I think Pat senses his time is coming to an end here. I feel bad for Mum and Dad but awkward about asking him to leave.

One morning Pat heads out to make some calls. When he comes back he tells me I have to rent a car. His C/O has given him a job while he's here and he needs my help. I'm afraid and excited.

'What do you want me to do?'

'There's an old pub in Peckham, there's a package that's been left there for me. I need to go and get it.'

'Right . . . Um, sure.'

'There's a house. We need to park up the street and see who comes and goes.'

This seems way above my pay grade but he seems to know what he's doing so fuck it. I'll be a spy for the day. I hire a car. He tells me it has to be powerful in case we need to get away. I squeak a bit inside. We drive down to this old boarded-up pub. I don't fancy talking very much.

'Pull in here. Keep the car running.'

'How long will you be?'

'Don't know.'

Pat leaps out. He looks around to see if we've been followed. Classic spy stuff. He walks off and disappears behind the back of the pub. I need to shit so badly. After ten minutes he comes out holding a small package.

'Drive!'

I leave at pace revving loudly. After a while I ask him what's in the package. He tells me it's a handgun. My shit comes out. This is way too much for me. I'm actually properly afraid. The next day he tells me he doesn't think I should come on the stake-out. I'm thrilled. He leaves very early and comes back late afternoon. I ask no questions and he tells me nothing but seems happy. He wants to celebrate. His treat. Cool. I'm still on edge but a night in London makes me feel better. It'll also give Mum and Dad a chance to have the place to themselves for the night.

We spend the night tearing it up in town, this is great, this feels like we're back on kibbutz. This feels like the old Pat I know. I relax into him again. At one point we cross a packed Leicester Square when a rangy kid, all ribcage and long arms, approaches us.

'Pills pills pills . . .' He's got pills apparently. I make that kind of 'hmmm, yeah, um, sure' face. I pull some money out. He pulls some pills out. I look at Pat to see if he's up for it. I've forgotten the job he does. I turn to see him grabbing hold of this kid round the neck. Balls.

From out of nowhere two of the dealer's mates run towards Pat, he gets hammered by flying haymakers. Pat grabs the dealer even harder, his head deflecting the fists of these kids. I see others approaching.

Pat screams at me. I am literally shitting myself. 'Run to a phone and dial 999. Tell them Anti-Terrorist police officer needs back up.'

I do not need asking twice. I fucking sprint out of there. I'm being followed. I find a phonebox on the east side of the square and dial 999. I tell them what I'm told to say. Even before the phonecall is finished I start to hear sirens. The door to the phonebox is jerked open, I'm punched. I grab the door and pull it closed. I'm shouting down the phone. Three youths, mates of the dealer, associates, are trying to get into this phonebox. Through the window I can see police vans and cars and officers pouring into the square.

It offers little or no relief to me. These kids are tearing at the door to the phonebox. They've seen me in the square with Pat. The door's flung open, I pull it back closed, through the gap, fists, punches and knives are trying to scythe their way in, trying to cut me. Street vengeance. Four coppers pound their way towards me. The kids see them and bounce. There's a brief scuffle outside, I see my chance and head out, running. All around me the scene is absolute mayhem. I can only estimate the number of Old Bill but I'd have to say more than fifty. Easy.

I find a copper. My hope is they'll stick me in a car and take me away. My fear is I'll be followed and stabbed, killed in an alley outside the back door of a theatre. I'm so fucking mad with Pat right now.

I explain to the policeman what happened and that I was the one who made the call. Instead of taking me off the street and out of danger he tells me to run to Vine Street, 'it's where they're taking everyone.' I don't pause, or wait or hesitate. I just run and run and run. My feet snap against the concrete, my heart pounds, my lungs are so fucking mad with Pat right now.

I leave the din of shouting and screaming and sirens and fury behind but I don't stop until I find the Nick. I run in headlong and burst into words. Pat is here. He's bloodied and bruised. We're taken into a custody suite. We sit in silence. I can't even look at him. The door begins to open.

He spit-whispers at me, 'Don't say a fucking word.' I couldn't be any more sober right now if I tried.

A detective comes in and he and Pat speak for a moment, it's terse and business-like. It makes me nervous. Pat reaches into his pocket and pulls out his warrant card, the thing that identifies him as a policeman. The detective softens at this. I relax by 4%.

A conversation happens, it's full of language I don't or won't understand. A document gets signed. I sit and say nothing. Then it's over. The cop stands, Pat stands, they shake hands. It's done. We can go. What has just gone down? What the fuck is going on? I'm so afraid I avoid Leicester Square for almost six years. I feel bad for the dealer.

When I get home I'm angry and confused. We don't talk. I think I want Pat to go now. I know we're mates and shit but enough is enough. I'm not a copper, in fact at this point I'm probably completely the opposite. Pat senses this.

The next morning he heads out to make his secret phone calls. When he comes back we're all there. I sense something is really wrong. His eyes are red.

'Are you okay, mate?' I forget about last night. He stumbles and stammers.

'My mammie's dead.' He releases a noise like a fat boar struck by a javelin and falls into my mum's arms crying like a baby. Shit. Poor him. There's no way we can ask him to leave now. I watch him grieve his way through the nice bottle of scotch he bought Dad upon arrival. We leave it for a while, imagining he'll go home and take care of what needs to be done. He doesn't though, not immediately.

A couple of days later he gets up and goes to make his daily phone calls. Strangely, after two hours he's not back. Six hours later he is still MIA. He doesn't come back that night, he doesn't come back the next day, or the next, in fact he never comes back. He never comes back. I never see him again. This, to me, is the most frightening thing of all, the not knowing.

After a couple of days my parents decide to search his bags and phone the police. He left everything he had at my house. Left it all. Just ran. He even left his passport, one of three he had which are all in different names. What the fuck was going on?

My mum is genuinely concerned, she files a missing person's report, the police come round, take his stuff and promise to make enquiries. Mum decides to let his work know. His work being the Anti-Terrorist police in Northern Ireland. She makes a lot of calls and tracks down, eventually, a man who Pat claimed was his C/O. This man knew nothing about Pat. He had never heard of the man Mum described.

I thought he was either a spy or a member of a terrorist organisation. A sleeper. Either was bad for me. For a long while I truly believed someone would knock on my door and I'd be killed. I'd seen too much. Also what was all that bullshit when he busted the pill dealers? How the fuck did that go down? The coppers there treated him like one of their own. And the scar! What the eff was that? Who was this man I'd befriended in Israel? I didn't know him at all.

It didn't help my conspiracy paranoia one bit. The trail then goes cold. Days become weeks become months. My fear subsides. My mind quietens. Years later and I mean, like, six years later, I get a phone call from Mum. She'd heard something about Pat. The police had contacted her after all this time. Pat was not a copper. Pat was not a terrorist. Pat was a professional conman. Holy. Fucking. Balls. A conman.

It turned out I was not his first stop after Israel and I wasn't his last. After he fled mine, leaving everything, he made his way to Sweden, obviously with another fake or forged passport, to hook up with a girl he'd met in Israel. She was a lovely woman. She was gentle and quiet, and suffered from a severe lack of confidence, probably due to the fact she was really quite big.

He seduced that poor girl, told her he loved her. Once she was in love that's when he closed the trap, got her poor gran to sign stuff over, lend him thousands of kronor. Then he left. I don't know who he went to after that but it went on. Eventually he'd been caught and ended up going to prison for a fairly long time.

Part Three

At some point Mum and Dad get the nod from the council to say their house in Wales was ready. She was going home, I was homeless. Nice. I know it wasn't as cut and dried as that but that's how it felt then. But despite the fact that I was soon to be on my own, I was thrilled Mum and Dad had the chance to leave Ray Lodge – a stark, modern construct and a reminder of their failings as people and as parents.

Rachel, the free spirit, had come to live in London, in a kind of squat-thing in Golders Green known to me simply as 'Golders'. I want to be near her so I head there. I've no friends and no mum and dad back in Woodford Bridge and I need somewhere to live, somewhere to work and I definitely need some cheddar so I go to Golders Green.

The house was a big old lump of a place sitting on top of a kosher bakery. It was a madhouse and a shit hole, but it smelled nice. It had four large bedrooms and a kitchen that was usually the centre of high jinks. The loft had also been converted into a living space. I never went upstairs and never met anyone who lived up there. I knew they *were* there because at night I could hear them moving around, whispering.

All in all I think twenty-five people lived in that place, crammed inside on top of one another. Each room had five or so people plus the whispering loft dwellers. That meant the house was always happening, it was noisy, the place never slept. (Except at night.)

The people who'd been at Golders the longest got the best rooms; when someone left everyone moved up a space, better room, bigger bed.

I was the last to arrive so I got the smallest bedroom although it wasn't actually a bedroom, it was a cupboard. It had no windows and instead of a door a kind of plastic shower curtain. It was a shower curtain. The room was so narrow that the thin single mattress which was my bed bent up the sides of the walls. I felt like a hot dog sleeping in a bun.

I wasn't in that cupboard long. There was a fairly swift turn-around of folk with people coming and going. It's what I'd become used to. A space came up in one of the rooms and I took it. I was enjoying life at Golders and my on-again off-again thing with Rachel. There were five of us crammed into a bedroom, but a good five. Me, Sarit and CJ, Lauren and, I think, Jo, Rachel's mate.

Sarit was a beautiful but very fiery Israeli. CJ was a tall, beautiful male model from Socal with an easy smile and big booming laugh. They were girlfriend and boyfriend. Like a lot of beautiful Israeli women, she was hard work. She often sent CJ out at three o'clock in the morning to get treats. He always obliged. What a good egg. I'm not sure I would've.

Lauren was nice, she was a London girl through and through with West African heritage. She was chippy and had a laugh that always made me smile.

For a young man, living with Lauren could be tough. I'd never met anyone who was so brazen and open about their body and nakedness before. After showering she'd come back into the room where I was trying to plough my way through Solzhenitsyn's *Cancer Ward* and towel dry *and* oil her bare, lovely, giant African breasts. It was amazing. I didn't know where to look. I was barely out of my teens at this point and although Israel had opened my eyes I still had a lot to learn.

One night Lauren and I decided to take a shit load of mind openers and explore the mysteries of the universe, laughing like fucking idiots. We sat in the kitchen looking at each other change and morph as the sun came up. Briefly I became an African girl and briefly she became an overweight white man. How we laughed. The door to the house opened at about 5.30 a.m. and a complete stranger walked in. This wasn't odd, the door was never locked and people would often come and go.

This stranger was a woman in her thirties, pencil thin with a big helmet of bright orange hair. She smiled and joined us at the table. Was this happening? It was. Cope. Breathe. I'm African once more and I cluck and suck my teeth. We both look at her, eyes wide, she fumbles uncomfortably. One of my eyelids droops down and briefly obscures my view. I lift my eyelid up with both hands and the woman then makes a noise. It is long and it sounds like she is saying the word *buuuuuuuuurrrrrrrrrrddddddddddddooooooo*. There is no such word in my language. I don't think there is such a word in any language. I look to Lauren for reassurance and support and discover she is no longer there.

Lauren runs away screaming at about the third 'u', leaving me sweating and trying to lift my big floppy eyelid back over my head so I can see. I smile and back away into a cupboard; the cupboard is tiny and it forces me to re-emerge briefly. I smile and a tooth falls out. I turn and run up the stairs. Later I sadly find out the poor woman was there to meet a friend who was taking her to the airport, she was also profoundly deaf. It was too much for our brains to take. Poor girl. What idiots.

* * *

I began working at Chiquito Mexican restaurant at Staples Corner when I was twenty. Let me, off the bat, state for the record that when I began working there it served the finest Mexican food to be found anywhere in London. All the sauces were handmade fresh every morning by an army of brawny Ugandans. Now, sadly, it's an absolute abomination, just my opinion you understand. What a shame we live in a shitty world where the phrase 'Brand Standard' is commonplace. Anyhoo . . .

I began working on the bar at Chiquito sometime in the summer and really liked it. I only planned to stay there for three months until I got my shit together, whatever that meant – it felt more like something to say to convince myself that I wouldn't be there for five years, which of course I was.

It would also be the first place I actually set eyes on my heterosexual life partner, best friend and godfather to my son, Mr Simon Pegg. I'm jumping ahead of myself though.

Restaurants, like kibbutzim, have a high turnover of staff or 'Fresh Meat' as we liked to call them. At this point I was fresh meat. At first I was partnered with another bartender, known as Wavy Davy. An angry Kiwi who seemed to hate his job, his life and especially the customers. That said, he was a good egg at heart and certainly fun to work with. I'd never known anyone be so cheeky to customers. It was all about the tips. I loved his catchphrase 'you flaming ball-bag', it was a real winner.

Dave showed me around the big walk-in fridges and freezers, it was a place I'd get to know intimately over the next few months. Sometimes if I was mega hung-over I'd pull a chair into the fridge and sit there wishing I was dead.

The first time he showed me round the big freezers he pulled out a tray of frozen ice cream balls covered in cornflakes and bit into one like an apple. These were the deep-fried ice creams, an important part of Chiquito's elaborate birthday treat that all customers got if it was their birthday. He bit into it and stuck it back on the tray. I'd never seen lunacy like it. A few days later I found myself alone in the freezer. Wanting to be as cool as Dave I grab an ice cream and stuff it in my mouth. Sadly though it wasn't an ice cream. It was a ball of frozen shrimp butter. It was horrid and I vowed I would never randomly eat frozen balls of unknown matter again. It's a promise I have never broken.

The most fascinating part of the whole place for me was the kitchen. As you kicked open the flappy 'In' door you came upon the kitchen proper, we called it the Line. It was not for the faint of heart. Many was the time I'd seen bad waitresses made to cry by good cooks. A bad waiter can fuck shit up very quickly in a busy kitchen. A couple of times too I'd see some low-level violence, angry waiters pulling cooks through the line. People would have to jump in to stop it going any further. When, years after, I worked in the kitchen myself, I lost my shit with a waiter one Sunday and ended up pulling him through the line! The key is to strike fast, get a nice tight grip and then lean back and stand up. The waiter comes right through; if you're lucky you drag them across the beans and sauces and they end up looking like an oil painting.

On the far right of the line was starters, next to that the section where all the dishes were garnished, and just behind was the heart and anus of the kitchen, a very big, very hot griddle. Next to this there's a section where soft tacos and burritos are prepared. Throw in a couple of big ovens and the odd salamander grill and you get a picture of what the line looked like. On the far left was the pot wash. This was the home of Karim, a stick-thin Ugandan man who had the sing-ing voice of an angel and spoke little or no English. The only thing I ever heard him say was, 'Can I have cheeseburger' – they fed us a staff meal every day and a cheeseburger was always his. I caught him lots of times eating scraps off the plates, something we'd all indulge in every now and then. Who could resist a juicy shrimp?

The only other interaction I had with Karim was a curious one: he'd hunch over like an old man and shuffle towards me in his ever-present Wellie boots, he'd then grab me in his thin but exceedingly strong arms and pretend to jerk me off, while making this noise, *dibbydibbydibbydibbydibby*. We'd all howl with laughter. Why?

But for now the bar was my realm, it'd be three more years before I made the move back of house. There were two sections to the bar, customers and service. Service meant you only made drinks for the waiters and their tables. On the weekend it was bedlam. The little bar printer would beep and puke out a ticket and another and another and another; if you weren't fast enough you'd end up with a bunch of very cross waiters all demanding their drinks first.

Wavy Davy never had a problem with demanding waiters, he was more than happy to tell those 'flaming ball-bags' to get fucked. On a busy weekend I liked it very much, I liked the buzz and the pressure. Double shifts were cool but long as it was busy most of the day. The bar was not the place to legally make a lot of tips. If you wanted to potentially earn £100 a day for a busy double the floor was where you needed to be. That's where the action was, the glamour.

I started working for £1.92 an hour plus tips. It was nothing but I didn't need much as I paid hardly any rent. Any money I earned went on weed, drinking and cabs. I never went on holiday, I didn't have a car or kids, I didn't really need or want much. Chiquito was my life right now, I needed nothing except what it gave me.

Unlike people I went to school with, faces from the old neighbourhood and even most people from kibbutz, some of the people I met in Chiquito became friends I still know today.

Big Red was a man with the words 'Fuck You' tattooed inside his lower lip. Red was a cunning little silver fox, he always had an angle, a way to make a quick buck, a way to stick it to the man with a scam. He was with a girl called Chicky, a real beauty with a great laugh, she was lovely and we got on well. She was like my big sister. They were a great couple, great people and they really looked after me. Chicky and Rachel were great friends who knew each other before Israel, so we all hung out a lot. I think I attended my first dinner party in their house. It was a very mature thing for me to do, I may even have managed to wear trousers. They had a small flat down Kilburn way crammed to the rafters with cool shit. They were stylish, cool people.

Chicky was there the day me and Rachel split up for good. Rachel was going to LA to pursue her dream of becoming an actress. The day before she left there'd been a horrible misunderstanding about a used condom she found in my bedroom. She accused me of cheating on her. I hadn't but she found my 'posh wank' excuse hard to swallow.

Racked with sorrow, me and Chicky sat up all night drinking in their flat. Red, who'd left the restaurant to become a milk-man, got up at four to do his round to find us still up. At about five and after many tears Chicky convinced me that going to Heathrow to say goodbye was a good idea, a grand romantic gesture. Yes! I was all about those, great idea. I have a vague recollection of us being in a car at one point, and then we were magically at Heathrow.

Rachel was really happy to see Chicky. Not so much me. It could've had something to do with the ironing board and bottle of Captain Morgan I'd insisted on bringing. Rachel's mother was also there. She hated me. I hid, trembling behind the ironing board until Rachel had gone. That board definitely had its uses.

On the way past, her mother hissed at me, 'I feel really sorry for you.'

I wasn't sure what she meant but I took it to heart and cried all the way home. What was I crying about? Stupid drink.

Sometimes on busy nights Chicky, a trusted employee, would work in the cash booth, a little cupboard in the corner of the kitchen where we'd drop off the bills and money after the tables had paid. Once you were in there you had to stay in there. Security, you understand.

One particular Saturday, and this was rare for me, I had the whole day off. I arranged to meet a mate who also happened to be my general manager at the time. We went to drink in a shit pub up in North Finchley, pints and pool being the order of the day. After about an hour a shifty cunt approaches and offers me a magical and ancient laughing compound. I gratefully accept.

He limps off, returning ten minutes later, and discreetly drops the package into one of the pockets of the pool table. Real cloak and dagger shit. The package rolls into the body of the machine and is lost. He returns ten minutes later and, forgetting all the subterfuge, decides to simply put it in my hand. We consume the HaHas and wait for Christ to arrive.

At one point my GM suggests we go back to the restaurant and drink free shit and have a fajita or two. The Toucan and me agree this is a good plan and we float off into the sky. When we get there the place is calming down a bit, still busy but manageable. I wonder for a moment if anyone else can see this Toucan?

We sit in a corner of the bar. He drinks beer and I gulp a giant strawberry margarita. Delish. Someone comes and tells me Chicky wants me to go and say hi. In the kitchen it's bright and hectic and all the Ugandans shout the word 'Woomla' at me. This is actually true. The Ugandans on the line refer to me as the Woomla King. I can't remember why but I like this alter ego.

My big dumb grin arrives before I do and knocks on the cash booth door. Chicky opens up and beckons the rest of me to come in.

'How fucked are you?' she howls, laughing.

I loved Chicky's laugh, part dockworker, part geisha. My eyes roll and then focus on a button sort of hidden under the cash desk.

'What's that?'

'Panic button.' Hahahahaha . . . we laugh.

I'm panicking a bit so I jab at it. Janine now panics a bit too, but she's laughing and is quickly calmed by my confidence that it doesn't do anything. As she's laughing I jab at it again and again. We chat briefly and she reminds me I shouldn't have my spirit bird in the kitchen. I understand. We have a little cuddle and I move out to finish my giant red drink.

As I kick open the swingy both ways door I'm met by the sight of twelve armed policemen steaming through the front door of the place. The button worked. I look to the boss who seems really cross with me. The Toucan stifles a giggle and pecks a nut open on my head.

'It was me! I leant on it by mistake!' I fess up immediately. Honesty is definitely the best policy when confronted with firearms I find.

I'm frogmarched outside and given a very stern dressing down. I'm so glad they can't see the Toucan. A rare and endangered bird such as this could bring me a shit load of trouble. The Toucan winks at me and pops a nice ripe berry into my mouth and we smile, he nuzzles my ear with his beak and right then I know we'll be okay. They buy it and leave. Sorry SWAT team, totes my fault.

This sadly was not my last brush with armed police, there was to be what has now become a legendary story – when I say legendary it just means I've told it a lot. In terms of the timeline I'm jumping way ahead here but what the fuck, I like telling it.

We were shooting series two of *Spaced* and there's a scene where Mike Watt TA strips an MP5 sub-machine gun blindfolded. Being a bit Method and knowing Edgar would take great pleasure from me learning how to do it properly they got one of the on-set armourers to take me through the process of stripping and rebuilding the weapon. He'd even kindly taken some Polaroids at every step for me to follow when I got home. They were letting me take this home . . .

I shoot the first scene of the day and then wonderfully I'm wrapped. Incidentally, the word WRAP on a film set is an acronym for Wind Reel And Print. A throwback to the early days of film-making. Yawn. Sorry, but I find all that a bit cool, some continuity in film-making that runs across the generations. That sound I hear of film running through the gate, or used to hear before film started being used less and less, is the same sound Harold Lloyd or Buster Keaton heard when they filmed. I think there should be a button on the new digital cameras that reproduces that sound. Anyway . . .

I stuff my sub-machine gun, spare clips and a handful of dummy rounds into my bag and jump into my car to head home. I discover the house – a big, ground-floor flat I share with Michael Smiley and Simon – is empty. It's right next to Highgate Station and the back garden is huge with an area of woodland beyond that's a real hotspot for European Jays.

It's a very hot day, the kind a tabloid might refer to as 'a scorcher'. I open the back door that leads directly into our lovely back garden and allow some much-needed breeze in. I change into some tiny house shorts and mince around with the gun for forty minutes or so. I take turns raiding the other guys' bedrooms. Tossing a balled-up pair of socks into the room, stunning the terrorists inside with a flashbang before moving in and cleaning up with a series of devastatingly accurate double-taps. PapPap! Tremendous.

After a while it's time to put some time in on the task at hand, stripping this firearm. I retrieve a giant bag of icky, smoke a bowl and get to work. At first I follow the pictures, slowly pushing out the pins in the correct sequence, stripping the receiver out, barrel, ejector port etc. It's going well and I decide to start stripping it with a blindfold on, hone my martial skills properly. I blindly strip and rebuild the weapon three or four times. Pleased with the way it's going I decide to smoke another bowl and take the rest of the day off.

I remove the Bluetones scarf I'd been using as a blindfold and straight away something feels wrong. My spider-sense tingles. I look to my left as it feels like someone's watching me through the window. I'm right – someone *is* watching me. Actually six someones, six armed police officers.

Two of them are already in the room pointing Glocks at me. Great handgun. The other four, armed with rifles and, ironically, actual MP5s, are outside. Once we'd laid eyes on one another it was on. I tensed. They tensed. This is really bad and very dangerous. One wrong or quick misplaced move – hell, even a deep breath – could end in me being killed.

They see their opportunity and stream in like a big blue tsunami. They holler various things at me, like 'don't fucking move' etc. I'm now working on instinct, my anus clenches and a small cough is released. I, slowly and in one silken movement do two things: I take my hands off the replica and raise them, palms and fingers spread, high into the air above me. I then shuffle backwards away from the shooter and further onto the settee. I couldn't have been more submissive if I'd tried.

I'm hauled off the sofa and hogtied. Once immobilised they stop pointing their killy guns at me. Still, I'm not allowed to move or speak. They search the house methodically, laying out everything they find in a logical and pleasingly symmetrical manner.

Mine was not the only firearm-shaped thing we owned. With the weed and still smoking bong, the table now looked like a snapshot from a raid on a Triad girl farm. I was oddly thrilled.

By and by the mood lifts. They'd set out ready to kill a lump with a skinhead and having not had to kill anyone they relax slightly.

I could hear them shouting and talking to the girls in the flat next door. I was embarrassed by what they were saying, I'd rather they'd lied and told them I was some kind of hardnut. I heard snippets of this conversation . . .

'What's going on?'

'—blah blah blah—'

'Actor.'

'Silly little boy . . .' etc.

Some laughter, they were clearly flirting with these girls – still if it kept them from shooting me in the mind then go for it.

Forty or so minutes passed. My voice, which at first had been high-pitched and squeaky, returns to normal. When they'd streamed in, and while I was sitting back and opening hands up to the heavens, I was also shouting, 'Don't shoot me, I'm an actor!' but in the highest possible voice. I called it the übersoprano.

The lead officer screams back at me, 'If you're an actor what's your Equity number!!!' I stumbled, I did not have this information to hand. That was when shit was bad. Since then I'd recovered somewhat and my story had checked out and shit was less bad. That said, I never in a month of Sundays with the replica and the big lump of green believed I'd stay out of custody. No fucking way. I imagined the call to production from a young, court-appointed lawyer. Not good.

I then wondered how they'd known about the gun. Apparently a poor old lady had seen the barrel sticking out of my bag as I got out of my car. They'd blocked the road off and had sent scouts in to watch me hop around the house like *Die Hard*'s John McClane but in short shorts. What a dick.

The team's chief told me, with some jollity, that in their pre-raid briefing they'd decided to take me down, to shoot me if I'd had the gun in hand. It was so close. I actually think in this rare instance being stoned helped me.

The guy in charge picks up my 'erb bag, sniffs it, zips it back up and leaves it on the table.

'You'll deserve a nice stiff drink after this, son, and you may want to knock this shit on the head, eh?'

Police laughter. I couldn't believe this, it actually appeared that I would not only escape custody but get to keep my 'erb bag as well. What the fuck!

They stride towards the back door from whence they came and leave me with a final piece of wisdom . . .

'You did well, mate, a lot of people piss themselves.' Much laughter from the Blue Tsunamis. I was thrilled I hadn't pissed myself.

* * *

When I wasn't setting off security buttons in cash booths I was still working on the bar. Wavy Davy had gone and in his place were two South African guys, Dion Sampson and Tony Lindsay. I still know Tony, he's one of my best friends, I was best man at his wedding and godfather to one of his children. He looks like a skinny, white Dwight Yorke. His initials are tattooed on my arm (along with Simon Pegg's, Michael Smiley's, Danny Brown's, Edgar Wright's and Nira Park's). Sadly I don't really see Dion any more. It's one of those horrible drift-aways where six months becomes a year and a year becomes five becomes ten. I regret this.

I'm a pretty good mimic of accents, particularly South African, and for two days with the help of my voice skills I completely fool Tony into believing I'm from Durban. It's a story Tony still tells today.

I don't remember leaving the big lump of a house in Golders Green but I do. I move in to a house on Cricklewood Lane, number 142. I live there for a long time. With whom and in what order I have no idea.

It's a small, three-bedroom maisonette with a wonderfully large balcony. I had a great time living there and again people come and go and rotate but I finally had my own room and I loved it. Number 142 was a revolving door of lunatics, alcoholics, actors, singers and artists. I'm not sure which tag suited me best, definitely not actor though. I never wanted to be an actor. The thought of being an actor was a terrible nightmare to me then. Having people watching me show off seemed a horrendous notion. Don't get me wrong, I had my moments but usually that was in small groups of high friends, not un-high in a studio watched by eighty people. I really had no idea what I wanted to do. I had no long-term goal.

Down the way at 148 lived the wonderful Kiwis Keith and Michelle and Michelle's sister Rebecca. I still keep in contact with them to this day and occasionally see them when I'm down in Wellington. I invented a thing called the Cheese Eagle, a raptor that only eats cheese that Michelle used to love. I'd swoop down and grab her Edams. That sounds weird. Sorry, Keith.

At work I'd moved from the bar onto the floor and found that I was a great waiter. My unflappable, logical mind found it easy to prioritise sometimes up to twelve tables. (Not easily, waiting twelve tables is very hectic.)

I've said before in interviews that being a waiter was how I learnt to become an actor, that and my long training since I was a child in pretending and mimicking accents and doing impressions and copying what I saw on films and adverts and television. I quickly understood that if you wanted to make big money as a waiter you had to adapt to every customer that came through the door. I think generally there are only seven or eight different types of people in the world so it wasn't too difficult.

If 'Geezers' came in I was a farkin' cockney barrow boy, I was a chirpy, cheeky, cockles and friggin' mussels 'big old boy outta Repton' kind of toilet. They loved it. If a rich Indian family came in I'd bow and scrape and only talk to the oldest man in the group or the most glamorous lady. If businessmen came in there would be lots of 'yes sir no sir'. Out of all the groups I served, businessmen were by far the rudest. I was literally shit to them. Their self-importance was boundless. I had to frequently remind myself they couldn't be that big a deal otherwise they wouldn't be having a shit hamburger at Chiquito while discussing unit cost on lengths of PVC piping. Anger at rudeness aside, I started to make some pretty good money.

I liked working in the restaurant. I never had a thought about my future. I never really had, even as a child. (A trait I hope my son doesn't inherit.) That said, this stupidly blasé attitude has served me well over the years.

At this point I had little or no contact with Mum and Dad. I was too angry and too sad. I'd been left alone when they moved to Wales and alone was how I considered myself mostly. Of course from time to time there'd be phone calls. As soon as I heard Mum on the other end of the phone, literally the first two words she spoke, I could tell that she'd been drinking. I hated it. As soon as I heard the tiny slurs of speech I turned off. 'Is Dad there?' I'd talk to him instead and usually I was pissed off with him for letting it happen. He didn't let it happen by the way, he had no choice. Mum's all-powerful character and illness within meant it was easier to go with it than fight against it. I feel ashamed that I treated them this way but I didn't know what else to think or do. So usually we just didn't talk.

Being a dad myself now and knowing what they'd gone through I can't imagine how hard it must've been to not see or speak to your son for months at a time. I think it has and will kind of haunt me for ever now they're not here. 'I could've done more.' In reality though there was nothing more I could've done.

What I really wanted to do was write novels. Thanks to Rachel I'd discovered a love of moody Russian literature, the works of Milan Kundera and other eastern European existentialists. I longed to sit in a chilly, carpetless garret eating a watery potato soup, itchy blanket slung across my shoulders, writing about lost love and how grim and pointless life was. Thank you, Comrade Solzhenitsyn.

Copying Red's example I trawled through the myriad junkshops and secondhand places in Edgware and Golders Green hoping to strike gold. What gold meant was a first edition hardback book. I think in all my time doing it I found three, one by Norman Mailer, one by Aldous Huxley; the third one, my prize possession at the time and more so now I've worked with Steven Spielberg, was the first edition novelisation of *Close Encounters of the Third Kind*. I loved that book. Still do. I love the film and I loved the soundtrack that fifteen-year-old me used to listen to at night to frighten myself.

Years later I find myself on the set of *The Adventures of Tintin* directed by the lovely Mr Spielberg – Uncle Steven as Simon and I take to secretly calling him – I've got the book with me and on the last day of the shoot he signs it! Such a nice personal inscription. Funny how things work out. That first edition I found in a junk shop is now priceless, to me anyway.

When I wasn't trawling secondhand shops for rare first editions I was working. I worked most of the time. Thing about that sort of existence is if you don't work you don't make money. Simple as that. I had a vague concept at the beginning of my foodservice career that I'd save some money and travel again but it wasn't working out that way.

What I earned I spent. After most weekend shifts and some weeknights we'd end up in a Nepalese restaurant in Cricklewood called the Pink Rupee. To this day I still think about the perfect Butter Chicken they served. We'd sit there sometimes until three or four in the morning pissed and laughing.

There was a lovely old man who looked a bit like Fu-Manchu who'd come in late at night and read his paper, he was nice, we'd chat to him and mid conversation he'd fall asleep into his curry. Fu-Manchu was the only person I ever knew with bona fide narcolepsy. It was so shocking it wasn't even funny. It was a bit funny, obviously not funny if he were piloting a container vessel, but here in the relative safety of the Pink Rupee, sometimes it could be a bit funny. A couple of times I had to fish him out of a particularly saucy Pasanda to stop him from drowning. I'd gently lift his face out, move the plate away and pop his head down on a napkin. Seconds later he'd be awake again, wheezing his sixty-a-day laugh and tucking into his supper.

I drank, I partied, and I worked serving mediocre hamburgers to fucking horrible businessmen. This was my existence and it was a rut that I liked being in.

At Chiquito we had a thing called the Birthday Song – if someone came in and it was his or her birthday we'd be forced to sing the following ditty:

> Happy happy happy birthday,
> Happy happy happy birthday,
> Happy happy happy birthday,
> To you, to you, to you, Olé!!!

Some fucking genius got paid to write this. I'd heard it was Chris de Burgh but I've never received confirmation on that. We used to have a better birthday song but TGI Friday's took them to court for infringing birthday song copyright. It was basically the same song but someone had cunningly changed the word 'Friday's' to the word 'Chiquito'. (Probably the same genius that got paid a Trillion Turkish Lira to write the new birthday song!) Who knew the rules surrounding theme restaurant birthday song law could be so tricky to navigate.

The birthday song generally made me sad. For someone who got embarrassed easily and had/still has a little working-class chip on his shoulder, having to sing for rude dickheads who were essentially lauding up the fact they did jobs where they weren't forced to sing for a stranger's birthday made me cross. Busy Friday and Saturday nights were the best for the birthday song. All the waiters would grab spoons and pans to use as percussion instruments and we'd really belt it out. Part of this was about defiance, not wanting to be broken. Sometimes instead of the last 'Olé' we'd mumble the words 'fuck you'. It was so quick and hidden among the rest of the cacophony people never twigged. Hardly ever.

The birthday song was very popular, punters lapped that shit up. Sometimes annoyingly customers would pretend it was someone's birthday even if it wasn't, just for the embarrassment factor and the free fried ice cream.

On a quiet Monday afternoon having a couple of young kids demanding the birthday song when I'm the only waiter and Wavy 'Flaming ball-bag' Davey was the only bartender was another matter. You had to do it so you'd suck it up and belt it out. If you were lucky they'd leave you a thirteen pence tip.

Tiny tips were always given back. At first I didn't have the balls to do this but after a while getting a pound tip off twenty women who'd eaten and drunk 400 quids' worth of burritos and margaritas, who also received great, fast, efficient, friendly service, was too much to take. Sometimes I'd follow them out and give them their pennies in the car park . . .

'Oh, thank god I found you, you forgot your change.'

They'd smile, confused . . .

'Oh, it's fine, it's for you.'

I'd smile . . .

'I think you need this more than me. Thanks though!'

Outrageous behaviour. Waiters live on tips. Fact. But . . . As a waiter, to expect a tip is wrong wrong wrong. It needs to be earned. Tips is actually an acronym – To Induce Prompt Service. I think Dr Samuel Johnson, the inventor of the modern dictionary, coined this.

Late one night almost as my shift was about to end I was given a table of surly Middle Eastern gents. Getting a table at the very end of a long shift was a pretty mean thing for the host/hostess to do. If you'd been cross and shouted at the host you were generally punished at some point.

A clever host has the power to make your shift very easy indeed. It's about gently filtering tables into your section bit by bit. If you've twelve tables all at different points in their meal it's easy to cope. Sit four tables all at once and you have a problem. I wasn't generally a shouter but illogical people who are shit at their jobs make me cross.

Tonight it was my turn to face the hostess's wrath. I'd snapped at some earlier lunacy and I was to be punished. Or not, as it turned out. I'd almost finished cleaning my section and just about to ask my GM if I could close when the hostess, Melissa, who was actually pretty good and absolutely lovely, sat a group of surly men at my table. It essentially meant that a half-ten close would now become a half-twelve finish. Maybe later. The repercussions were great, it meant that I wouldn't be smashing the granny out of a Butter Chicken and eight pints until at least one in the morning. Not cool.

Middle Eastern businessmen want one thing from a waiter: to be treated like kings. If you can identify the richest one in the group and pander to his needs then you might hit the jackpot. Pander too much though and you're perceived as a snivelling worm and they're more likely to set their hawks on you at the end of a meal than give you a big tip.

They sat and drank bottles of spirits; the thing about buying bottles of spirits in a restaurant is you get charged by the shot, thirty-three shots per bottle at £6 a time, that's almost £200 a bottle, and that was the cheap shit. They drank jug upon jug of margarita, they feasted on nachos and fajitas and delicious, deep-fried chimichangas, in fact everything on the menu, and everything good Texaco-Mexico cuisine had to offer.

They ran me ragged. After the desserts, which they were too pissed to eat, Prince Money Bags, who smells of deep Italian leather and Aramis, raises a perfectly threaded eyebrow that denotes he'd like the bill. It was £2,400! The biggest bill I'd ever seen in that place. He pulls out a pack of fifties big enough to

choke a pig and rolls off three grand in cash. I thank him, nod
to the party and leave the table. I'm stopped, I feel a firm, manicured hand on my arm. I turn, his deep mahogany chocolate
eyes blaze and crackle, he smiles gently. I think I'm in love with
the handsome Omar Sharif-a-like, he mutters the words every
waiter longs to hear: 'Keep the change.' He just told me to keep
the change! I am in love. He just gave me a £600 tip and I didn't
have to suck ONE cock. Not one! KER – FUCKING – CHING!!!
That was the biggest tip I ever got and like most of my money
at that point it went pretty quickly. Six hundred quid buys a lot
of beer, green and king prawn madras.

At some point along my meandering timeline a girl came to
work in the restaurant who would eventually and inadvertently
change my life for ever. She was a wee Scottish thing I'll call
Charles Mouse. I really liked her a lot. She was quick to laugh,
funny as fuck and so smart. At that point I'd never met anyone
like her. I must admit for a moment my heart sank when eventually I found the nerve to ask whether or not she had a boyfriend.
She did. All the best ones do. I caught a glimpse of this sexual
Tyrannosaur one night. It was the first time I'd ever seen a man
under thirty-five wearing elbow patches on a corduroy jacket.

A few weeks into knowing her we had a party at 142. A big
sound system was brought in, the front room was emptied of
all our shit-brown furniture and a big bag of crisps was opened.
This party promised to be a roadblock.

I'm a bit nervous to be honest, her boyfriend – her stand-up
comedian boyfriend – was coming. I'd heard a lot about this
guy, I felt any man would have a problem living up to this kind
of expectation. The Mouse felt sure we'd get on. (As an aside,
if you want me to dislike anyone tell me we'll really get on.)
Happily though this was to be the exception to my brain's

stupid stubbornness. I wasn't working that night so we began the party a little early, with half-pints and shots first in the pub across the street. By the time people start turning up I had become, with the aid of Red Stripe, either a charming bon viveur or a lumpen jelly bag, I can't remember which – no matter.

I was actually really nervous waiting to meet Mouse's boyfriend. Sure I was funny, perhaps in the top five, maybe even top three, funniest people at Chiquito Staples Corner. That's no mean feat when I was working with Flea (the template for Mike Watt). And Harry, a Nigerian arms dealer who looked like Rango.

We offered an open-door policy at 142 and at some point Mouse walks in, I crane to look, and there he is. I hide in the crowd, I'm not ready, I flit from inside to out, I host, I avoid, I spread confusion, a little fear. Mouse catches up with me in the kitchen and we say hello.

'Are you coming outside to meet him?'

'Sure.' I'm hammered and think WTFN.

She leaves, I follow. He's there chatting to some of my friends and they're really laughing, some of the girls are even tossing their heads back, really guffawing.

I realise, oddly, I now have a toothpick in my mouth. No idea how or where it came from. I gob a foul brown liquid from my chewing tabbacy into a bucket, it dings loudly. The crowd part and that's when I see him for the first time, Simon fucking Pegg . . .

For the next two hours we spar, jab and comedy counter-jab, our eyes narrow as we size each other up, we drink and, at points, we go separately to the toilet. In truth I remember very little of this meeting. I know we laughed a lot and that there, on that balcony in Cricklewood, was where our (at this point) twenty-one-year best-friendship began. We did impressions, Rick from *The Young Ones*, Matthew the kindly Nigerian from *Desmond's* and of course sports commentator David Coleman.

Things then get dark and blurry, party business takes over, and in the confusion and flirting with Simon I've neglected my job as host. Other faces come and go, drink is quaffed, girls are kissed or not kissed, people become shapes and silhouettes and eventually sound is the only sensation to remain until that gradually drifts away and I die.

I'm glad people were there to tell me what happened. Apparently and actually pretty early in the night I drank myself to a standstill. Sitting to take a breath and to gather my thoughts I fall asleep, cross-legged, leaning against a giant Bass Bin and that was where I stayed all night. People had to step over me to get out. Simon tells it that I was slumped against the speaker while the speaker rumbled me to pieces, reggae and Red Stripe will do that to a man.

HAHAHAHA!!!

'Stop laughing, Nick! It's not funny. Didn't you realise you had a terrible and burgeoning drink and drug habit?'

'Stop shouting at me!'

Peggy Poo and me see bits and pieces of one another over the next couple of weeks. A drink after work here and there, the odd house party, but it was at the Pink Rupee where our love truly blossoms.

A bunch of floor staff had gone out after work one Friday night for a nice Butter Chicken and a few cold ones. The management had pushed together a number of tables and Simon and me found ourselves sat opposite one another. We'd reached a place, pretty quickly actually, where we could make ourselves laugh like drains. We still have that today. We'll find something funny and work the shit out of it until it reaches its zenith comedically and then it dies. Game over. Next!

As we talked and laughed drunkenly that night Simon did something that would change me for ever, change us for ever. He picked up a condiment and moved it across the table making this sound: *Birbirbigitt Birbirbigitt bigitt*. I knew exactly what this was. Time slowed around us, a warm bubble of light inflated and for a moment I couldn't see or hear anything but SJP. He was making the sound of the mouse droid that Chewbacca roars at in *Star Wars*. It was as if we were the only two people in the world. He got it, whatever *it* was. I understood him completely and he understood me.

I'm not sure how long we were in that golden bubble of self-indulgence but once it popped our mains were on the table. It must have been a while though as my naan bread was floppy and cold. This was the beginning. From this point on, me, Simon and at first Miss Mouse were pretty much inseparable. I didn't know what was happening but I'd made a new friend really quickly, and I wasn't afraid or nervous, it didn't feel weird – on the contrary it felt great and it's been that way ever since. I guess one could argue we fell in love that day. It's never really left us either, it's obviously changed and evolved as all long-term relationships need to do if they're to survive, but we still make each other laugh more than anyone else.

We can also fall into fits of laughter without talking which some people find unnerving. I always know exactly what he's thinking. An eyebrow cocked or a brow un-crinkled at just the right time can be like an A-bomb going off for us comedically. Not talking can be just as effective as repeating over and over again the phrase 'Would you like a white eel?' Let me explain.

We were on a plane a couple of years ago coming back from the Dublin leg of the *World's End* press tour. We were sat together at the front of the plane, we'd been delayed for some time so by the time we boarded we were tired and emotional. After take-off a lovely old flight attendant shuffled up to us and almost whispered in the softest Irish brogue, 'Would you like a light meal?' We both declined but there was something about the phrasing that got us going – once it happened it couldn't be stopped. I imagine it's probably how David Banner feels before turning into the Hulk; it can't be stopped so the best thing to do is to embrace it and enjoy the helplessness that comes from laughing so much you cry, laughing so much that eventually no sound comes out accept the odd 'Eeerrrrffff'. I turn to Simon: 'Would you like a light meal?' The change begins. We have a thing that others call 'Rainman', it's where we say the same thing or a variety of the same thing over and over again.

'Would you like a light meal?' suddenly became 'Would you like a white eel?' And on it went. At one point we imagine that she's vigorously woken us from a deep sleep to offer us refreshment.

'Oh, I'm so sorry to wake you, I noticed by your eyelids flickering that you were in a deep state of REM sleep but . . . would you like a grey seal?' We had this from the start and it's something that's never left us. Some of the in-jokes and lols we have now are based on and evolved from things that started all the way back then.

* * *

We were a cool little crew at the restaurant round about this time. Being a waiter was good but unrewarding, it was easy, I was good at it and it was never much of a push. I was a big fish in a small pond and that was cool. I was cool like this. It was enough for me. At that point I wasn't sure what I wanted, I never felt like I had to make a decision in terms of something long term. My parents never pushed me to get into a career. It literally never came up once.

Every Thursday Miss Mouse and I would rush back to the place she shared with Simon. Expecting our arrival he'd set up a kind of nest in the living room and we'd run in full of excitement, open some wine and watch *Northern Exposure*. We loved it. Even now if I put on an episode and see grumpy Dr Flieschman or Ruth Anne in her 'Born to bingo' jumper it takes me back to that nest. It makes me happy.

It wasn't just *Northern Exposure*, it was *Reeves and Mortimer* and *The Day Today* as well. I'd never seen things like this before. I'd felt them, felt that they were possible and that they might exist out there but I'd never seen them. I guess this is what happens when a university-educated Rik Mayall-a-like and a Dagenham bell-end hook up. The pot gets stirred.

The three of us really were inseparable. We did everything together. Mouse and me would work, Simon would gig and come to meet us, and we'd eat and drink and fuck about and laze around in Soft World and laugh. It was like *Y Tu Mamá También* without the rimming.

This was also the time where the character of Mike Watt TA, or roly-poly gun-mad Mike from *Spaced*, first fell out of my mind. He was a bit different at that point though, older, an actual veteran whose combat experience had driven him underground, a woodsman with advice on a million different and exciting ways to kill a man. Covering a foe in Tizer and then letting fire ants eat the flesh from their bodies being just one.

Another was finding an enemy asleep, cutting his legs off, while still asleep, replacing them with table legs and letting termites do the rest. That kind of stuff. Simon and me laughed a lot at Mike. We loved his misogyny it wasn't really a fear or dislike of women, it was more like they didn't ever show up on his radar. He didn't know how to deal with or talk to them. 'How you doing, little lady? Mike Watt TA.' This was Mike's seventies-style greeting to Woman.

Mike was a mixture of two people I knew at the time, one was a really close mate called Lee, although people called him Flea. He was a curious one. A big, giant, baby of a man, tall and heavy with long greasy hair. He was bonkers and made me laugh a ton. I know he wasn't a Nazi but he liked Nazi memorabilia. It confused me. It was wrong but he was a lovely man, kind, gentle, an alcoholic lunatic but definitely not a racist or a fascist and absolutely not an anti-Semite as I'm sure his Jewish girlfriend at the time would attest. He just liked the design of the stuff. We hung out and got drunk together a lot, sometimes we'd head out to some dark shit hole in Camden and drink two bottles of JD while listening to some band called Stinkpipe or Ovaryfart. I once saw Flea slide down the middle ramp-like centre between two escalators in Camden tube station. He probably flew fifteen feet off the end of that thing.

The other man responsible for the other half of Mike was a brawny lump we called Kippy. He was a member of the TA by day and a mediocre bartender by night; someone my dad might've referred to as a Bullshit Merchant. He was tall and muscular and the girls loved him. Me and Tony and Dion would tease him about his part-time army career. Kippy was to have the last laugh though: years after our time together he actually made the regular army and went on to do several tours in Iraq and Afghanistan. Who knew? All that bullshit was actually true. I opened the paper one day and saw our glorious leader David Cameron being protected by Kippy. He had dark Oakley shades on, a PLO neck scarf and a fat M4-style battle rifle. Amazing. Good for him. What the fuck do I know?

Pretty early on in Simon's, Mouse's and my time together I casually mentioned to Mouse, in a moment of reflection, that maybe I could be doing something more with my life. Simon had moved down to London from Bristol to pursue a flowering stand-up career, and she suggested I try stand-up too and that Simon could help. I wasn't sure. The very notion of performing made me immediately frightened.

Simon kindly wrote me a note, which I still have somewhere, telling me where I should go to do open spots. (Open spots are the little five-or ten-minute bits that new stand-ups do.) This unpaid gig was the chance to hone your skill. To feel real terror in a relatively low-pressure environment. I remember on the note he'd written, 'Don't be afraid. Audiences smell fear like sharks smell blood.' It was so fucking true. I didn't like the idea of doing stand-up, it filled me with unease, but I went home and began thinking about writing a set. I had no idea where to start.

* * *

I'd called a bunch of the promoters and comedy bookers on Simon's list and secured my very first open spot at the Cosmic Comedy Club on Fulham Palace Road. I'd worked on a little set and was as ready as I would ever be. This seemed very unlike me, putting myself out there, but I'd reached a point where I kind of said, 'Why the frig not?'

Simon thought it would be a good idea to go and see some stand-up before I dived in. I'd never seen live comedy before, naively I didn't realise it even existed, or that as a scene it was so big. I had no idea, apart from *The Young Ones*, that there was an alternative comedy scene. Yeah, I knew about Bernard Manning, *Wheel Tappers and Shunters*, Norman Collier and the like, but my life up until that point had been deals for tiny amounts of hash in shitty pubs, watching Irish men fight, a father who was a workaholic cum nervous wreck and an alcoholic mother who died a bit more each day. I had never before tasted these delicious little cutlets of culture that were now, thanks to Simon, being served up to me. I liked it, they tasted sweet like barbecued lamb.

The Cosmic was a big place, much bigger than I'd been expecting. I thought most comedy was done in grubby basements or upstairs in shit boozers. The Cosmic was part of the new wave, built using the swelling coffers that a hungry audience desperate for a laugh brought in. It was like a small theatre but instead of rows of chairs facing the stage there were long benches and tables. It was pretty dead that Tuesday night, twenty or so people, maybe thirty if I squinted my eyes a bit.

The room was really quiet too, the only noises I could hear were the low rhubarb of chatting and the clatter and squeak of knives and forks as the sparse audience hacked their way through chicken and chips. These are perhaps some of the worst conditions for comedy to thrive in.

We stood at the bar and the guy who ran the place came to say hello to Simon who was fast becoming a major player on the London circuit; they chat for a bit and he bustles off. Simon and me have a couple of beers. It fills up a little more but it was no way what you'd call busy. The booker came back over, another chat. He heads off again, Simon turns to me.

'The compere hasn't shown up. They want me to do it!'

I would've been so nervous but he took it all in his stride. He left me at my booth drinking beers and disappears through a door, emerging on stage five minutes later. There's a polite ripple of applause although some seem cross that a comedian would spoil their supper by coming on and trying to do some stand-up.

After some classic Pegg-style jovial banter he brings on the first act. I've no idea who any of the stand-ups are that night but they were all pretty brutalised. It certainly didn't make me want to do stand-up. Simon returned looking down. He didn't think it went too well. In fact he states that he died on his arse but I thought he was good. I don't remember him dying.

Tomorrow I'd be on the same stage doing my first ever stand-up gig. What an idiot. Don't do it!

The details of how and why it happens elude me now but for some idiocy I'd been entered into an open-spot competition as my first ever gig. Sadly, lots of people from work had been invited – I don't think inviting people would've been my thing at the time. I would've been happy doing it quickly on my own and running off into the night from whence I came. No, inviting people sounds like it might've been Chicky or Jo's doing. The kind of thing where you tell them quietly looking for some gentle support, and before you know it most of the restaurant was involved. Looking back though it was a good thing. I was glad of the support.

My lot take up two whole benches, maybe twenty people give or take. After my gig we were having a big party back at 142 no matter what the outcome. I couldn't wait for the party. Several hours before the gig I'd begun to feel something I had rarely felt before, nerves. Real terrifying, shit your pants nerves.

It made me sick to my stomach. The only time I think I'd felt anything near this was the moment before the referee blew his whistle to start a rugby match. This wasn't a rugby match though, this was going to be much rougher.

I was there predictably early. I'm always early. I can't help it. I stand around not being able to talk or eat, friends come and talk to me, I barely respond. I smile weakly and shake a hand, my hand, why am I shaking my own hand? In the end I hide behind a curtain silently going over my routine in my head. Simon's there but knowing what I'm going through he keeps his distance and advice to a minimum, he watches me like a great corner man, assessing me, geeing me up where necessary.

The lights go down and the competition begins. This is the first competition of any kind I've ever entered. I'm second on the bill out of ten or so terrified souls like me, which is something at least. I think it's always best to get it over and done with. I develop a mantra at this point, it's a kind of countdown to release: 'this time tomorrow it will all be over' becomes 'in twelve hours it will be over' then an hour, then ten minutes, you get the idea. I still use this method today if I'm ever going through something stressful or unpleasant. I never quite understand why all the speeches at a wedding come after the meal. It's stupid. I've given two best-man speeches and one groom's speech in my life and they both took place after dinner. Like all the other A-list top-table speechmakers, I'm too nervous to eat. By the time you finish and you're hungry again everything's cold.

'Nick Frost . . .'

The food was nice too, at Simon's there was haggis and I love haggis. Love it. All oats and stomachs and pepper. At my wedding we had Moroccan lamb, crispy on the outside and pink in the middle with a delicious tzatziki-style thing. Not traditional wedding fayre but fuck it.

'Nick Frost . . .'

At Tony's wedding in Africa I think we had dik-dik, at least it tasted like dik-dik – that said, it could've been any number of gamey bush meats. I was best man at that wedding and I think it's safe to say at that point the first best man in the world to give his speech reading from a BlackBerry. I'd never seen so many one-armed men at a wedding – I asked and was told something about drunk driving. Terrifying.

'Nick Frost . . .'

'What? Stop shouting!'

'You're on!'

I *was* on. The compere's calling my name. It's now or never. The ref blows the whistle and the ball is coming straight at me through the glare of the sun. I take a deep breath.

Backstage is a cheap plastic and metal chair, the type you get on hospital wards and public libraries. I pick it up and throw it out across the stage. Why? I pretend, using the microphone offstage, that I'm having some kind of unseen fracas. After a moment I run on, looking offstage, and make some shit joke about me owing Mother Teresa some money. I'm embarrassed just writing this, to be honest.

It gets better. My material wasn't great but I was enthusiastic and showed no sign of nerves once I'm on stage. Simon's advice about sharks and blood still rings in my eyes. I'd decided that if I wasn't going to be the best comedian in the world I'd be confident and in these situations maybe confidence can get you pretty far. If you can't be good be lucky. I wear a pair of white Nike Hi-top trainers, jeans, a white fifties-style bowling shirt kind of thing with a slight beige stripe running through it, and a pair of terrible thick-framed Ray-Ban glasses. Buddy Hollies I think you can call them. As a young waiter I got a lot of shit for those glasses. Shit from tables of lads. Pricks. Now they're being used as part of a comedy uniform.

I'm trying to remember parts of my routine now, and like most things in my mind it's pretty hazy. (It's not, I'm just too embarrassed.) There's some cutting edge stuff about a man who has a Treet for a face (Treets later went on to become peanut M&Ms); there's also a 'joke' about stealing an orangutan from London Zoo and hiding it in my rectal cavity and that's all I'm willing to tell/can remember.

It seems to be going really well. There's a lot of warm applause and, more importantly, lots of laughter and not just from my noisy lot, although I'm sure their infectious noise helps grease the wheels. After eight or ten minutes I reach the end of my material. I'm so happy it just about bursts out of me. I say thanks and say my name, I pick up the chair Mother Teresa's thrown at me and that was that. I did it. I can hear people clapping and a whooping and I couldn't help but beam. I was so happy. Simon's there waiting for me and he's smiling. The look he gives me was one that I've seen him replicate many times with me over the years. Pride. He was proud of me.

I come off stage and feel the tension pour out of me like a sonic bleat. It was amazing. I get a weird rushy migraine. I got a migraine after every gig. I think it was a release, a relief of getting through this most alien of things. Even though people say I was funny, getting up on stage and being judged was still difficult. Still, I'd finished and I could sit back and relax with the gang, who were now quite pissed, and watch the other poor saps.

I'm not really a competitive person, at least I pretend to myself I'm not. I've never trusted people who are overly competitive. I don't get it. I get the drive and commitment needed to see something through, a work ethic, what I never got were those people who are desperate to win at any cost. It's just not in me. I think also when it comes to something as subjective as comedy or literature it's difficult to accurately pick a winner. I feel if you're willing to put your heart and your all into something as emotional as art in all its facets and forms then you're a winner from the get-go.

After the stand-ups finish we all have to endure a nervous wait while the scores are totted up. I go and have a piss, it stinks, I gaze into the metal trough and I'm joined by a man who comes and pisses next to me. He waggles his eyes suggestively; this, I discover, is the chief judge of the competition. His waggling puts me off. I'm not sure what he expects. I finish and wash up. He joins me at the sink, waggling.

'I shouldn't tell you this but . . .'

'What?'

'No, I shouldn't.' He turns and dries his hands. I don't push.

'Okay, I shouldn't tell you this but between you and me . . .'

'Yeah . . .'

His face softened . . .

'You've won the competition. Congratulations!'

He leaves and I lean on the sink. I can't believe it. I'd won a comedy competition at my first attempt. It meant that I'd now go through to a regional heat. What. The. Fuck. I went back to Simon. Sat down, he noticed something.

'What's up?'

I told him what had happened in the bogs. He was so happy. I think I made the mistake of telling someone else, and before long all my lot were coming up and congratulating me.

The lights drop and the compere takes to the stage. This was it. This was my night. It was the first time that I could actually, justifiably call a night mine. There was applause and the room fell silent.

'Blahblahblahblahblah. Comedy. Comedy, blah blah, comedy, and the winner is . . .'

I smile, it's totally Robbie Williams in its smugness. My leg muscles get a premature message from my brain. It says:

'Prepare to stand and receive your accolade, bigman.' They twitch. This is it. Here we go . . .

'And the winner is . . .'

A girl on the table next to mine stands – no, leaps – into the sky. She's screaming, her crew rush to embrace her. It looks like the famous Iwo Jima flag pose but with chicken in baskets on the table.

What the actual fuck. Boos ring out around the venue. People are angry. My legs are angry that they even bothered getting their coats on. They go back to bed and I slump into my chair. I watch the girl skip onto the stage and collect her book token. My spirit sags.

I'm told later by an impartial third party that there was a great deal of impropriety and vote rigging from the winner and her posse in the final moments of the count. I'd been robbed. Cheated.

A similar thing happens years later at some kind of shitty comedy award. We're sat near the stage, always a good sign. A producer tells us minutes before the show that *Shaun of the Dead* has won. I'm so fucking proud and happy. In between that premature announcement and the award being handed out they'd managed to secure Jack Black on a live video feed from LA.

Desperate to add Hollywood credence to the event they'd given the award to *School of Rock*. Gutted. Not that *School of Rock* won, it's a great film, but who doesn't like to win every once in a while?

Me and the crew leave the club. I'm crestfallen but happy, I'd done my first ever gig. I was proud and I proved to myself that I could do it. There was a big party at mine and everyone came. They all made me feel like a winner that night. I think I even signed an autograph for Keith and Michelle, just for fun like, but it was nice.

This was the start of my career as a stand-up comic. I did twelve gigs in all. It was a short career. Six were great and six were, perhaps, the lowest points of my life. The good ones generally went very well except for my post-gig head pounder. Some were just okay – did the open spot, got a few laughs and off I went. The bad ones were really bad, really terrible. I think my problem with stand-up was this: I was a funny person but not a good stand-up. I find it hard to explain. It was mostly the same material give or take but the reactions of the audiences were completely different. There were so many variables, not least of all the confidence or lack of from gig to gig. Stand-up for me was a bit like golf. I wanted to be good straight away and when I wasn't I lost heart. Like everything in life these things take time and effort.

Although I had great gigs I never once found my own voice. Being a fan of *Reeves and Mortimer* and the stand-up of Harry Hill, Sean Lock and Simon Munnery, I really wanted to be a weird surrealist and the problem with that is I wasn't using my own voice. Get me in a small group and I could be frigging hilarious. In a room full of people looking at me expecting something funny I found it tough. Often my voice would crack or when heckled I'd forget where I was and stand there saying 'ummmm' for what felt like six hours, blood pumping out of my ears until the slow handclaps would begin and I would die a terrible terrible death.

The shortest gig I ever did happened at a pub venue in Ealing one Tuesday night. I was on a day shift at Chiquito and from early in the day I could feel the panic rising, 'In twelve hours this will all be over.' The day shift was busy so at least I could throw myself into the work. This coincided with a time when for some reason I was taking a lot of Pro Plus. Not a good idea. The day shifts were always chilled out, more or less, there'd be a slight rush from noon until three and then you had a couple of hours to kill until the evening staff came in. Once you had a tidy-up and a restock of clean, polished cutlery, you'd stand about doing fuck all – hopefully there'd be a bartender on so you could have a chat and a laugh but usually you were on your own. Sometimes a couple of very young Indian lovers would come in and you just knew they were not meant to be together. They'd naughtily giggle and laugh in fear that they might get caught at any time. I liked that. Young love will always find a way.

This day there was boredom and, thanks to the handful of Pro Plus I'd fisted down with four cups of strong espresso, anxiety. I had to leave at five o'clock sharp. There was a saying an old manager of mine used to have. It was fucking annoying but sadly true and I was always early anyway so he never aimed it at me, but hearing it would make me want to strike him in his fat ginger head with an oar. It went like this:

'blubblubblub early, blahblahblah, on time, blah blah bluch, late'.

I struck him hard and he fell backwards into the turbulent ocean. He blubbed, his wide, white face fixed with an 'I can't believe you did that' look. He jolts and is pulled down. He rises back to the surface briefly but is wrenched downwards once more by an unseen Goliath, he smiles, not at me, it's just his brain turning his mouth up at a sweet memory long forgotten. One more jerk by fuck knows what and the foaming water blooms deep red, his sweaty ginger bonce was gone for good.

I once watched this mirthless Honeymonster of a manager give the chefs and me an early morning masterclass on how to make the perfect green tomatillo sauce. He made us stand around and watch while he stirred a massive cauldron with a giant metal spatula. That day four poor Ugandan men and myself were forced to witness six litres of salty fluid drip off his nose and forehead into someone's meal. He was so wet by the end of it that he had to go home and change. And what had we learned? Nothing. We had learned nothing. Those men had fled Idi Amin's brutal dictatorship only to be met with this new, more sinister brand of fuckery. Poor men.

At a quarter to five I had still not been relieved. The phone rings and someone in the office answers before I have a chance to. It's also getting busy. I can feel a rage building within me, a tiny baked bean-size rage.

A voice shouts from the office, 'So and so can't be in until six!'

Fuming! More Pro Plus, another triple espresso, more tables, more ear steam. Where in the human body is ear steam generated? At six-ten the waitress saunters in, I change out of my uniform that smells like old milk and I bolt into my pre-booked cab.

We turn left out of Staples Corner and slam into a traffic jam three hundred miles long. A hiss of steam pisses out of my brain. I sit still for as long as I can, I pay angrily, and run out of the taxi. We'd travelled less than a mile. My head pounds, fists itchy with rage. I run and try to board several buses that are bulging at the seams. It begins to rain heavily. Balls.

I eventually find a bus that takes me to the tube which then takes me to another bus, and then from there it's a simple thirty-minute walk to the venue. This is not going well. I should've turned round and gone home there and then. I should've known that this was a bad sign. An omen of the most terrible portent, like a crow shitting on your hat. I was so fucking cross. I'm soaked to my skin. I take a breath and try and get my shit together.

The venue was an old hall attached to a shitty fucking pub. From inside I can hear a noise that begins to fill me with dread. The noise sounds like an inexperienced compere starting a vicious heckle war with twelve cunts all from the same Sunday league pub football team.

As I push through the swing doors I see an empty hall save for an inexperienced compere starting a vicious heckle war with twelve cunts all from the same Sunday league pub football team. A crow shits on my hat. The compere sees me, understands who I am and waves me up. I'm not ready for this. I'm totally unprepared. I haven't even taken my coat off. I scamper towards the stage, I can feel angry low-browed meat bags eye fucking me. I may not even get as far as the stage. The compere introduces me as Nick Roast! I should run, that's what my eyes and legs are compelling me to do. I don't.

I still have my jacket on as I mount the stage, the compere passes me, thrusts the mike into my hand and whispers, 'Good luck.'

I look at these hate-filled baboon-rapists and open with a tried and tested goodie.

'Hello!'

I notice a big man stand up from somewhere in the middle of the pack. He must have something really important and insightful he needs to share. I'm all ears. Two ears. Here goes . . .

'FUCK OFF, YOU FAT CUNT!!!'

Oh. He seems so very cross. I slowly clip the microphone back into its stand and hop down off the stage. I feel deaf, it's a mixture of intense rage and heart-crushing grief. A terrific heat flash ensues. I trudge out of the hall still soaked and out into the deluge. Inside I hear them laugh and roar.

It was gigs like this that made me want to stop. A half-decent stand-up would've taken those men to pieces. After the day I'd had and the build-up and the transit and the rain and the Pro Plus, it was all too much for me.

I had another gig where two businessmen sat in the front row chatting and laughing at me. Not with me, at me. Throughout most of my set. It got so bad that at one point I dropped my microphone and leapt into the crowd. I managed to grab one of them round the throat and subdue the other with my big right leg before security put me in a choke hold and bundled me down the stairs. I wasn't asked back. There were one or two more gigs but my heart wasn't in it. I stopped. I was disappointed in myself. At that point I wasn't what you'd call a starter finisher. That came later.

During this time though Simon and I became closer and closer. We really were a mismatch in terms of background. It worked though. I was a bit rough and had no idea what PC was or meant. Simon went to Bristol Uni and was all about feminist cinema. He even knew what an acronym was. He showed me things and I taught him that it was okay to say the word 'black'.

While my stand-up career died, SP's bloomed and I was happy to be along for the ride. I loved watching him gig. We worked out that one year I saw him gig over two hundred times. We'd drive all over the country in his little white Renault 5. One wintry afternoon we were about to settle in for the evening when Dawn his agent rang to make sure he hadn't forgotten his gig in Hull that night. He had forgotten. We threw our shoes on and ran out of the house. This was a time long before sat-nav. We used maps. Maps are basically static versions of a satnav but printed onto large sheets of paper and bound into a big book and, do you know what, they actually worked pretty well.

It took us an age to get to Hull. Part way up the country it started to snow really heavily; eventually we got to the gig at Hull University students' union, which sadly was virtually empty. He still did his gig, the show must go on darling, and he put just as much effort into this as any he did, full or not. Good lad.

He finished, we jumped in the car and fucked off. On the way back the snow was so thick and heavy we were forced to pull over onto the hard shoulder. While there we began to get the fear that a lorry, unable to see us in a small white car in heavy white snow, would plough into the back of us doing one hundred and forty miles per hour. The car and everything inside it, us, would be completely obliterated. They'd have to identify me by using my dental records. It was close, lorries would thunder past us and we'd scream and grab onto each other. We became hysterical and laughed till our tears froze.

We couldn't stay there. Eventually we got the courage to start the car and drive home.

Simon would soon be going up to Edinburgh to do his first Fringe solo show. It was a really big deal. He put a lot of effort into that tour. It really took it out of him but predictably he smashed it. While he and Mouse were in Edinburgh I got to stay in their little flat in Cricklewood. Absolute bliss. The only job I had apart from taping *Reeves and Mortimer* and *Northern Exposure* was to look after Simon's lovely big goldfish, and what a noble beast it was. I'd never seen a plumper, longer-tailed, more beautiful fish. I think he'd had it for a long time, a firm friend and confidant throughout his university education. What a fish.

They were due to return on a Monday; I returned home from a day shift on a Sunday to find the fish dead. It was dead. Oh god. Any pet looked after by a friend or relative will always die the day before the owners return. Always. One day before. So it was the case with mega fish. I fell to my knees and sobbed, more for me than for the fish actually. I pulled it out and gently blew into its gaping mouth hole. Nothing. I placed it back into the tank and used my hand to create a turbulent current with the hope I could push some oxygen through its pale, lifeless gills.

It's still dead twenty minutes later when I give up trying to bring it back to life. The fish was well and truly dead. I slump onto the floor exhausted by the efforts that went into the revival attempts. After a while my pragmatism wakes up. I need to arrange the funeral. How does one deal with the earthly remains of such a stoic aquanaut?

I lift him (I'm guessing it was a he) onto a piece of newspaper and mummify him ready for his journey down the toilet to his spiritual father, Poseidon. When push comes to shove I can't do it. I evolve my plan slightly and I decide to bury the beast.

I look for a suitable coffin. I empty the curdled liquid from a milk carton and gently lower him in. He doesn't quite fit, his tail is so long and beautiful that it sticks out of the top of the carton by a good three inches. What to do? I grab a pair of scissors and neatly cut the tail off, plopping the two long fins in either side of his body. I close the carton up, Sellotape it shut and bury the poor mite. I say a prayer in the beast's own tongue and that was that. Simon wasn't happy and I think a small part of him believed that someone murdered that fish on purpose. I guess we'll never know for sure.

Him and me spent more and more time together, Mouse not so much. She got a job touring with a play and off she went. When she came back terrible things happened. When the considerable ash plume settled Simon and I were all we had left. I never saw Mouse again. I got him and he got me. It was imperfectly perfect. I picked him up and he picked me up, so began our time living together.

After moving out of Mouse's flat Simon had nowhere to go so he came and moved in with me at 142. At first he lived on the couch for a bit, then he slept next to me on the floor but soon he became chilly so we topped and tailed. One of our favourite things to do was sit up in bed and read a big book together, usually a big glossy atlas or a book about Christmas. He'd hold one page and I'd hold the other. After a while he'd just stay in the bed. It was cold at night and we'd just snuggle down and sleep. It felt right.

So much has been written about us sleeping together like some kind of modern Morecambe and Wise that it now feels pretty boring talking about it. At the time though it felt nice.

There was never once a sense that at any point we'd start making each other's bananas cry. We often use the phrase 'Some mornings I didn't know where he ended and I began.' That makes me laugh so much. I think it made it into our wedding speeches.

I often get a suspicious narrow-eyed look from 'Real Men' who hear we used to sleep together in a single bed for nine months, but we were great friends and then like now we've never had a problem showing affection and love for one another.

This arrangement didn't last long though, thank god, for as much as I liked it I enjoyed the nights I got the bed to myself. Simon was offered the opportunity to travel to Australia as part of a comedy tour. He took it. I was sad for me but happy for him. It was exactly what he needed. Of course I was still working in Chiquito. I must have been twenty-four by now, I was starting to get bored on the floor, starting to yearn for something else, what that was I had no idea.

It's tough sometimes when you deal with the general public and you realise there are a lot of fucking bell-ends out there. One lady asked if I could put more ice into her drink, as it was too cold! Whaaaarttttt! Another man complained, as he'd found a bone in his rack of ribs. It is bones. Ribs is bones. The bit that's delicious is the bit between the bones. That's the bit you eat. Sometimes there was a strange phenomenon where once one table complained about the food all would start to complain. I think it was a kind of shared psychosis.

On a couple of occasions someone would complain about something small. This is how I'd deal with it. Big smiles. Big bowing apology. I'd take the offending plate back into the kitchen, count to five and bring it straight out again. Exactly the same meal. Sometimes I'd regarnish it, sure, or stick it in the microwave but in essence it was exactly the same meal. They'd tuck in happily, chuffed a waiter, someone of lower status, had apologised to them. That's the key to dealing with complaints at the table. Many apologies.

You have to make them think they're completely right, apologise, remove the offending dish straight away and offer something else. Nothing should be too much trouble. If they're really acting up sling them a free pitcher of margarita. No one can resist a free pitcher of margarita. Even if one of their party dies choking on shrimp a free pitcher of margarita makes everything okay.

Some people though were absolute monsters and deserved to be punished. One man who was so disgusting got his car scratched to fuck with the two pence tip he'd just tossed at me. I stood in the window and watched him discover the offence. Fuming. Good. Don't fuck with the waiters.

If the person I was serving was both a monster and a vegetarian, I'd handle it a little differently, I'd take a different tack, a silent revenge if you will. While their burrito or soft taco was being made I'd nip behind the line and pop in the tiniest, microscopic speck of beef into their meal. They never knew a thing. I'd smile while they shovelled it down and abused me knowing they'd be turned away from their heaven by their vegetarian god once they'd passed. Sometimes revenge tastes just fine served piping hot.

Late one Saturday night I receive a table. I was very not happy. I was six minutes from closing and they get sat in my section. I must've really pissed Melissa off that night. Fifteen rowdy drunks who are loud and aggressive, lots of swearing, lots of nipping back and forth to the toilet, lots of sniffing. When it comes to the food, some order one starter between two people as a main course. This was not going to be a good table tip-wise. On top of everything else these folks were finger click-ers. I was tired and pissed off. I took all their shit knowing there'd be little or no reward at the end of it.

No matter. Suck it up, do your job, get rid of them, go to the Pink Rupee. After a while I get clicked at by a belligerent old fucker wearing stained tracksuit bottoms and a dress shirt. Not a good look.

'Oi!'

Fuck, here we go.

'Oi!'

He repeats it again but this time louder. His angry relatives have taken some kind of offence that I didn't react immediately to what I imagine is their elderly father and they are now giving me a kind of death stare that makes my feet ache.

'Yes, sir, what can I get you?' His voice stumbles and cracks, his eyes close then flicker, he seems way fucking gone.

'Get me a fucking beer!' Woah.

This man's far too pissed, he's so pissed it's actually illegal – no, morally *wrong* – for me to serve him any more alcohol. As a waiter I have a responsibility to this poor man and his family while he's dining here at Chiquito Mexican Bar and Restaurant plc.

I also think it's a great way for me to get them out as quickly as possible. At first my voice shakes. I know the reaction to this will be bad. British people tend to react really badly when you accuse them of being drunk. Even if they're so pissed they're shitting in a hat.

'I'm afraid I can't serve you any more alcohol, sir, I think you've had far too much already.'

His son looks up at me with half a chimichanga hanging out of his mouth. His eyes fixed wide with a disbelief his brows never knew existed. The women at the table tense up. It'll go like this: first the kids get chippy and call you a cunt, then the big-armed women wade in and attempt to smother you with their bingo-wings, lastly the men punch you in the temple with a Clipper lighter until a fluid that smells like freshly cut hay dribbles out of your ears, all this for the chance of a £1 tip.

I grow more confident. Legally I have the law on my side. Rumbles around the restaurant at my denial of alcohol mean my GM has come out to watch, to observe from a distance this family killing me.

'I'm afraid I can't serve you any more alcohol, you're too drunk.' Silence.

The stick-thin dad with the stained tracksuit bottoms, drunk and so angry, struggles to get to his feet. He stammers, fuming.

'I'm not pissed . . . you, cheeky . . . prick . . . I've . . . had a fucking . . . stroke.'

Oh. My. God.

Some heck breaks out. The women stand and tuck their war-gunts into the top of their jeggings. The men get their stubby Clippers out ready to jab into my paintwork. I edge backwards really slowly and turn, running into the kitchen. My manager follows me at pace. I can hear shouting.

'Just go quickly and hide in the break room.'

My plan has worked perfectly. Sure people have been stabbed but I'm out of there by midnight with a great story, noshing down on a Butter Chicken.

* * *

Rachel had gone and I'd been single for a while. Sure there had been kissing and second base visits but it wasn't very fulfilling.

I'd never been the type of man to just fuck around, not then, not later. I didn't like it. It felt weird and I always ended up falling for one-night stands. I'm a romantic at heart and I think what I was really looking for was love.

One afternoon, a bright, clear spring day, a girl walked into the restaurant, a new hostess who completely blew me away. This was Stevie and she was amazing. Tiny little floral print dress, long bare legs, glossy brown hair, rich chestnut-coloured eyes and the most amazing smile. Butterflies and bluebirds surrounded her. She was the most amazing girl I'd ever seen.

'Hello.' She was Scottish. She bit her lip. (She didn't but it adds to the erotic charge.)

I just stare at her. She giggled a bit and I scurried off to fetch the manager.

That's how it began. I was completely enchanted by her. I'd never felt anything like it before. Over the next few days and weeks I played it cool, well, cooler than I had during our first meeting. She was so out of my league. To use one of my lines from *Cuban Fury*, 'It was like a butterfly going out with a parsnip.' Again I was the parsnip. I had something that the parsnip didn't have though, I had the funny, I could make her laugh.

I flirted with her so outrageously over the next few weeks she felt compelled to tell me she had a boyfriend. I was sad, she saw I was sad too. I'd played my hand too soon. She knew. I didn't care. The dance begins. We up our flirting. I can't believe this. It never goes this well. Never. She told me she wasn't in love with her boyfriend any more. That made me happy. She saw I was happy. That was a green light to me.

The usual way of courting here in Britain involves alcohol and lots of it. You go out. You have a drink, a dance, another drink and then you try and kiss, then you decide to go out or not at a later time. It can be that simple. It can also be a fucking disaster. A few times you'd get too pissed to close the deal or you realise that she's a complete helmet when she'd had a few. Or I was, entirely possible.

The problem I had was this. A year or so before meeting Stevie I'd decided to stop drinking. Holy Fuck. Big shout. I did not see that coming. It'd just got all too much for me, the hangovers, the anger, the aggro, the crushing shame of a wet bed. I couldn't do it any more. I went to AA but chose a really hard-core meeting in Hendon. The people there, the brave people, frightened me. Their stories and tragedy frightened me. These people were at the end, they'd hit bottom. I kidded myself that I wasn't like them, that Mum wasn't like them. I honestly never made the connection between what those people at that meeting had and my mum's own illness. Later down the line Mum attended two AA meetings in Fishguard. After the second someone pointed out two women there who came not because they were alcoholics but because they wanted to gossip about who in town had a drink problem. I wonder how many people those two blabbermouths drove away from help. I never went back to those meetings. I decided to try and do it on my own.

So far I was a year dry and as such I didn't have the tactical advantage of using alcohol to woo Stevie. No matter. We still laugh a lot, our hands brush together, the air between our fingers ignites spontaneously. She bites her lip. (She actually did this time.) It was too much to bear.

Eventually after weeks and weeks of intense build-up it happens. We lie on the floor smoking joints (I know, I know) and reading passages from *The Prophet* to one another, what a cliché! At one point I turn and kiss her. She kisses me back. It was amazing. And that was that. We fell in love. I fell in love. We were an item.

Stevie became my girlfriend. The more I knew about her the more I liked. We walked around London hand in hand, lay in the park, laughed, went to museums, the lot, proper boyfriend/girlfriend stuff. I told her about my exploits in Israel and promised one day I'd take her there. I told her I intended to write a book about my adventures, she liked that, liked the fact I wanted to be a writer.

Some afternoons if I wasn't working I'd take the bus into South Kensington and wait for her to finish university (she was studying biology). I'd never been to a university so it was always a thrill to push through the big old doors and enter the Gryffindor Quad from the east side. I'd watch the boffins running here and there with their abacuses. It was nice. For a moment I regretted my absence from tertiary education.

Stevie and I hadn't moved in together but I spent a lot of time at hers in Cricklewood. We planned our trip to Israel and worked hard to pay for our tickets. We were actually in love. It felt amazing. She was fresh and funny and fit and beautiful and every day I was with her I found myself a moment away from fighting with perverted men. Going out with a hottie has its downside. The letching chimps hanging out of vans making 'fuck' noises at her was too much to bear. Poor woman. Poor women. If you go out with a hottie you better be good at looking like you're good at fighting.

At one point in our sexually frantic courtship I began to write my book. I called it 'The Alcoholic's Guide To The Holy-Land' and it was a fictitious account of a boy's time on a kibbutz. It was based on my own time there but trippier, more psychedelic, with a really tragic ending. It was also tragically, really shit. When I tried to read it a few years ago I was struck by how infantile it was. The imagination was there but everything else was truly awful. Leaving school at an early age hobbled me slightly, grammar wise. I still don't know what an adverb is. True. The only reason I wrote that book was to impress Stevie.

I had no table to sit at and certainly no such thing as a laptop. I wrote it using a creaky old typewriter with an ironing board as a table. I didn't plan the thing out, instead I wrote the whole book like a big story a child might write at school.

With our lovely young relationship getting more serious it was time for us to pay a visit to her parents in Glasgow. I began to sweat at the thought of parents. My last parent hadn't gone so well. The rum and the ironing board shit. I planned to learn from my mistake and be cool. Be on my best behaviour. I'm not drinking so this should help a lot. We took the train up and we're met by her mum and younger brother at the station. It's my first trip to Scotland and with Stevie on my arm I felt great.

Even though her family are Rangers fans they live in the shadow of Parkhead, the home to the city's traditionally Catholic football team, Celtic. This, I sensed, was a secret pain for her father.

Stevie was greeted at the door the way you'd expect a returning daughter, the apple of Daddy's eye, to be greeted. I was also greeted the way you'd expect, a sharp nod, an impossibly firm handshake and that was about it. He knew, as a father and more importantly as a man he knew, and as a younger man I knew he knew and he knew I knew he knew. It was unsaid and it simmered. She was eighteen, I was twenty-five and we were boning like rabbits. I was a scummy, overweight English waiter who smoked way too much weed. She was a porcelain-skinned ray of light receiving a fine university education with the aim of becoming a scientist, a fucking scientist for godsakes. She was gorgeous and clever and saucy and I totally understand her dad's negative vibes.

It was cordial to begin with, the first inkling of an issue arises when I refuse a beer. Suspicious. They have a few, we chat and then Dad decides to put *Braveheart* on. He goes upstairs and returns wearing a fine Glengarry with a long feather stuck in the top. I was beginning to feel uncomfortable that said, the DVD player's sound system belted out a tremendous noise with an impressive depth of clarity. I could literally hear every drop of English blood spilt on the battlefield in crystal clear 5.1 digital Dolby surround.

I'm definitely in the spare room that night. At one point the door opens and Stevie creeps in. I'm terrified our angry noiseless fucking would wake Dad and he'd come in and cleave me with *his* fat broadsword.

In the morning Mum introduces me to the wonders of the square sausage. Ironically I'd been doing exactly the same to her daughter the night before. (I have no idea what that means.) The Saturday was nice. We visited the sight of the battle of Bannockburn where Robert the Bruce routed the English, then we drove to Sterling and I was forced to climb the William Wallace monument, erected to the memory of a man who'd spent years routing the English. I started to get the feeling I wasn't welcome.

We drove through the Highlands and Dad stops the car and makes us all get out. I'm forced to drink from a small stream running off the heather-clad hills to prove Scottish water was the cleanest and best in the world. It gave me terrible diarrhoea.

I still sensed a simmering anger from Dad. To smooth things over I ask if I can cook them dinner. My mum's fantastic recipe for Beef Stroganoff is sure to smooth over any cracks. Food and the eating of it I feel can be a great weapon in the war for peace. I've been cooking the Stroganoff since I was twelve and feel its soft beef and rich sautéed onions would work a treat.

Me and Stevie hung out and laughed while I cooked. Her brother keeps an eye on me while Mum and Dad laugh like drains watching an old video of English people being killed in car crashes. As I was about to serve up there's a slight issue: unknown to me her brother has a weird phobia of people touching food with their hands. I wish he'd said something while he stood and watched me cook it. Mum fortunately intervenes and makes him something untouched by me. This was the beginning of an uncomfortable dinner.

They sniffed the food with suspicion while me and Stevie hungrily tucked in. The conversation gradually turned to the future, our future, a future that included our forthcoming trip to Israel. We'd mentioned it in passing the day before, enough time for the parents to cogitate the information. I was now grilled about my time there and the current security situation, I could tell they weren't happy.

They put their collective feet down and insist Stevie would not be going to Israel with me. A loud argument begins between Stevie and her parents. I'm blamed for this, this change in her. I'm the scapegoat. At some point Mum pushes her chair back and storms upstairs. Dad stands.

'See what you've done?'

I try and make it right but my flustered assurances about terrorism and separate beds only seem to make things worse. Mum's upstairs crying, Dad is fuming. It's then I notice his left fist is clenched and leaning in the rice, poor Stevie is in tears. This is terrible.

Father's last words to me as he thunders up to bed were these: 'I want you gone first thing.'

I think I'd be out with a rice-fist in my ear that night if Stevie hadn't liked me so much. Why did parents hate me so?

The next morning a cab arrives at 8 a.m. After much arguing Stevie insists on coming home with me. Her parents are angry about this. I want her to stay, I think this would be for the best but still we leave together. I could see she was sad and I regretted this. There were tearful hugs on the doorstep for Stevie, she breaks away and walks to the cab, I smile weakly and look doe-eyed, maybe we can salvage something from this. I hold out my hand, the front door is slammed in my face.

I lean down, open the letterbox and shout through, 'Bye then!'

This does not go down well. Dad opens the door and thunders out. I leg it into the car. It was only Stevie's plea for leniency that stops me eating a gob full of his angry rice-covered fist. Why was it still covered in rice?

At some point over the next few weeks I move in with her, much to the annoyance of her flatmate Edna. At first we're blissfully happy, at least I was blissfully happy. Sometimes Simon would ring me from Australia and we'd bullshit and talk and it'd remind me how much I missed him. He wrote me a really long letter once but customs opened it and took out several pages so it made little or no sense.

Things had got past the honeymoon stage and Stevie was in class at uni more often than not. I hated not seeing her but we were arguing a bit and my policy of non-drinking was really beginning to put a strain on our relationship. She and her best friend Tim would spend more and more time drinking together. I grew jealous and suspicious.

Being forty-three now I look back at that time and curse myself for being such an idiot, for not seeing the signs, the blatantly obvious signs. I was blinded by love. If someone I was seeing spent the night out with a boy I think I'd be very cross and absolutely suspect the worst. Then I was just desperate to keep hold of her. I wrote her a book for fucksakes, a really terrible book. God, I fell hard for her. Often the compulsion to hang onto something so badly leads it to slip through your fingers like a separated egg yolk, indeed this was the case here.

Stevie had gone to a weird science camp in Surrey to study worms. I was invited to spend a night there. It was awkward and she was a bit cold but then so was I, I think fearing the worst. I'd drawn back a little bit. I watched her drunkenly flirt with Tim all night. You know when you watch two people and can just tell something has been shared. A line has been crossed. If not physically then certainly emotionally. We argue and I leave the next day.

When she gets back it's pretty awful. She says she wants to move out, even though it's her place. We agree I'll take the flat over. That said, I didn't think she meant moving out that day. Her 'friend' Tim comes to help her. After a bit of persuasion I get her to admit to me that she'd been having an affair. Heart. Crushed. I was so sad I wasn't even sad. Again I was numb.

With tears in my eyes I sniffled out a final thought: 'Just fucking leave, take everything but my books and go.'

What a pretentious art-helmet I was. I had about ten books. I stormed out to work and when I arrived home six hours later she was gone. She'd literally taken everything in the flat except my ten books which were in a neat pile in the bedroom. I cried as I made a cup of tea in a wok. It was the last time I ever saw or heard of Stevie.

I was left in that flat on my own. I hated that place, you had to walk through the communal downstairs hall to get to my front door. The place stank and a drunken, aggressive Irish loony lived there. He frightened the shit out of me. Creeping in late at night was the worst. The lights would be off and the hall illuminated by the silent TV that was still on, flickering. If you were lucky you'd hear him snoring. Perfect, unlock the door and go home. If you were unlucky he'd stumble into the hall and threaten you with his thick, Irish Hulk hands. My mate Dion got hold of him one night and threatened to fuck him up. He slumped to the floor, terrified. Good. I hate bullies.

The other downside of Stevie leaving was our trip to Israel. I'd booked our tickets and I couldn't get them refunded. I was still keen to go. Ten nights in the sun was exactly what I needed right now so fuck it, I went.

I've got a lot of thoughts about this holiday. Maybe holiday's the wrong term, I went there to mentally convalesce. I decided to keep a journal and get down all my thoughts and feelings about what happened between Stevie and me. Being alone was tough, I loved and missed her so much, and Israel wasn't how I remembered it but that was my problem not Israel's. I went up to the old kibbutz. It was nice to hang out with some old Israeli friends but my heart hurt and I felt really lonely. After a couple of days I said goodbye and bussed it down to Tel Aviv.

The rest of my time in Israel was spent walking around the city, trudging down the beach to the Arab section in old Jaffa. It was nice and cool down there near the sea. I'd sit in a café and write my journal for most of the day. As ever I was pretty much skint. At lunch I'd walk over to the bus station and have a falafel. Fortunately they were still offering that great deal – if the pitta was intact then you could get it refilled with fresh, hot falafel as much as you liked. Remember, the key was to keep the first couple relatively dry. Once you reached the ultimate tummy fullness you could moisten (sorry) the whole thing up a bit with tahini and other exotic Middle Eastern sauces.

Falafel aside, I was sad and skint and bored. My diary however makes for very interesting reading. I looked at it fairly recently and was surprised by the amount I wrote. I filled up a whole book with my filthy melancholy. You can see as it grinds on how my emotions change. The first half of the book is me, grief stricken and broken physically and spiritually. Then there are some juvenile ramblings about life and love. Then about halfway through there's a passage where I break away from my sadness and ogle at a passing girl's lovely bum. Naughty. My spirit picks up from there. I begin to write about other things not connected to Stevie.

When you split up from a girlfriend or boyfriend, things like life tend to get in the way of truly understanding what's just happened to you. It slows the healing process. I found the good thing about being away and alone was I had time to think about Stevie and us and the break-up. I had time to work it all out. And as a result I think I got over it pretty quickly. Don't think for a second that was that. It still hurt like fuck but I could see a way out.

My boredom and depression and no fucking shekels got the better of me however. I go to a travel agent on Dizengoff Street and tell them, using some fabulous acting, that my grandmother has died and I need to get back home immediately.

They couldn't be more helpful. They mistake my tired eyes, light beard and the shadow on my spirit for actual grief. The next day I am on a flight.

Years later not long after my dad died I went away on holiday. I thought it would help. It didn't. It was a terrible mistake. I wasn't ready for it. Me and Chris (Baby Momma) argue terribly – completely my fault – and we decide to go home early. Before changing our flights the airline insists upon seeing my dad's death certificate. Karma in action maybe, too many Herberts pretending Granny has died. Still, heartless pricks, also who carries their dad's death certificate with them on holibobs?

I get home from Israel and go back to the empty house with no furniture in it. I boil a wok, sit on the floor and decide what to do next.

* * *

My first brush with House music had been as a sixteen-year-old. Basically, apart from the odd flirt with indie, metal and alternative styles, it lasts a lifetime. Don't get me wrong, I love all types of music except ragtime but House music, and in particular Hard House, is something that has stayed with me until now. While at Chiquito and through my friendship with Tony and Dion I hung out with a lot of South Africans and Kiwis. We all had a shared interest in Hard House. These were Tony and Dion's mates from back home, all in all a good bunch of girls and boys. We started clubbing a lot. It was the boom time for Hard House in the summer of 1997 and I was there at the front blowing my little horn. Hard House was everywhere and I had no idea after my first brush with the embryonic scene back in 88/89 that it was still happening – not just happening, but absolutely going off.

Dion and Tony started going out almost every weekend after shifts in the bar at Chiquito. At first, and I'm not sure why, I didn't really fancy going clubbing. I think I had a weird kind of agoraphobia. Simon was still away in Australia on tour but I was happy in Cricklewood and the thought of leaving it and going into London put the willies up me. Still, after hearing about this thing happening my curiosity eventually got the better of me. It was safe to say I was hooked from the start.

The first place I went to was a club called Sunny Side Up. It was set in a long wet tunnel under a viaduct in Vauxhall. It was frightening and amazing in equal measure. This was not strictly my first brush with HaHa beans but it was close. I never had it during the Second Summer of Love, too expensive back then for me. The sum of £25 for one dose seemed like lunacy. No, back then you needed something weird and long lasting. Lysergic acid diethylamide. Cheap and cheerful.

A few months before my first Sunny Side Up I went out with a mate of mine called Sean. He was tall and impossibly thin with long glossy black hair. He looked like a Navajo. We puffed a bit together and he suggested we go to the Ministry of Sound. I was nervous but thought fuckit, why not. While in the massive queue to get in he gave me a small glowing pebble. I take it and, using my watering fear-spit that was pooling in the depression under my tongue, swallowed it down.

I was so frightened about taking this new rave canape, after hearing bad things about them on *London Tonight*, I thought my heart might explode there and then. By the time we got to the front my feet were tingling. The security apes look us over and tell us to fuck off. Oh. There's clearly no waggle-room in this statement. We trudge away disappointed. Sean knows another place but I feel sick and trembly so I decide to head back. It's still early to hook up with the team at the Pink Rupee.

I'm sitting on a night bus passing through Kilburn when something strange happens to me. The 'thing' has dissolved inside my tummy and is now giving my brain a gentle massage. I rush as it jets up from my feet and into my brain so hard it makes my eyes roll backwards. It was like someone had flayed me alive and was blowing a fan over my freshly exposed nervous system. The old fella next to me shifts nervously. He gets up and stands by the door. It was my stop too so I get up and stand next to him.

He's a small well-dressed Indian man, I begin to notice the jacket he's wearing, it's so nice, a soft brown tweed-like fabric. Really lovely and so inviting. It pulses and throbs at me. I rush again slightly and I realise I have this man by the arm and I'm rubbing my face on his shoulder. My eyes are as wide as bin lids. He's frightened and I'm horrified and apologetic. I let go of him and he jumps off the bus and runs up the street. I follow briefly but my heart's not in it. Instead I cross the street and stumble into the Pink Rupee. It's bright and people look afraid of me.

That was then. Things felt differently now. I'm not on a bus on Kilburn High Road, I'm here at Sunny Side Up under a viaduct in a drippy tunnel. It felt right. It felt like home. That night on the bus opened my eyes. It was the beginning of a long relationship with that scene with its smiling people and the myriad possibilities that mind-altering things propose at three in the morning: world peace, laughter collectives the government couldn't touch, chemical stasis and what have you. It started off great. I wanted to be frozen in these moments. Eyes rolling, cuddling strangers to the most amazing music imaginable. We were the few. Our scene was underground and people were afraid of it and, by association, us. Me.

This was a dangerous time for me. It'd be my undoing. Not just yet but eventually. Tony, Dion and me would work our arses off in the week, skimming a little off the top here and there, at weekends we'd smash it up. The whole gang. We'd start Saturday night, then onto Sunnies at eight o'clock Sunday morning. After that we'd maybe head into Soho or go back to 142 Cricklewood Lane.

The girls would have baths or showers and change into warm, fresh clothes and the boys would smoke and continue to greedily ingest powerful chemicals. Sometimes we'd go to the Spotted Dog in Willesden and I'd watch them drink the edge away, usually though we'd just lie around talking and trembling. The girls would look after us and play with our hair, give us massages, feed us orange juice. It was nice. I used to sit, eyes wide, and watch the juice inside the glass transform into a pint of rice.

The spirit liberators always made me see the weirdest things, things civilians would've found frightening. I wasn't frightened. I liked it. I yearned for it, yearned to be in that place where anything and everything happens. I embraced it fully. At the height of the lunacy I'd often get a thing where everyone I looked at would be wearing glasses. I'd have to run my hand over their faces to know if they were real or not. People didn't mind, they knew what was happening. Unless they were real glasses and then I'd have to apologise profusely.

Once I saw a hot glow like a laser or a spot welding arc under a man's skin in the middle of his forehead. It just hummed and crackled while I looked at him. Another time a beam actually broke through and shone an intense light out of a man's back.

I followed him. The thin beam moved across his shoulders, slowly tracing a shape I couldn't make out at first. The faster it got the easier it was to see as an image. Have you ever seen pictures of the Nazca Lines in Peru? It was that. It was one of the hummingbirds drawn on the floor of the desert, so big they can only be seen from the air. It didn't freak me out. I considered it a spirit guide. I smiled and it told me I should eat another peanut. So I did.

These were my weekends. It wasn't just Sunny Side Up either. We went to a place called Sunflowers, we went to the Aquarium in Old Street, a club with a swimming pool in it! Disgusting. We went to the O bar in Soho and on and on and on. My favourite DJs were Tony De Vit, Pete Wardman, Skol, Roosta, Darren Poole, Darren Pearce, BK, The Tidy Boys, The Sharp Boys, John 'OO' Fleming, Tall Paul and Luke Brancaccio. These were the gods on the scene at the time. You didn't just go to specific clubs, you followed the DJs around. Wherever they played we went.

Tony and Dion decide they want to go to the States, that was always their plan from the start but the mayhem and the rut one inevitably gets into working in the food service industry meant they'd been here longer than they'd envisaged.

They left and went to live in Huntington Beach, California. Shit, I missed those jerk-offs. I enjoyed hearing of their exploits and was jealous I couldn't be there. Girls, surfing and getting high seemed to be the order of the day. Simon had left Australia and had gone to spend some time with Tony and Dion over there, then travelling around on his own and getting his shit together.

When Simon got back we begin our lifelong 'I love Agent Dana Scully' phase. God we loved that woman. By this time I'd sourced a TV and a cupboard and we were pretty happy with this. Simon and I would lie around watching endless *X-Files* box sets dreaming and hoping that one day we'd watch Mulder and Scully kiss. That's all we wanted.

This was the time of the infamous Piegate drama. Piegate's something bad I did to Simon. Something I regret. Even though he says it's cool I know deep down he's never forgiven me, probably never will.

We'd spent the day puffin it up. We're at a point, between episodes of the *X-Files*, where we get the munchies something rotten. I'd invented a meal, which, apart from the staff food at Chiquito, was the only thing I seemed to eat for years. It was called simply, Pies in a Bowl. It consisted of two Findus chicken and vegetable pies, cooked, in a bowl. I'd then mash the pies up, add Bisto gravy, lashings of white pepper and ketchup. It was fucking lovely. I miss Pies in a Bowl. It was a big hit, it was cheap, nutritious, and suited my lifestyle perfectly. We were Pies in a Bowl kinda guys back then.

I don't know what made me say the thing to Simon that I said. I think it was the Devil or Hitler. Yeah, that's it, it was Hitler. I found myself taking a loud breath like I'd just remembered the most important thing in the world, his ears pricked up!

'What?' Simon was mine.

Slowly I drop my knowledge bomb on him . . .

'I've got chicken fucking pies in the freezer!!!'

His eyes widen. We both cheer! What was I doing? Stop this now. I didn't stop. We got to the kitchen and we pause, harvesting the anticipation. In forty-five short minutes – just enough time for another *X-File* – we'd be feasting on Pies in a Bowl. Simon looked at me. I egged him on.

'Go on . . .' I pushed him to open up the freezer. His little face looked so young and excited. It was like watching eight-year-old Simon open up his Stretch Armstrong on Christmas Day. Simon opens the freezer. Once the icy fog clears he sees nothing. There is nothing in the freezer but an icy emptiness. It's like a diorama of Hoth. There is nothing at all in the freezer. There are no pies. What's more I knew there were no pies. He looks around with a weird smile on his face, understanding perfectly what was going on yet at the same time understanding nothing. He can't believe that I would've, that I could've, done such a thing.

'What's going on? Where are the pies?' He's clearly heartbroken. What have I done? I've completely misjudged this,

'There are no pies,' I regretfully advise.

He slumps, spirit crushed. I begin laughing manically, taken by the evil spirit that inhabits my kitchen. It instructs me to scream and rip my shirt in half. So I do. Simon looks terrified.

Simon didn't stay with me for long in Ivy Road. In Australia he'd met and toured with a Northern Irish bloke called Michael Smiley. They'd decided to move in together as they were both stand-ups and had become very good friends. The first time I meet Smiley I'm terrified. He has a skinhead, bad teeth and scars from a bicycle crash on his face. He's by far the most energetic, aggressive, funny lunatic I have ever met. I loved him and still do. He's one of my best friends sixteen years on. Michael was a great stand-up, audiences loved him and were frightened of him in equal measure. He'd escaped the ravages of eighties Belfast and moved to London and fell into the world of cycle couriering. He loves cycling. Me and Simon used to tease him about what gear he had on his bike, he'd laugh because we were idiots.

The first time I saw Michael do stand-up he started his set like this: 'I'm not actually a stand-up comedian [ripple of laughter], I'm just here to tell you you've got fifteen minutes to clear the room!' With his thick Belfast accent it got a big laugh. Sometimes when he did it the laugh was a nervous one at first that developed into a relieved roar when people realised he wasn't from a terror agency. I think Michael was a bit suspicious of me to begin with, two working-class men circling around each other, I understood.

Somewhere in the mishmash of my timeline Michael and Simon find a flat in Kentish Town and move in. It's a cool place. I still wallow in my Ivy Road flat for now. I'd moved from being a waiter on the floor and into the kitchen. I started working on the line. I was the only non-African and I loved it! I'd known a lot of these guys for a few years when I was a waiter, now though I was part of an elite crew. The kitchen brigade.

I began at first in the prep kitchen. I'd come in early each day and start my shift at 8 a.m. I'd check in all the deliveries, put them away and crack on preparing the sauces and salsas and marinades the restaurant would need for that day. By far the best thing about that job was the fact I didn't have to deal with customers. It was bliss and I actually felt like I was learning something. I'd spend hours slicing and chopping vegetables. Stirring sauces and preparing crispy tortilla shells for the nachos.

Being in the restaurant first thing with just the cleaners and the duty manager was sweet. We chatted, we had music on, we drank coffee, ate stuff we shouldn't have been eating and laughed. During my time in the kitchen I really got to know a lot of those lovely Ugandan men very well. At one point a year or so in I'd picked up enough of the language to be able to do a small stand-up routine in Swahili. They bloody loved it. I'd watch them clap and howl with laughter as I portrayed a man, stopped by police, having to explain why there's a monkey in the boot of his car. Monkey in a car boot comedy must be pretty big in the comedy clubs of downtown Kampala judging by the level of rich African laughter it would elicit.

Me and my friend Yusuf, a Ugandan ex-international foot-baller turned line cook, worked on an elaborate and very false backstory of my time as a child in the remote Ugandan town of Mukono. The story revolved around the fact my father used to be the manager of the Mukono Collins Hotel and this is where I grew up. It would freak out new Ugandans when they arrived at the restaurant. I loved that game. I guess it was like acting. I loved Yusuf. We went to a party one night where I met the wife of deposed and exiled Ugandan dictator Idi Amin. She was all right.

There was a big manual at the back of the kitchen, it told you in very simple steps how to make every sauce they used in the restaurant. That was my job and eventually I didn't need the manuals. Sadly for me that knowledge no longer exists inside my brain. It's a shame as I often yearn for the rich and creamy queso sauce or a sharp and spicy green tomatillo sauce for my homemade burritos. I can make my own versions but they're not quite the same. The only recipe I remember is the one for guacamole, I love it and it's something I still make to this day.

I was moved out of the prep kitchen and onto the line. This is where I really wanted to be. Cooking, although it was definitely not cooking. Not really. Not in the truest sense. It was putting together pre-made elements of a dish, not doing every dish from scratch. It was still tough and needed a great deal of skill on certain sections. I started, predictably, on the starters section. The waiters took a while to get used to the fact I was now a Linepig. Some of the sneakier foodservers, the ones who'd do anything for a tip, would try and approach me to sort them out free shit for their tables. I didn't. I couldn't.

A tiny machine would beep and puke out an order. It was then my job to gather all the bits together. Easy. I moved from appetisers to mains and from there onto the grill. The grill was where the action was. The weekend on that broiler, Friday to Sunday, was crazy. It was so busy. From 12–4 p.m. you were slammed and from 7–11 p.m. you were slammed.

One of the differences between the bar and kitchen was you could shout and swear in the kitchen and no one in the restaurant could hear you. Some of those poor waiters got sworn at so much. Bad waiters could potentially put some really bad fuck on your night. It could take the kitchen a long while to recover. I was responsible for anything that was cooked on the grill, steaks, fajitas, ribs, and every kind of burger. It's the kind of stress I like. The whole kitchen can fall or thrive on the strength of their Grill Man. At times on busy nights you could have fifty things on that griddle all at different points of readiness.

Like most things that involve a lot of people, communication is the key. When it's flowing and going well it feels amazing. We're all one beautiful Ugandan hive mind moving as one, making sure all the items the waiters need find their way onto one big tray all at the same time. When it wasn't that, you were fucked, hard and quick.

Although I liked working in the kitchen more than I'd liked working on the floor, it had its downsides. The worst one was the clean-up after a busy night, having to degrease that griddle and the floor and every other bit of your section was a pain in the potty-hole.

I'd done every job possible in that restaurant and for the first time in five years I began to have an itch I needed to scratch. This was something I'd never thought of before. I began to think that maybe I should leave that place and move on.

I was living a weird double life at this point. Working in the place had now taken a back seat to hanging with Simon and Smiley and other loonies, watching tons of stand-up and meeting good, funny people. My mind was being fed and this new sense of possibility made working at Chiquito more and more of a drag. There were so many great comics at the time and London culturely, comedically felt so fertile.

I was definitely different back then to the person I am now. I felt comfortable and relaxed and myself with Simon and Smiley and my friends at the restaurant, people I'd known for a while and trusted. Anyone else though and I retreated into myself. I became the silent shadow on Simon's shoulder, ever present but hardly talking.

I'm not sure why. Chip on my shoulder maybe, a suspicion of these types of flamboyant arty folk? I think the simplest answer was probably the truest. I was a bit shy and I thought, wrongly it turned out, that all these funny, smart people would just not be interested in what I had to say. Not true.

I think my working-class thought processes were a lot different to theirs though. A lot of the time I was silently working out whether or not I could take these people in a fight should push come to shove. How would I escape should there be a small fire? Does anyone have drugs? That kind of thing, but mostly it was just shyness.

This was the time I met Edgar Wright, the sweetest little ball-bag you'd ever wish to meet. I remember going out with Simon one night to the Battersea Arts Centre to see some stand-up and afterwards we stood around drinking in the bar, and that's where I saw him – a small and delicate little hair bear with skin as fine as wedding porcelain. He was a young director doing stuff with Alexei Sayle and Lenny Henry. He talked a lot and quickly (this has never changed), his passion and knowledge of all things TV and film meant it took me a while to fully get to grips with him. Not that I didn't like him, I just couldn't find a gap in the conversation to say anything, and even if I had I wasn't sure at that point if it'd be valid or funny enough.

As well as Edgar I met cool young bands and musicians, editors, costume designers, actors, writers, comedians. I was really lucky. I felt myself growing inside. Something had been awakened. The restaurant didn't seem enough, it was basically all I knew but I just couldn't do it any more, so I left. There was no fanfare. I just left. Five years. Goodbye. I knew I'd only leave to go to another restaurant but it felt good anyway. It was positive.

After five years of stability now came a time of job-hopping. Moving from restaurant to restaurant. Work was no longer the most important thing in my life, it was raving and comedy and Simon and Smiley and my mate Danny and Maxwell and all the other new people I'd met who'd enflamed my throbbing art gland. That took money though. I think if the truth were told I was a little bit embarrassed that I had to wait tables while my new mates did comedy. I had no reason to moan, these guys were skilled and worked bloody hard.

Simon and Smiley were living together at 9 Busby. It was a fantastic place. If you could avoid the violent racists or dangerous street gangs that littered the walk from Kentish Town tube you were laughing. It was fine in the day but coming home from work after midnight was sketchy. My trick when walking past groups of youths on bikes, hoods up, spitting, is always to either be totally invisible or act like a loony. I'd much rather mime eating some of my own fudge than get myself all stabbed up.

The house, if you ever made it, was a big lump of a place and because of Simon and Smiley's generous souls they took pity on me and let me live there. I paid very little rent. This meant though that I was morally obliged to get a Smiley talking-to about the virtues of 'Pulling your own weight, big lad!' I've had lots of these, even fairly recently – we call it getting 'Smiley'd'!

Michael had the room at the top of the house, he was very Bohemian and had his bike hanging on the wall and a pair of Technics 1210s set up, no bed just a mattress, bongo drums, big record collection with the odd picture of George Best in his prime here and there. It was mostly off limits but we were allowed to go up and play records when he wasn't about, which was often – Michael was a very good, in-demand stand-up who'd tour the country most weekends.

Simon had the big room downstairs next to the kitchen, two big floor-to-ceiling windows illuminated the place and there was a lovely original Victorian fireplace on one wall next to his futon. It was really nice, he too had a banging sound system.

My room was the place where the other two left boxes of shit they didn't want or need any more. In fact you could be fooled into thinking that freezing, damp room was a storage area for a tramp's mortuary. If you pushed aside some of those boxes and made your way past the binliners full of shoes and faux furs, you'd see that some poor soul, me, had made a rudimentary bed. No mattress, just cushions held together by a thin cotton blankey, two flat, yellow pillows without cases and a duvet without a quilt cover. This was the Crab Pit. This was the bedroom where I lived. A sordid shit hole.

The room was so cold in the winter that when I woke up an icy fog would hang low, hugging the floor like mist in an Arctic pre-dawn. I think this is where I got my superhuman resilience to the cold. I have to be cold at night. I know human beings are split into two camps in this matter, warm room or cold room, but I am definitely firmly encamped in the latter. The colder the better. What's the duvet for otherwise?

My need for extreme cold has driven wedges between me and some girlfriends in the past. I say wedges, we argued about it and then in the night they'd die of exposure. I lost three of them like that. Shame.

I went to a wedding in Ireland once with Chris and was forced to stay in a B and B, first and last time by the way. Don't get me wrong, lovely little place, new build though, the owners were nice, very welcoming but the house was like a fucking sauna and the windows were locked shut. It was immense. I awoke at 6 a.m. so hung-over and hot that I had to walk four miles into town topless in the rain to cool me down.

* * *

After three years of not drinking I have a weird notion pop into my head. I'd been really strong up until this point and hardly ever thought about alcohol. Still, the voice in my head had now begun to tell me it would be all right to have one beer. Just one little ice-cold pint. It can't hurt, can it?

I had to push these thoughts from my mind remembering the friends' rooms I'd pissed in and the countless times I'd borrowed a hairdryer to use on yellow, wee-stained sheets. There's a kind of shame we don't have a word for in English, I suspect the Germans do, they have a word for most things grim. It describes the embarrassment one has at being caught dumping a wet mattress in the street. Combine this with fights and anger and the dreadful quilt of fear that frequently hung over me days after heavy drinking occurred and you can see why I wanted – no, needed – to ignore this voice that had begun to crackle inside of me.

I don't know what started this man ringing his bell in my head but I felt like I needed to have a drink, just one, just to try, just have one. Okay? Just one. No! Yes, do it. Stop! I can't stop. The din and screaming of my Weakness being fucked loudly in the room next door by a young stud with a giant dick became so loud I fled the house to escape its wanton moans.

I left our house in Busby Place and walked past the old Jewish school that's not there any more. A few times after massive benders we'd find ourselves standing on the balcony in sarongs and balaclavas drunkenly toasting the horny sixth form girls who'd laugh at us as they went into class.

The din turned into a sinister whisper as I wandered into Camden Town. The shouting made me angry. The whispering made me frightened.

I stood and paced up and down outside the World's End. I stopped and looked up, the name of the pub was not lost on me. I spent an hour outside cogitating on what was the best thing to do, all this time the hiss building in my head like the rumbling in Tommy Lee Jones's 1997 hit film *Volcano*. I went into the pub. I'd never been in it before and was struck by how shit it was, how the clientele were either down and outs or stick-thin Italian tourists with futuristic haircuts.

I walked around that pub looking at those people, those guilty day drinkers, and I go to the toilet to do a quick line of tears. Standing at the bar now with that noise roaring out of my brain I start counting out change and finally order a beer. A Foster's of all things. The barman places it on the counter and turns to put my sweaty coins into the till. By the time he turns back I'm gone. I left the pint on the bar and ran outside.

All in all I spent nearly two hours in turmoil at the thought of that Foster's. Fighting this urge. I was tired and it laughed knowing how unrelenting it could be. I'll fucking show you. I strode back in and the Foster's was still there. The barman has put a beermat on top to denote the pint is still active. Oh god, it was still active. I took the hat off the glass and looked into the golden column. The crescendo of noise was deafening now, but as I lifted the jar up to my lips the noises and clatter, clank and chatter, ceased. Anne Heche and Tommy Lee Jones look up, it's awfully quiet?

BOOOOOOOOOOOOOOOOMMMMMMMMMMMM!!!

I drank that pint down in one go, it was cold and it was fizzy and it was amazing and the guilt and disappointment I felt at that moment tasted fucking great. What had I done? Emperor Yamamoto looked up from his map of Pearl Harbor and uttered his now legendary words, 'We have awoken a sleeping giant.' That old, dead Japanese bastard was right. The AA has a saying: One drink is too many and a thousand's not enough. I ordered another. This time I watched the trace as the bubbles fled up, it was a real *Ice Cold in Alex* moment.

I gulped that one down too, not as quickly as the first but in four big shunts. Then another. I needed to call Simon, racked with guilt and excitement I wanted to tell him about what I'd done. I was still a year or two away from getting my first mobile, my main Christmas present from Peggy that year. I'd made a massive Christmas error by searching the house looking for my pressie haul. I'd found a bag under some coats deep in a cupboard. I shouldn't be doing this but I can't stop myself, I open the bag and holy fucking shit the Ericsson mobile phone of my dreams! Bosh!

Sometime between that point and Christmas Day Simon made a decision to change the phone so when I opened the gift, full of excitement, my crestfall was plain for all to see as I set my eyes on a giant lump of a Samsung mobile. A lesson there for every naughty boy and girl.

But this terrible moment was still a couple of years away. I go outside and call Simon Pegg from a red phonebox. He came straight away. I think he was pretty pleased I'd started again, to be honest. It meant we could now get right on it.

After four or five pints we stumbled back through Kentish Town with our trousers round our ankles. We got home hungry for more and smashed up a bottle of Blue Label Smiley had been keeping for special, he wasn't in so we went for it. That next morning I woke up with one of the worst hangovers ever. I find a large, rabid badger has shit into my brain and down the back of my eyes. It's horrible. That was the beginning of my second coming as a drinker. If you're expecting a PS to this where I go through some kind of primal pissmageddon then you'll be disappointed. Things were different from then on with drink for me. Yes I got pissed and beaten and swore at people and got sworn at and puked, passed out and blood-farted bacchanalian havoc all over the place, but I wasn't the same person I was when I stopped four years previously and that made me happy.

The house at 9 Busby Place had a garden that we couldn't access. We could see it but we couldn't get to it. The only access was through the downstairs flat. We'd been told that the place used to belong to our landlord's father who'd sadly died there. I can't really remember our landlord but I remember a feeling of dread if we knew he was turning up. I feel like I want to say he was a mean skinflint who never wanted to spend any money on the place but he had it in his power to let us have the key to downstairs and in turn the garden, so we played the game. Smiley, our working-class hardnut and spokesperson in residence, put the shit eye on him and the landlord tentatively agreed. We were thrilled. It meant we could have a garden for the summer.

There were a few of us at the house that morning when we first decided to use the key to the Dead Man's flat. We'd heard noises drifting through the floorboards before but I put that down to the 'erb I'd been smoking. We used the Dead Man as a thing to frighten us, he was a cautionary tale, a fishwives' yarn. We knew it was rubbish and stuff we'd say just to freak each other out but standing there at his old front door making a spooky *ewwwwwwwwhhhhhheeeeoooohhhhhh* noise I couldn't help but feel anxious.

The door stuck and we all pushed it open, our noses assaulted by the whiff of things old and foul. It was day and the sun struggled to make a dent through the brown net curtains. As we stepped inside the yellow-dark room our eyes strained to focus on the horrors within.

The Dead Man's flat was exactly as it was left the day he died. Nothing had been cleared. It was a mausoleum, a memento mori covered in a thick layer of dust and it was fucking creepy. There were still plates in the sink, food in the fridge, clothes, cutlery, pots, pans, dusty hats, furniture.

Poor bloke. We walked around for ages like CSI: Kentish Town, we looked in every drawer and every cupboard, on a calendar he'd marked dates well into the future when he'd be taking his pigeons to their next race.

We'd forgotten all about the garden. Our focus had turned to a very dusty but completely functioning La-Z-Boy recliner. Smiley was brave and gingerly sits and uses the sturdy lever to recline, fully. Simultaneously our minds link and we all accepted that in spite of its creepiness this would be a great addition to our house. This was the green light for low-level looting to begin. It felt like a bad idea, I could feel the dusty spirit fingers of a pigeon fancier jabbing his bones into my eye. We survey the garden for a second and all hastily agree on what needs to be done to make it nice and went back upstairs.

The chair was dusted and hoovered and it was good as new. We had a fucking La-Z-Boy recliner! This was the best day ever! The chair though had the last laugh, the chair and the Dead Man. The malevolent spirit of that old pigeon keeper sadly haunted the chair, we should never have taken it. People who slept in that chair, and there were many, all shared a similar dream. They awoke in our front room in the chair, unable to move, the Dead Man would be on them, over them, moving and looking into their eyes. If it was a girl asleep in the chair he would often rub himself off on them; once he finished the spell was broken and the girls could finally wake up. Weird and horny shit I'm sure you'll agree.

Over the years Simon and I had many other brushes with the occult, it was something we loved to flirt with. We loved the fear. We loved the spirit world. Often the pair of us would head into the wilds to hunt for ghosts and ghouls.

The first time we did this was deep within the Essex country-side. We pulled up outside a thirteenth-century Saxon church he'd read about. The church sat in a freshly ploughed field and we switched the engine off and sat in the cold dark, our breathing, shallow and quick, the only thing that could be heard. We got out of the car eventually after winding each other up a lot and tried the door to the ancient church. It was locked. Lights from a slow-moving vehicle on a nearby lane and my terrible overwhelming urge to wee forced us to run back to the car and drive away at high speed laughing like idiots.

When we lived in Highgate our house had a massive garden that bordered on a piece of woodland. For months we didn't really pay it much mind other than it was a nice thing to look at and the busy comings and goings of the cheeky European Jays was most cheery.

Simon and I were alone one night drinking litres of strong cider. It was dark and drizzling and having discovered a hole in our fence earlier in the day we decided to go through that hole and see what was in the forest. It was a mistake that almost cost one of us our life.

The forest was dense and the ground covered in a tangle of logs, vines and slippery ivy. We could see the lights of the cars on the Archway Road and hear the *clickclack* of the pedestrians streaming out of Highgate Station. It was exciting to be an unseen watcher, it pushed us deeper into the woods.

Eventually we find ourselves alone in the rain in a forest in the middle of London. We'd left the noise of the road behind. It felt like we were the only people left alive. It was a feeling we liked.

That house in Highgate was where we talked about what we'd do, how we'd cope during a Zombie outbreak. It took us a while to refine our plan but eventually we settled on this:

Using the backs of the houses we'd garden hop down the Archway Road until the houses became terraced with balconies along the front. We'd take to the balconies fifteen feet above the undead horde and silently make our way to a place called Pax Guns. A shop we'd reccied many times. It sold high-powered air rifles, optical scopes, ammo etc. but we suspected it had tastier stock out back for naughty little bastards like us. Climbing down through their extension skylight we'd raid the shop for whatever they had and arm ourselves with shooters.

Our plan has changed and evolved slightly over the years to include the use of edged weapons and pieces of pointy metal. The last thing you need when you're facing a gang of bitey fucks is to run out of ammo, then you got wampum big problem. A knife does not run out of bullets. That said, using a rifle as a club or stabbing a long blunt barrel through the eye bulbs and into the brain would also do the trick.

Once we'd secured our weps (weapons) we moved on to stage two of the plan. Heavy weps. (Heavy weapons.) You can't have too many heavy weps. (Heavy weapons.) I'd heard of a British army base in Enfield, which was essentially a giant arms cache. This was our second destination. After finding a truck or large van we'd head there to raid it hoping we were the first. Other desperate survivors will kill you just as quick as a mindless Z-Bag.

With the guards either changed or long since gone, it would be easy to break in and upgrade to the standard British Infantry L85A2 assault rifle in 5.56mm, its troop support version the L86A1 LSW and a long-barrelled .50 cal sniper's rifle for weekend field clearance. Then our plan changed gear. We needed to think about friends and family and a long-term solution for living the rest of our natural lives in relative comfort.

The answer was an easy one. We'd use one of London's many stadiums. As we were closer to Arsenal this is the one we chose. Once inside it gave us everything we needed. The stadium was a circle of lockable gates. Security was assured. The many hospitality boxes gave us somewhere to set up a kind of home, there'd be supplies, food and plenty of bottled water. More importantly for our long-term survival, half the pitch could be turned into fields for the cultivation of fresh food, wheat, corn, potatoes, apples, pears, plums, tomatoes, and the other half could be used for the grazing of the livestock we'd need for fresh meat. Easy.

However, this plan was a long way from needing to be utilised (2029) and right now we were soaking wet, pushing through an urban forest looking for goblins. What we found was a tad more exciting.

The forest clears slightly and we see the big brick arch of an old tunnel. It was caged and gated but in the far distance we could see a tiny speck of light. An entrance or exit depending on which end you're standing. We turn and follow what used to be the train tracks deeper into the woods. After a couple of minutes struggling through the forest we both stop, our mouths fall open. We have just unearthed the find of our lives. An old abandoned tube station. The remnants of the old Highgate High-level station, closed in 1954.

We stood in silence not quite believing that this had been here all along and we never knew. After a moment we climbed up off the tracks onto the old platform. It was amazing and perfect in every way. We patted ourselves on the back, finished our big cider and opened the back-up we'd brought in case we ran out, which we had. Good fucking times. Running around that place peering into the locked rooms and rattling the old platform dispensers selling things long forgotten like Hutchinson's Original Phlegm Pastilles and Miss Cunty's Titwax felt like heaven to us.

The rain began to lash down and fearing we'd soon run out of back-up cider we turn and head for home. It's heavy-going on the way back, muddy, slippy, very treacherous indeed. I lag behind with the dwindling cider rations. I could hear Simon in front telling me to hurry up. I pick up the pace and seconds later I slip on some wet ivy and smash my head on a log. I'm out cold. I think I'm unconscious for thirty seconds or so. When I wake I can hear an angry Simon calling my name. He thinks I'm fucking about. I can hear him shouting.

'I'm not fucking about, Nick! You better answer me!'

I couldn't speak or move.

'Nick! Fine! I'm going home and I'm ordering Chinese because I'm really hungry and I will see you later.'

He pauses . . . Nothing.

'Okay, I'm going. Seriously.'

I hear him tramp off into the woods towards our house. I cannot move. I'm badly injured and slump into unconsciousness again.

When I come to it's raining heavily still. I'm drunk and hurt and wet, this is a very dangerous triumvirate. I could kill or severely maul someone to death in this fragile state. I pull myself up into a sitting position and from there the next thirty minutes is spent dragging, tumbling and crashing my way through the forest towards home. Falling face first again I sleep for a while. A hundred metres or so in front of me I can see the welcoming lights of our front room burning in the darkness. I compel myself towards them. Finding the hole in the fence I crawl through and

I'm in my own garden. I roll onto my back, relief floods through me. The wolves turn back, afraid to pursue me any further.

I hoist myself up onto my feet and stagger, jaeger-like, up the garden and towards the house. I can't believe he left me. He bloody left me. Could this be revenge for Piegate? I fill the window soaked and covered in leaves and mud and shit and blood. Eventually Simon tears his eyes away from the TV and cheerily waves me in. I'm speechless and stumble into the front room, Simon sits happily watching telly and eating a massive Chinese. I'm angry and try to tell him as much but I'm stammering badly.

'Sorry bud, I thought you were joking. I was really hungry.'

I wasn't joking. I was also really hungry, hungry for medical assistance. Next day at the hospital it was revealed that as well as the massive lump on my head I had suffered a heavy concussion and a light hypothermia. This was the penultimate time we ever hunted for ghosts. Like Piegate, my near woodland death is a section of our lives we rarely talk about.

The last time we ever messed with the occult was in December 2002. We'd read about an old abandoned stately home in Surrey called Tilford Manor. It was the seat of the Duke of Guildford until a fire gutted the place and killed the fifth Duke's wife and his six children. After the tragedy the house was left to fall into disrepair.

This sounded perfect for us. We drove down late in the afternoon and arrived just as the sun was beginning to set. The main gate, at one point a fine structure, now dilapidated and dense with weeds and brambles, had a space large enough for the both of us to push through.

The forest on both sides seemed untouched and completely overgrown, no birds sang, no wind blew, this was the perfect storm for both horror and the desperate need for me to do wee wee.

We walked up the drive, now pierced by grass and weeds, until we got our first glimpse of the shattered remains of Tilford Manor. I felt a surge of cold from my feet up to the top of my head and we stopped, briefly unable to move. It was the creepiest place I had ever seen. Me and Simon discussed just going home but eventually, laughing like drains through terror-nerves, we decide to push on. I'm not sure we were ever going to go in, I think we were just going to walk around the outside and look through the windows, shit ourselves up a bit, that's what we enjoyed.

The windows on the ground floor were boarded up. We made our way around the back through a tangle of overgrown hedges and trees. The back of the house stops us in our tracks. It was absolutely beautiful, with a half decent gardener this place could be knocked into shape in no time at all. A vast, over-grown lawn spread out downhill from the house to a lake now covered in weed. A frog and newt haven for sure.

We walked down the lawn a little and turned to look back at the house, it was only now we see the place in all its glory. In its day it must have been fabulous. Now it's remembered only as a house where six children died.

I began to feel we'd done enough on this ghost hunt, we should go home, my almost constant need to wee was begin-ning to change into a solid yearning to make a plop. If push came to shove I could dump in one of the outhouses and use my pants to make clean and it'd be blamed on a loose-bowelled junkie.

Hidden in among the bushes was a set of stone steps leading to a battered old door. Simon pushed at it and with little effort the thing shuddered open. We deployed our head torches. *Paul* anyone? When ghost hunting we'd always have our head torches, it was a great way to leave both hands free if you needed to punch an amorous hobo.

The wind howled and the door slammed behind us. Inside that room was freezing cold. We stood in what I believed to be an old servants' kitchen or pantry with stone floors, butler's sinks, hooks for cloaks and on one wall, high up near the ceiling, a long row of bells. Underneath these shiny brass flowers were little handwritten notes to tell the old maids what room was ringing what bell. Down here, this place seemed untouched by the fire.

I assumed it had started in one of the bedrooms and spread, sparing the lower levels. Our fear was briefly overwhelmed by our curiosity about this piece of forgotten history we found ourselves in. Pushing through another door and up another set of stone steps we arrived at the foot of a great wooden staircase, ahead of us was the old front door, massive and boarded up with planks. On the left double doors leading to who knows what.

Here, there were signs of both Mother Nature's seizure and the fire which had taken six young lives. The ornate plaster cornices above the great staircase blackened and charred, had cracked. The wooden balustrade wrapped in long tendrils of ancient ivy. At this point one of the kitchen bells tings. I piss and we spend an age looking at one another. This is a shared aural hallucination, right? We wait. The fear subsides and we begin to theorise in whispers. It rings again, this time it's slightly more insistent. We hold hands and drops of sweat pitter patter fear all over our trainers.

We sprint back into the pantry and look at the panel of tiny bells, willing it not to ring. It rings again. This time it is long and angry and sustained. The sign beneath the bell reads Miss Emma's

Room. It honestly feels like we're possessed because we both make the decision to go and find her room. To this day I wish we hadn't. We should've run there and then. We should've run away.

We creaked up the stairs. Branching off the first floor landing there are two corridors leading to the back of the house. Each corridor has five or six doors. We walked down the first corridor, downstairs the ring of the bell, angry, insistent, continued. Every door is locked. Turning back we hear a loud creak coming from upstairs. We feel compelled to go up. We find charred wood, smashed brick and plaster; here half the house had given up and slumped in on itself.

Trees and bushes spring out of the brickwork making this part of the house look like Shockheaded Peter. We see the clouds racing by. Peering down into the hole we see what must be a hundred dolls and teddies littering the rubble beneath. All are headless.

Towards the back of this burned and broken corridor we see a door. As we approach it we see it has a cracked chalkboard hanging off the black door handle; in spidery, faded writing we see the words, Little Miss Emma. Simon and I look at each other and the bell downstairs stops ringing. I know what we shouldn't do but we do it anyway. My hand, trembling, reaches out to the dented and smoke-stained knob. I turn it and the mechanism inside the lock clicks and the door swings open.

The room inside is black with soot, the remnants of a fierce fire evident. There is a cupboard, a bed, burnt and charred, and a small dressing table, its combs and brushes melted and warped, its mirror cracked. We enter the room and kick and stand on what must be a hundred dolls' heads. The fear shakes itself loose and jangles up my spine and into my brain. We shouldn't be here. Once again the bell begins dancing down in the pantry. Whatever, whoever, is pulling that cord is in this room with us.

I turn to look at Simon. His eyes are wide as saucers, his mouth is agape and he trembles. I cannot see what he sees. I don't want to see what he has seen but I must. I have to see what he's seen. I turn and look at the spot on the wall where the bell pull dances and after a second I see it. It is black on black. The burnt wall here is not flat and it is not a wall but it is burnt and black, her nightie is black, charred, her face is black, her hairless head is black, her hands are tiny and black. She stops pulling the cord and the distant bell falls silent. Her face crinkles and her burnt, brittle eyelids spring open. She looks at us, right at us, her eyes, white as box fresh cue balls, are the signal for us to go. Flee now . . . RUN!!! And we do.

The wind roars through the house. We hear Little Miss Emma laughing and laughing, it is loud and terrible. It vibrates inside me and I slump against the wall and vomit. Simon grabs me and heaves me down the main staircase, we turn and head down the steps into the pantry. All the bells begin to ring, the inhabitants of the rooms long empty, angry and now pulling with all their might. We claw at the door and surge outside into the garden. The pantry door smashes closed behind us and inside the bells stop.

We don't stop running until we reach the car. We get inside and Simon revs the engine hard and we spin away as the wheels struggle for purchase. We don't say a thing and eventually we have to stop. Simon shakes so much I'm afraid we'll crash, he pulls the car over and we cry. It is uncontrollable. We never speak of this again. I will never forget Little Miss Emma's white eyes.

* * *

At some point two friends that Simon and Smiley had made while on tour in Australia came to stay. I'd heard a lot about these two. Greg Fleet and his then girlfriend Janei Anderson were both performers, actors and comedians. Greg was the person responsible for killing Daphne in *Neighbours*, he played a drunken yahoo who killed her in a car crash. Janei can be seen as Jacqui in the film *Romper Stomper* screaming up a right storm when the Koreans start handing out revenge beatings to the nutty skins.

I liked those guys from the start, I mean really loved them. I was struck by the amazing relationship they had at the time. I say amazing – it was terribly co-dependent but I'd never seen anything like it before so to me it was amazing. He was so naughty. He'd been a heroin addict for years and years by the time I met him but she just forgave him any indiscretion. Janei had so much bloody love, she was a sexy, funny, den mother. She cleaned with a finger of spit, she'd advise, she'd listen, cuddle, kiss, whatever was needed. She was also fucking funny. What a gal.

Greg, or Fleety as he was known, and me got each other immediately. We understood, not just each other but also the need to push things to their very end point, both socially and chemically. I'd never known anyone who did heroin before. I was frightened and fascinated and, to be honest, pretty confused at first. I think I was taught to be afraid of 'smackheads'. I didn't think they could be normal, amazing, beautiful, creative people who just happened to do heroin. Then again my tolerance for addiction and addicts was pretty high anyway because of my own experiences with it. I was more than ready to accept people for who they were, not what they did.

I didn't realise at first what was happening with the heroin, Greg would slope off to the loo and stay in there for ages. When he came out he was so sleepy. We'd sit and watch the morning cartoons, Greg would sit in the Dead Man's chair and smoke, he'd nod off and would come to as the hot end of his ciggie burnt him awake.

With Smiley and Simon and our two new arrivals the house bloomed and blossomed. It felt amazing being there, it was like a Lars von Trier collective but with less trumpets. Some mornings we'd all put faux fur coats on and shoot music videos. We were always creating something. I still had to go to work and wait tables or shake Martinis but it gave me a reason to forget my folks and my sadness and enjoy myself. This, of course, meant drugs, although I never tried H. I always hated needles so for me injecting was way beyond my limit.

This was my Camden Town time and I loved it, I looked forward to it, it made me feel special. Every Sunday I'd get up at whatever time, shake off whatever was still in me, and dress up. I'd try and look cool to impress Janei, it was difficult for me – the others made it seem so effortless. Janei was a very stylish woman and I tried to impress her whenever I had the chance. We all did. Smiley has always dressed well. He has a great sense of style. He's one of those fellas where clothes just hang so well on him. Greg was an H pony so he seemed not to care much about fashion, yet in his not caring it made him very stylish and cool. Lucky prick.

After breakfast/brunch/lunch we'd stroll into Camden Town. Camden Town then on a Sunday was very happening. It still is but now it seems more corporate-sponsored, cleaner, less dangerous. It's still nice though, even a little edgy I guess if you're a Danish teen on an exchange trip. Back then it was a dirty, dangerous breeding ground for bands and drugs and laughter and fighting.

We'd walk around the stables for ages, buying T-shirts or new screens for the bongs or sunglasses. It made me feel like an extra in *Blade Runner* walking under the railway arches that heaved with tourists, Rastas, wide-eyed Ravers and back-combed Goths as we trawled the stalls looking for nice fresh falafel. It was exciting.

Under the bridge by the lock was the place to go if you wanted to buy the shittest drugs in the world. The dealers were men used to cutting at thin tourists looking for something to blaze up through the window of their two-star Paddington flop house. I'd been burned a couple of times but sometimes after a few drinks on a Sunday it was hard to resist the temptation.

One afternoon I pushed past a group of Polish kids who were waiting to be threatened. A frightened young Swede with deep cuts to both his arms bumbled back up the towpath crying. In the canal there were two corpse-shaped things floating just beneath the surface. It seemed quiet for a Sunday. No matter, I fancied a smoke and this time I had a surefire way to not get burned.

As I neared the stick-thin one-eyed Rasta I took an approach I was hoping they'd never seen or heard before. Honesty. I was going to be honest and just lay it all out there.

'All right?'

'Whauwan?'

So far so good . . .

'I need some bush.'

I'd heard some white Trustafarians in an earlier exchange say 'Me need some bush, mon.' They got cut and rightly so. The exchange progressed and I see One-Eye reach into his jacket to fish out Sir Stabsalot. It's at this point I spring the trap:

'Wait!' He tenses up. I continue:

'Can I be honest with you?' A fog of confusion descends upon the trader. His hands tremble as he works out what's happening. I think he thinks I'm Old Bill. I'm not. I continue:

'I'm from London, born and bred as, I think, are you.'

'Fucking right, blud. Islington.' His patois drops for just a second. This is good – for the moment my body remains watertight.

'Can I be honest with you?' I repeat.

'Go on but be quick I got Spanish kids to slash at.'

'I understand. I live in Kentish Town, I'm here every week and I've been burned in the past by people that trade under this bridge. I'm a bit pissed and I'm desperate for a smoke, I don't want to spend £40 buying something that'd be better suited going into cannelloni.' I hear someone drop a knife behind me in utter disbelief. There's a long pause, he's debating how to open me up: tummy jab maybe, bleeds a lot, takes an age to die if it's shallow enough I guess, how about a . . . facial slash? Facial slash is good because it sends out a very visible warning. Maybe a few short sharp stabs to my bum and upper thighs – I'll shit standing up in the shower for the next eight weeks but I'll live. Who knows. Let's find out, he stares at me . . .

'Yeah, okay, fair enough, follow me.'

I follow One-Eye back to his flat on the outskirts of Camden. I'm slightly nervous but we've begun to chat and like a trusting fool I go with him. The atmosphere lightens somewhat when he lifts his patch to reveal another fully working, bright clear chestnut eye. I shouldn't have but in the atmosphere of honesty and trust I do. He invites me in, I accept. By and by we have a glass of semi-skimmed milk. He pulls out a carrier bag of stinky shit, I hand over dollar bills, he hands over the fat buds and the deal is done. Simple as that. We shake hands and drift back into town together. As he nears the bridge he explains, pulling down his patch, he has to put his game face on.

'I've gotta get back to work. It was nice to meet you though.'

'And you, mate.' I go to shake hands, he pulls away.

'I can't, the guys are watching.'

'I understand. How do you want to play this?' He thinks for a minute.

'I'll shout loudly calling you a Bumbaclart, I'll go through my pockets looking for my carnival knife and you flee into the crowded market place.'

'Sounds like a plan. Thanks, Ian.'

'BUMBACLART!' He winks. I run.

Sometimes honesty is the best policy.

Camden on a Sunday was something all the crew liked. Usually it was me, Fleety, Janei and Simon, later we'd hook up with Smiley and his lot, the stand-ups, proper stand-ups, dark, edgy, wonderful loonies. Later still Dion and Tony and the South Africans would roll into town and shit would get weird. These were not exclusive combinations. For a long while we'd hit the World's End, the place where I broke my neck falling off of the wagon, and sit there for a long-time session. Once hammered we'd drift off into the market for fun and cheap Chinese food that made us all need to do semi-solid toilets really quickly. We loved it.

There was a club in the market on a Sunday evening run by the legendary DJ Goldie called Metalheadz. We weren't into Drum and Bass that much, Hard House was our thing, but we weren't snobby and after fifteen pints it was nice to have a joint and a jump. The guys came a couple of times but their hearts weren't in it. Mostly – and when I say mostly I mean the five times we went – I went on my own. I loved the music but the clientele seemed a bit too serious, they seemed to want to be seen, it didn't feel like anyone was having that much fun. Not like Hard House, that shit was all about fun.

Sometimes, and I liked these sometimes, I'd have a mooch with the gang and we'd stop to drink a coffee under these arches deep at the back of the market. Dub reggae would rattle my eyes, my nose assaulted by the smell of 'erb and incense. We'd sit and watch tourists drift through. It was so nice sitting there, it felt like being in a futuristic space souk.

Afterwards we'd bowl over to meet Smiley at The Stag's Head pub just across the street. I liked it here a lot. It was a proper Irish boozer, packed with hipsters and locals. It also had an amazing Thai kitchen. Like I said, traditional Irish. It was always exciting in that place. Smiley obviously bossed it, he's so fucking cheeky and gets away with absolute murder, it's thrilling to watch. He'd often leave me open-mouthed by his naughtiness. The first time he met my mum he goosed her slightly and asked if she had knickers on. Lolz! She loved it. They all did.

As well as Smiley he was often joined by a big dangerous northern man called Danny Brown. Danny quickly became a good mate to me. He lives nearby now and I see him all the time. Danny, along with Smiley, Simon, Nira Park, Tony Lindsay and Edgar, all have their initials tattooed around my arm around a crown. Kings and queens among men. I couldn't have done any of it without them.

Danny and Smiley were the two toughest sons of bitches I knew and I couldn't help but feel slightly indestructible when I was out on the piss with that pair. There was also a small wiry fella called Andrew Maxwell who could talk the back legs off a donkey. He's funny as fuck and sharp as a razor, smart and dashing to boot. Great stand-up. When I had my stag night Maxwell turned up with a massive glass bottle shaped like the Eiffel Tower, it was full of absinthe. Pandemonium ensued.

Often other friends and family would turn up at the pub, children too; naughty and mischievous, smart, loved and clever, they would run around stealing sips from pints. It felt like these people in this place were my family. It was all I had and it was enough. After drinking and doing whatever else, the crew would walk back through Kentish Town back to Busby Place. We'd wind down listening to Smiley mix or watching new episodes of *The Simpsons* smoking fatties and sitting in the Dead Man's chair. I'd often snuggle up and nod off with my head on Janei's lap, she'd stroke my hair and call me Bubbie. I think it was the happiest I'd been.

This was the time me and Simon started to make our first little films. They were shit and amazing. Little horror films we shot on Simon's video camera. Our films, shot on location in 9 Busby Place and almost entirely in French, had the potential we thought to rock Hollywood to its very core.

Aniseed Du Peril was the story of a man killed by a possessed bottle of the antacid drink Gaviscon. Thrilling stuff. *Il Slash Mon Guts (He Slash My Guts)* was a grizzly stalk and slash which became an advert for Gaviscon. Smiley had a plastic retractable knife that we used in the film, and in the thrilling dénouement when a bad me killed a good me, the blade snapped. During the only take we filmed you can see how frightened I am exactly at the moment the knife breaks. It adds a dimension of realism to the scene if you know that Smiley will be so mad when he finds out you went into his room and took something without asking which you then broke.

Me and Simon rewound that moment about a hundred times and screamed with laughter every time we watched it. It's funny when my dying screams turn into a 'oooh' noise when I realise how much shit we'll be in.

Our last horror short was a black and white effort called *Dinner For Two*. A tense psychological thriller starring the excellent Greg Fleet and the Alluring Janei Anderson. There was a chilling twist at the end which I won't give away. The funniest part of that film was watching Greg trying to stick an LP record into a CD player. What a wally. So simple but boy we laughed.

My double life continued apace. I'm never sure what me I was. I know there were lots of naughties in my life. I was clubbing at every opportunity I could and spent my time planning for weekends or getting over the weekends. This had gone on for so long that I was beginning to feel jaded, dirty, even a little bit bored of it. My head was everywhere. The fantastic and magical had become the grubby and malignant. I was paranoid and the consumption of more and more was beginning to feel like a hollow mission. I never stopped to enjoy or breathe.

I found myself one night in a club somewhere in South London. I'd heard stories, rumours on the scene, that government agencies had infiltrated circles of dealers and that dodgy bumbles were being sold to break the movement up. I didn't believe it. I was sure our government has better things to do than fuck with hedonists and independent thinkers. Right?

That night a packed club full of happy people became an empty club within three hours. Everyone became very ill. I stumbled around until I found an overground station. Getting onto a train that was headed fuck knows where, I puke onto the floor of the empty carriage. My eyes roll, I couldn't believe what

I saw. I was covered in a thick black foam. What the fuck was going on? I was puking thick black foam. What organ in the body is responsible for producing black foam? I was unaware of the black foam gland in the human stomach up until that point. What was happening to me? I passed out and when I came to I was standing on a beach looking out at the sea. It was flat and calm. I closed my eyes. The sun was shining and it felt lovely.

I realise now I had been deaf, the noise of gulls and children screaming tickle my eardrums and I fully awaken. I have no idea how I got there, what time it was or even where I was. In my hands I have two books, *Cancer Ward* and *The Gulag Archipelago*, both by Solzhenitsyn. No idea how I got them.

I'm in Brighton. It's the first time I'd ever been. I make my way home and spend the day trembling. This was the start of the end of that section of my hedonism. It continued, sure, but it was different. It took its toll on me. My glass shattered. I wouldn't call it a massive breakdown as such but it was a tiny bit of a breakdown. A Nervy B as my mate Paddy would call it. I had a little Nervy B.

When I was coming down off shit I used to feel sounds. Sounds would transfer into nerve commands and rattle up my pathways into my brain. It was terrible. I hated it. I always said to Simon it felt like my mind was a very thin veneer of glass resting on four old, red bricks. Every now and then someone would drop a piece of gravel on that glass. The fear I had of it shattering and its noise transforming into a bolt that raced up through my nervous system and into my brain was too much to take. One day my glass shattered.

I stopped working, I stopped going out, I couldn't really eat. I lay in bed or on the sofa smoking weed, feeling fucking sorry for myself. Feeling my brain frighten itself whenever it could.

Weed didn't help me of course but I never knew that back then, that's a fairly recent realisation. It's probably been the thing that fucked me up the most over the years and I failed to acknowledge it until it was almost too late. I think I refused to accept that it was the HaHa biscuits making me feel like this. How could something I love so much be hurting me so bad? I couldn't get my shit together. I was afraid and I was shit.

Simon and Smiley and a few of the girls I knew were amazing at this time, always popping in and bringing me Weetabix. I like Weetabix. The boys gee'd me up and financially sorted me out. I really owe them so fucking much. After a few weeks I started to pull up out of my dive, the darkness cleared slightly and something started to drag that big, wet quilt off my stubborn bonce. Smiley is always great in these situations. He Smiley'd me one night and told me how it was. It was exactly what I needed. In the absence of my own dad, due to our alcoholic exile and my sad bitterness at the whole 'Mum' situation, he was it. He was the kick up the hole that shook me out of my chemically induced mind funk.

Smiley was the guy who made me realise that it was all right to succeed. No one had ever told me that. It was something I'd never considered before. That's stayed with me ever since. It's okay to succeed. I knew what it felt like to hurt and fail, those things were familiar to me. But the thought that I was allowed to succeed was something new and scary and something I needed to hear.

* * *

I did not want to go back to working in restaurants. I looked around for other things first before I was forced back on the floor. A cabbie maybe? I liked driving but couldn't afford a car, I didn't have a pot to piss in. What could I do? Me and Dion thought about starting a garden-clearing business called Busy Bees. It never came to fruition.

I needed to do something so I took the first job that I saw. I spent a week working in a call centre off Great Portland Street. Telesales. It was not for me at all. It was full of *Wolf of Wall Street* wannabees. Guys with headsets on selling, selling, selling. At points they'd stop yabbering to use the telesales professional's greatest tool . . . Silence. Let the other fucker speak first. Take away every opportunity the guy on the other end of the phone has to say no until the only thing he can say is, yes. Boom! There's your sale. There's your commission. I hated watching those cocky twats. I lost count of the amount of smug winks I got from helmets about to make £50 in commission.

I found it really difficult. I couldn't do what they did. I didn't care enough and it felt like a scam. I'd sit in my booth, head down, cold-calling people, reading my lines off the ready-prepared script. People who'd been there a while didn't need the script, they used it as a frame and hung their own shit off it. There was a skill involved certainly but I didn't have it. I'd mumble into the headset and get hung up on. NO NO NO! I heard that a lot. I made no sales. In that business you live and die on bottom line. No sales? No commission? Then you're out.

After a few days chasing leads I sensed a sale was on the cards. I used the silence and chiselled away every opportunity for the customer to say no until he finally said yes! I leapt up and punched the air. I had my first sale. The company procedure for a sale was this: you took a sales form and faxed it over to the other company, got them to sign it, faxed it back and then boom! The sale and the commission was yours.

I gathered the documents together and rushed to the fax machine, I wrote the fax number on the back of the last sheet, stuck it in the machine and dialled. A moment, some squeaks, and the fax went through. I was about to get paid. Yes! I was chuffed to bits. Maybe I was cut out for this after all.

Colleagues now full of pride, and seeing my immense potential, came and patted me on the back. I did it. I shuffled the papers and re-ordered them, placing them in a little file marked 'Successful sales'. It was at this point I realised I'd actually faxed him my script covered in explicit doodles of giant helmeted dicks and big-titted women, legs spread ready to gratefully accept the aforementioned giant helmeted dicks.

The guy was furious and complained. I didn't come in the next day and was unemployed again. Good. I hated that fucking horrendous, windowless, smug-filled anus farm.

So obviously I went back to the only thing I was good at. I wound up back in a dining room having an interview at a restaurant called Frankie and Benny's. It was a bad interview as I still struggled slightly talking to people and being outside but I had to do something so fuck it.

* * *

Having to work in a restaurant again after hanging out with my friends who were my family, these funny, complicated, beautiful, creative, angry fuckers, and knowing there was another life I could be leading was a real pain in my helmet.

I got the job and was now working in East Finchley. I could do the work in my sleep but I began to enjoy it as I always seemed to.

It was the same drill. A fiery crew in the kitchen, this time all Portuguese, dishing out pasta and pizza, and a nice manager, Sam Baker, who swore like a trooper and laughed a lot. I liked her. One day I saved her life when we stole a pizza and wolfed it down laughing like drains out the back, she sucked a piece of sausage down the wrong hole, and choked. I intervened when I saw her lips turning blue, performing the Heimlich like a champ. We both watched the Frisbee-like pork assassin fly up and out of her throat. She gasped and we hugged and laughed.

There were a couple of boys on the bar who I became friends with. They were up to no good. By this time Autoglass had been round and replaced my shattered mindscreen. The Nervy B now long forgotten, I jumped in with both feet. As was my wont.

One day a new waitress came into the restaurant. Her name was Callie and she rocked my little world for a while. What is it with me and gorgeous waitresses? So silly. I think I was still quite shallow at this point. I didn't care enough about what was up top or in the heart, I cared about how they looked and something so superficial will only ever bring one thing. Pain. Pain for me anyhow. I've left this behind, now as I've gotten older but then I was crazy for the perfect nose and glossy red hair of this girl. This would be no flash in the pan. I fell hard.

Apart from a few bonkers parties with the hardest, naughtiest kind of chocolate buttons, Callie was the most memorable thing to happen to me during my time at that restaurant. That and *Spaced* of course. Callie had a boyfriend but I sensed they were off-again on-again quite a lot. She wanted to be an actress, I still had no idea what I wanted to be.

I made Callie laugh and I could feel us getting closer but she was still in love with her boyfriend. I knew from the beginning it would hurt, I suspected she was using me to get back at him, although I'm not sure he ever knew about me, thus defeating the purpose I guess. I wasn't the kind of hunk girls used to make other hunks jelz. He was, I imagine, a big, handsome fucker, to get her you'd have to be. (Unless you were funny, like me.)

I think the mistake I made was fairly early on telling her that I loved her. Error. I think I did. I felt like I did anyway. Now obviously looking back it was nothing like love. It was my balls trying to convince my brain that I loved her. As soon as I told her this it was game over and I'd lost. Again.

This affair went on for a while and coincided with a heavy consumption of dangerous and psychoactive lolflakes. The lolflakes I think helped and prolonged my 'relationship' with Callie, added another level of mystique to me. I may not have been a looker in her eyes but I was funny, smart, complicated and troubled. This was almost enough to keep her interested. Almost. I used a cracking technique when we first met, although to say technique would imply some kind of thought process behind it; there wasn't. What I did was I simply forgot her name. It made her mad that this plain lump would, could, forget *her* name.

We had some lovely days. Once in the morning I brushed her hair and we went to the zoo but I could see her heart wasn't in it. We worked and I made her laugh and I wanted her to love me and it was complicated and I guess secretly I liked it. The fact I ever got her to stay in the Crab Pit was amazing to me. How would any young lady in her right mind ever want to wake up in Tramp Henge? I knew how to treat a woman back then. Once I bought her a lettuce as a present. I woke up and she was gone. Only the lettuce remained. I panicked slightly.

I think if you took 9 Busby Place as a whole, its inhabitants, the vibe – sorry, me – it was a fairly attractive place for Callie to be. We had some amazing parties in that house. I don't remember much, which is probably for the best. I once saw two burly northern women holding onto each other for balance while they pissed off a high balcony onto the street below. It was a very dangerous manoeuvre.

That same party saw the police try and secrete a plain clothes officer into our rave. The police had come round earlier in uniform asking us to turn down the music. We didn't. So later in the night they pulled up the street a little way in a marked panda car and dropped off an undercover man. Silly tactic. We were all stood out on the balcony and watched the whole thing unfold. The young officer, wearing tight, stonewashed jeans and a fleece – what did off-duty police wear before the invention of the fleece? – hopped out of the vehicle and grabbed a four-pack of generic lager. He set off to infiltrate and realised he'd been rumbled. We laughed and barracked him from the third-storey balcony. He turned tail and got back in the car.

Some of my favourite times at Busby Place came on Sunday mornings when we had been clubbing hard. Smiley's records and deck set-up meant it was a perfect place to chill out as the sun came up. Sometimes twenty people would come back, the sexy Antipodean babes would bath and get into some kind of snuggie, while the boys smoked biftas and talked loudly.

We'd wake Smiley up and pester him to mix for us. He'd be absolutely furious for a second and then his spirit chimp would kick in and the need for him to create a little mischief would overwhelm his urge to kill us. Pretty soon after a Norn Irish breakfast (tea and a fag), he'd start to play records and the night would begin again.

NICK FROST

Eventually we'd run out of steam and we'd all lie in a heap, the girls in their snuggies and all freshly showered smelt and felt amazing. We were naughty, greedy boys and secretly the girls liked it. They'd play with my hair and massage my hands while my eyes rolled. They were perfect Sundays. I think this is a fine dynamic when you're in your twenties. The longer this goes on the more boring it gets. Especially for the girls. Girls don't want those types of guys into the mid-thirties and beyond. Very unattractive.

One afternoon Smiley arrived back from gigging upcountry, I hadn't been out and Simon wasn't in. Smiley was acting very weird. He was quiet, not like Smiley at all. He came in and made a cuppa. A few words were exchanged, not much though. He goes upstairs to shower, I light another bifta. When he comes back down his skinny little body is wrapped in a towel and he's wearing a big cardie. He sits down and watches telly not saying a word. Something bad has happened. I don't pry at first, the weed gives me a sixth sense that says 'not now' so I leave it. A little bit later my weed says 'now'.

'Hey, mate? Are you okay?'

He nods silently and gets up and leaves. My feet feel hot. Something's wrong. Ten minutes or so later he comes in again and turns the telly off. ALERT. ALERT. ALERT. I push my legs back and move the Dead Man's chair from horizontal into a high vertical position. The weed stutters . . .

'Don't, don't, please don't turn the telly . . .'

'I need to talk to you.'

'Right.'

'You know I said I was gigging up the country?'

'Yeah.' Oh god help me, I know what's coming.

'I wasn't gigging.'

'Oh. Right, where were you then?' I didn't want to know.

Me and Smiley have a long history, Smiley more than me to be fair, of flirting with Simon's lovely mum. It drives Simon slightly mad and makes Gill laugh, it's all in good spirits. She is absolutely lovely. She's one of the nicest people in the world and has been so good and kind to me ever since I first met her twenty-one years ago. We have a kind of mother/son thing going on, but Smiley's a big flirt and likes to make me and Simon feel uncomfortable so he always pushed it that much further.

Smiley continued but inside I knew what was coming.

'I spent the weekend in a hotel.' he said.

'Oh right.' I pretended to be dead but he continued anyway. Why had I smoked that joint?

'I spent the weekend in a hotel with Gill.'

BOOOOOOOOOOOOOOOMMMMMMMMMMMMM!!!

My left brain shuts down, my right hand shuts down and I piss-fit slightly. Smiley gets up, pats me on the shoulder and leaves me alone downstairs, terrified. My liver hurts.

I remain paralysed, shut down, dormant for over an hour until I hear the downstairs door open. Simon is home. I know the worst secret in the world and it's killing me. Our dream, our little collective, is gone and dead and I know and I can't say.

Simon senses weirdness from me and it's all I can do to stop myself grabbing a giant kitchen knife, touching the point to the place on my chest where my heart lives and falling forwards until it's sticking out the other side and one of my feet is twitching.

'What's up?'

'Nothing.'

259

'Smiley in?'

I nod. Simon puts the kettle on. I'm wearing a sarong and an orange shirt that I love, it has the legend 'Down By Law' etched on the back; being a big Jim Jarmusch fan I was very proud of this work shirt. I wear thick-rimmed black glasses and my hair is set in a high backcombed pompadour. The guys used to call it The Goose. I'm almost constantly high, something I'm regretting right now as I lie there unable to speak, hoping Smiley has somehow died in the last hour.

I hear his door open. I hear his bony little feet padding on the stairs. He's coming.

'Hey, mate.' Smiley puts on his butter-wouldn't-melt voice. Simon smells a rat immediately.

'Hey, mate.' They cuddle. Smiley pushes it.

'You wouldn't make me a nice lil cup o tea, would you?'

'Sure,' says Simon. 'Everything okay?'

A pause. I look at Smiley. He looks at me.

'Aye.'

Simon sits and we all drink our tea in silence. This is too much for me to bear so again I click into a vertical position, stand, retie my sarong and bumble around trying to act casual. Smiley's watching.

'Where are you going, big lad?'

Simon's slightly confused, he senses wrongness.

'What's going on?'

'Nothing, I'm going up for sleep.' It's one in the afternoon. I have to leave. I run into the Crab Pit and pull a box of musty towels across the door. I listen for Simon's grief-ridden cries as he finds out his best mate has violated not only the sanctity of a lovely friendship but also his mother. I pace and pound around my Crab Pit. Eventually I am forced to go downstairs. I ghost down silently and note the TV has been muted. Simon and Smiley sit next to each other in silence. Oh god. Poor Simon. Will Smiley eventually become Simon's new stepdad? That could be awkward.

I walk into the kitchen, fluids pumping around a brain, flabby and numb, make a whooshing noise every time my heart pumps, which, right now, is a lot. I do what I believe is the right thing to do. Let's have a cup of tea and talk this through.

'Tea anyone?' I turn to see them both smiling. Oh. Then Smiley waggles his eyebrows, Simon chuckles.

'What's happening?' I wish I was gone.

They both start laughing. This, it turns out, is a very cruel trick. A very cruel trick indeed. Smiley, seeing me high, had decided to play a joke of such life-rocking proportion I had internally peed into my own bladder. Why would you play a trick like that? Simon wasn't in on it but when I fled Smiley saw his chance to rope him in. What a willy. We laughed.

* * *

Our time at Busby Place came to an end. We knew our time was up one afternoon when me and Simon were watching TV. With no warning at all the ceiling of the kitchen/living room simply detached and fell onto our heads. We could easily have been killed. After a second, once an internal health diagnostic had been run, we laughed. The landlord never really had the drive or the gumption to do the place up. I think eventually he decides to sell that big lump of a house. So we move out.

Simon's career had gone from strength to strength. A couple of years before he found himself touring with Steve Coogan on his live show, *The Man Who Thinks He's It*. It was a great show. Steve and Simon became mates off the back of it and I guess, through him, me and Steve got to know each other a bit too. I like him a lot, he's funny and very generous.

When he found out we were being put on the street he offered us his mews house in Archway. What a Mensch. Next door lived either Pepsi or Shirley, from the band Pepsi and Shirley. They started out as a backing group for Wham! in the eighties but went on to have a nice little career of their own. I never found out which was which and we never really saw them very much so it didn't matter. It was a really lovely house and we paid very little for it.

I was still half seeing Callie, still in love, still working in the restaurant but something was about to change. Simon, along with an ultra-talented loony called Jess Stevenson, had been approached by Channel 4. He'd met her making a TV show that Edgar directed. They really enjoyed each other and Simon thought Jess and Edgar were friggin geniuses. He was right. They hung out a lot and came up with the idea for a flatshare comedy which became the show called *Spaced*.

It was great seeing Simon potentially get his own series, he was cockahoop. After a lot of meetings with the channel they agreed to commission seven episodes of network television. What a great thing.

Me and Peggy went to Camden one day to drink cocktails and meet Jess. Once she'd arrived they put a proposition to me: 'How would you like to come and be in our show *Spaced*?'

He wanted to use a slightly tweaked version of my character Mike Watt in the show and wanted me to play him. I'd never acted before and didn't ever think it would happen so I shrugged, 'Fuck it, I'll do it.'

That was that. Anything to get out of waitering. I never thought it'd happen and I'd ever have to do it so what was the harm in saying yes?

This gave me the chance to lord it up a bit over Callie at work, she wanted to be an actress so badly, she seemed amazed that I'd be so casual given an opportunity like this. Maybe she was a bit cross that this thing had flopped into my lap when I didn't really give a fig about acting or being famous.

I put the meeting in Camden out of my mind until I started to receive phone calls about costumes and sizes and my availability etc. What was happening? Simon would come home every night buzzing about what he and Jess had written that day, jokes they'd laughed at, characters they'd crafted. It was exciting. Still I waited tables.

In the evenings we'd sometimes all hang out together, go to a pub, party, dinner, drinks. I knew everyone more or less by this time and I wasn't afraid any more but I still didn't have much of a voice. Who cared what I had to say, what I thought was funny? I was good in small groups. Fortunately Edgar and Jess had seen me in small groups so they had got to know me better.

That said, it was only fairly recently that I discovered Edgar had had a conversation with Simon one day shortly before the pre-production of *Spaced* began. He questioned whether or not Simon was sure I could do it, whether I could act, whether I could perform in front of people. It's a perfectly understandable question to ask. I think Simon said yes – I think. What a gamble, what a risk to take. I hope I've repaid that trust over the years. I'm glad Simon was confident because I sure as shit wasn't. I didn't want to be an actor in any way, shape or form. No sir. It seemed too much like showing off for me and if there's one thing I'm not it's a show-off. (Maybe a little bit in the kitchen.)

What was I going to do? I'd never acted before. I say never – I did have a tiny part on BBC2's *Big Train*. Dressed as a builder I had to fall in love with a horny puppet bird as it bounced past me. That was it. It was short and sweet but I think Simon arranged it with Graham Linehan to give me a taste of what shooting was like. I got to meet the lovely Julia Davis and also a man who's become a very close friend over the last fifteen years or so, the very lovely Mr Kevin Eldon. Gosh he makes me laugh. He's the nicest Buddhist I've ever met. And that's saying something. Our children are betrothed to be wed someday.

It was only after I'd gone to my first costume fitting with a Scottish firecracker called Annie Hardinge that I began to real-ise this thing may actually happen. Annie and I have worked together a lot since then. She's a fantastic costume designer and a wonderful woman. Always well turned out with long curls of rich auburn hair. She's the kind of woman an American airman would've painted on the side of a B52.

Simon, Edgar, Jess and Nira Park – enduring friend, godmother to my son and perhaps the world's greatest producer – went into Channel 4 to have a meeting with someone high up. During the meeting my name was brought up, the exec wanted to know who I was, what I'd done and whether or not I was in *Spotlight*. (*Spotlight* for those of you who don't know is essen-tially lots of very big books with pictures and brief resumés of thousands and thousands of actors.) Simon and Jess lied and said I was in *Spotlight*. Fortunately for me there was another Nick Frost and we said he was me. The exec seemed happy and let it slide.

So this was me. A man with a complicated history, a past littered with overindulgence and family alcoholism, on the verge of making a TV show. The issue I have, and I think it's kind of a biggie, is I have no idea how to do the actings. Even though people had been calling me from the production office I still didn't think it would happen. I didn't want it to happen. I wanted things to stay as they were. I didn't really, I knew this was the change I needed, but I could've done without this ball of anxiety bouncing around inside of me.

Living with Simon I had the chance to get the scripts in advance and start to try and learn them. The thought of not knowing my lines and fucking up in front of people I didn't know made me want to die. I'm not too bad now, I just got better at learning lines, and after twelve years I'm pretty good. I still have that terrible fear of fucking up, but it's not all-consuming any more. Day to day I put a lot of time and effort into making sure this doesn't happen.

Sometimes though it just does go wrong. Actors are not computers, if a script has no melody or flow then it's tough to learn no matter how many hours you put in. Also, it's not live, it's not the end of the world. Audiences don't need to know how it's made, the process; what's important is the finished product.

Back then I was terrified. The Big Waiter on campus would soon be taken out of his comfortable restaurant, the place I knew and loved, the place that fed and housed me and supplied me with money for chemical vacations and an endless stream of horny waitresses to flirt with. Soon I would be thrown from the comfort of the above into the uncomfortable world of British Television. I didn't deserve it and I didn't want it. I did, however, need it.

About four weeks out from the beginning of production I was told to appear at so and so a place in town for my first ever read-through. Whatever the fuck *that* was. I had no agent although Simon's lovely rep Dawn Sedgwick (bloody good egg) agreed to take care of my paperwork. More importantly, I had no acting experience. Save for those 5 seconds on *Big Train*.

A read-through is something that's done around a big table with every cast member present. It's usually to help the writers get a feel for what's working and what's not. After the read-through the scripts are tweaked a little, sometimes more work's necessary. Then shooting scripts are released and you're ready to go.

I was so shy and nervous. I don't think I talked to anyone much. I knew Mark Heap and Katy Carmichael a little bit through parties and gatherings over the last few years but I didn't know them very well. We'd read through the script once all together on our own in a big room and then after that we'd grab a sandwich and then be joined by the big cheeses and heads of department, and other honoured invitees who'd all sit and listen to the scripts being read aloud.

These things never start on time. Actors, not all actors but some actors, are always a little bit – or in some cases a lot – late, often rushing in, cappuccino in hand, sometimes wearing a pompous hat or silken pashmina, items of clothing that alert potential street robbers to the fact that these people are actors and as such have no way to defend themselves whatsoever. It was ever thus.

I find read-throughs a lot of fun now. Unless the thing you're reading is shit. Also if none of the decision makers laugh you can leave the room feeling like it's your fault. It's soul crushing to see a Commissioner sending or reading an email mid read-through.

I've also seen the opposite happen, people laugh so much

that it's difficult to ascertain whether or not the thing is actually good. Actors love the sound of Commissioners laughter. It often means the louder the laughing gets the bigger the performance. It's an ugly thing to watch but completely understandable. Who among us doesn't like the taste of fresh laughter?

If you have the world's most amazing read-through it's often tough for the actual film or TV show to live up to the expectation of that read-through. I always think it's like spending a hundred grand on a dream wedding. Once the dust settles it's going to be tricky for the actual marriage to live up to the expectation of that massive knees-up.

We sat around the table and read the scripts. I don't think we read the whole series. I think we read three episodes or so. I was afraid but kept my head down and tried to interpret what Simon and Jess had written in terms of comedy beats etc. As Mike was my invention, written for me by two fantastic writers, directed by a hairy boy genius, I would've had to have been a complete fuckhead to not get laughs. I was funny, what I wasn't was an actor. Not yet, that comes much later. Right now I was a lucky waiter pretending to be an actor.

The first read-through with just us went great. It was relaxed, it was fun, and watching people, great people – great actors like Mark Heap and the sexy, beautiful Julia Deakin – work, and seeing what their process looked like, was exhilarating and fascinating to me.

I think throughout my whole life I've done a lot of this. Watching, seeing how things worked, seeing the shape of the food chain, who does what etc. I've asked a lot of questions too. As I never trained as an actor every department was equally interesting to me and I think that's really held me in good stead over the last twelve or so years. Especially as long term my aim is to direct and produce more. (Fingers crossed.)

After some light refreshment Nira, our fearsome producer, entered the reading room. She's not so fearsome now, not to me anyway and not after all these years, but back then I'm not sure she thought I deserved this shot or if I could even pull it off. I don't think she talked to me properly for two years. Many was the time in a pub after a few I'd turn to Simon and ask if he thought Nira liked me.

Nira's arrival means one thing, Big Wigs are en route. Assistants came in and set up chairs in a formation that was definitely gladiatorial. The chairs were shoved up close behind us. People filtered in, heads of department, well-wishers, agents, channel bods and other VIPs responsible for the show. Please note the most important person at a read-through will always be late. Always.

My heart begins to pound. I sit, frightened, quietly sipping on a water. This was the most alien thing I'd ever done. I think I remember catching Simon watching me, he looked nervous, we nod, he came and gave me some final words of advice. A light squeeze. It was all a blur. I must have looked like a frightened WWI tommy about to go over the top. Looking at it now I think this was the beginning of it all really, my career, this career that chose me. If I'd fucked up and the channel insisted they recast Mike that would've been that. I've no idea what I'd be doing today. Maybe I'd be an area manager for a chain of Mexican restaurants? Maybe I'd have a company car and play golf?

Nira stood and said some words, which is the one thing she hates doing more than anything. There's a little light applause, a laugh or two, and she threw it open to us. At the beginning of a read-through: words are said by the director and/or producer and then you go round the room saying who you are and what you do. I watched the introductions roll round the venue until it was three away, then two, one, now me! The blood pumps like fuck in my ears and I make these words fall out of my dry, baggy mouth:

'Hello. I'm Nick Frost and I'm playing Mike Watt.' That was that. Introductions over, everyone clapped and we were off.

The next worst bit was waiting for my first line to come round. Reading down the script and seeing it approach was awful, here it comes . . . here it comes . . . say the line . . . say it . . . NOW! And out it came. It got a laugh. Oh. Nice. They laughed, people laughed! That felt pretty good. The read-through finishes and people clap. Nice. Simon was giving me that look I liked. Pride, mutha-fucka, pride.

After the read-through there's always a little debrief, tea, pats on the back. I think after that, at least I hoped, Edgar and Nira might begin to believe that maybe, just maybe, I could do this.

Part Four

My social life and things outside of starting to make a TV show were still the same. Being naughty, powerful potions, and falling in love with fit girls who liked laughing but, long term, didn't see any future with me. The sex was cool, but I always wanted the love. I wanted them to fall in love with me. I wanted to properly love someone.

On top of that I still had my self-imposed exile from Mum and therefore Dad, which was a shame. Mum was a shame too, don't get me wrong, but seeing my dad look after this woman who was slowly dying was tough to take. It made me cross, therefore it wasn't too hard for me to exile the both of them.

It sounds hard I know. I'm not sure how it happened, me getting so hard, but it did. The more people died the harder I got. It was gradual, like the calloused skin on a builder's hands, the more trauma, the harder they become.

I've really had to watch this over the years, but therapy helped a bit. Everything's relative. People have a harder life than me. People have an easier life than me. After lots of mine had eventually departed, I'd find it difficult to hear someone bellyaching about the small shit. I had to work that out, that's my problem though, not theirs. It's big for them. All relative.

There were conversations with my folks semi-regularly on the phone, though yet again as soon as I heard that slur I wanted to hang up. I became impervious to Mum telling me how proud she was. It didn't mean anything and at the same time it meant everything.

By day I'd rehearse and by night I'd wait tables. It was an odd existence. Rehearsals were strange, reading stuff out, not knowing what was going on, what things meant. Learning my lines was the thing I feared most. I was also afraid of letting people down, and by people I mean Simon. If he thought I couldn't pull this off he never let on, which was either really clever or really nice. Maybe both, he's good like that.

The best thing about rehearsal was getting to hang out. Just sitting about, chatting, laughing like drains felt so good. I never felt I belonged, not at that point, but I felt welcomed. I had a lot of work to do to belong. I was meeting more and more new people and the prospect of having to leave ChickenPasta-McFuckheads or whatever it was called filled me with absolute joy. Once I left waitering to be an actor that was going to be it, fame and fortune awaited me.

My affair with Callie was getting complicated. I'd made the terrible drunken mistake of sleeping with another waitress, one who was actually pretty lovely. I mean as a person as well as being fit, which was a novelty for me. She was in a Spice Girls tribute act. I really liked her. What a shallow greedy dickhead I was. Maybe I got everything I deserved. I think I frightened the Spice Girl off a bit by being drunken and unpredictable one Christmas Eve. We worked in the day then got pissed once the restaurant had closed at 6 p.m.

We found ourselves frenching in the bogs. Then frenching on a night bus while a man dressed as a nun watched, then frenching on Simon's bed, frenching *in* Simon's bed etc. etc. etc. You get the picture.

I was in a bleak Russian novelist kind of mood. In between pumps and bouts of sobbing I'd swig from a large bottle of red wine. After we finished I threw the bottle across the room, it smashed. She seemed afraid and confused. I thought women loved that moody shit, that ennui.

The next day was Christmas Day, this was the best Eve I'd ever spent, all crying and sexing up a Spice Girl. I wanted it to go on. Tomorrow I'd be alone, Simon and Smiley were away, I couldn't be at home so I asked Spice Girl to stay. She didn't. I think the crying and bottle smashing mid-doggy was the death knell for that short-lived thing. I think I also might have told her I loved her too. Which got back to Callie. Shit gets complicated. Still, I have my work. My new work, as a TV actor. Ha Ha.

My friend Andrew Maxwell (the one that brought the Eiffel Tower of Absinthe to my stag do) calls me the world's luckiest waiter. Which I guess is right. Was right. Since the beginning, though I've always worked my cock *AND* balls off to make sure I didn't have to wait tables again.

I feel I ought to finish the Callie thread as when it actually finishes we won't be here. The book will be over by the time we get to that bit. I'm not sure I'll ever get the chance to write another one so I should end this now. I'd hate to think you'd never get to find out what happened.

After months of falling and chasing, hoping this could be the time a fit, shallow girl finally falls for a tubby jokesmith, we were approaching the end. It wasn't all bad which I guess made it worse. There were times when we did things that made me believe we could work. Once in the afternoon we went to see the film *Happiness*. She didn't get it and seemed offended watching Phil Hoffman jerking off. We left and sat in a café eating bacon rolls. It was so nice. We laughed a lot.

Please though don't imagine it was all her. Fuck no. I was far from perfect. My issues were many and complicated. Issues no pretty young girl from Leeds could or should ever have to cope with. This I understand.

There's one thing that happened that told me without a shadow of a doubt that I had to turn away and not look back for the sake of my own sanity and dignity, no matter how sweet this patootie was. I had to man up and bite the bullet.

One night we're lying in bed. In my new bed in the house in Highgate I'm to share with the boys. She utters to me words that have stayed with me for ever.

'I really like you but I wish you looked more like David Beckham.'

Wow. That hit me for six. It was the bucket of cold water in the face my dignity needed. All my instincts, finally singing off the same hymn sheet, hollered in unison.

'Get the fuck out of there,' they chorused. 'For your own sake, get the fuck out.'

I could barely speak, I looked at her perfect body for the last time. My balls wept, dropped to their knees, implored me to keep going, they told me things would change, she just needed more time. I'd heard enough, I slapped my dick round it's face. I was sick of listening to that fat liar.

I try to exit with a grand gesture, an overly verbose post-script she'll think about in fifteen years' time when she's wiping her tenth baby's arse and cursing the TV or cinema screen every time she sees my happy yet vulnerable face.

I need to say something which means I *couldn't* come back even if I wanted to. I think this technique was my psyche's plan of escape if all else failed.

In the end, as I struggle to pull my jeans up over my now striking balls (striking as in on strike, not visually stunning, although it has been noted before that I have very attractive Willy Balls. I digress), I manage to utter a shaky 'fuck you'. That's all I have, all I can muster. I leave at a pace, slamming doors, and stand on the street looking for a cab to take me away from all this heartache, when I remember that this is my house. She walks past me in the hall as I trudge back through the front door. And that's that. Well almost. I've never been one to just turn off emotions the way a fishmonger might simply turn off a running tap. For me shit lingers, which means small arguments tend to hang around. Shadows bang and holler upstairs as I try and work things through; things other folk would quickly forget tend to stick around a little with me. I need to learn to let things go, move on. Stop analysing every tiny detail. That shit be destructive yo. I, like you, am a work in progress. And I hope I'm never finished:

* * *

I have one more brush with Callie, in fact that's not quite true, there's two. A few weeks later I go and see her in a play. It's bad. She's okay but the play's not good. I think I'm drunk and sad she's shut me off so I leave at half time. I go back to the house in Highgate with Simon. We're watching REM live from Glastonbury. I'm drunk, I may have started into my first bottle of Night Nurse.

Me and Callie start texting, it's hard and cold. We're at that point where everything that went before, the niceness, the hair-brushing, Phil Hoffman jerking off, softness, laughter, they've all gone. They're replaced by a sharpness and a tightness of mouth. Silent tension reigns here now. I'm not sure how the end comes but it comes and I end up in tears.

I'm sitting on the sofa. Simon's watching me. 'Everybody Hurts' comes on. I cry solidly for an hour, my heart well and truly broken again. Simon fulfils the tricky job of cuddling me and telling me things I needed to hear right then. What a guy.

The second brush came years later, I'm in my house in Twickenham when a girl who looks exactly like Callie walks by pushing a pram. I don't move. Weeks later it happens again. I leap up and track her down the road. Nice arse. Days later I'm taking my bins out and she comes out of a house four doors down pushing a cute baby in a buggy. She's moved four doors down! From a completely different part of the city, Callie has moved into a house four fucking doors down. I'm amazed by this cosmic pull.

I don't run inside as my instinct tells me to. I stop and smile as she walks up. She smiles a bit too. Only a bit. It's awkward. I'm famous by this point so it must be hard for her. The man that never wanted it, never cared, standing there in house shorts holding bags full of stinky filth. Things are utterly different this time, there's no sense of a flicker, no match being held up to a short piece of fuse, no histrionics, no light flirt for old times' sake, nothing. We exchange a few words. I go in, she goes off. That's that. It's the last time I see her.

Days later a sign outside her house says 'FOR RENT'. Now I feel bad. Had I really been that bad? Does she really hate me so much? I have to believe this is not all about me. Months later I bump into a mutual friend. My suspicions are confirmed. It wasn't about me. It never is. Well, hardly ever.

* * *

All this was yet to come. Right now I'm leaving the restaurant and starting my career as a TV actor. Easy. The rehearsal process ends. The numerous meetings with hair and make-up and costume mean my character's look was now set in stone. Mike Watt TA would wear combat gear and polarised shooting glasses, the legacy of a childhood injury. He'd wear big combat boots and have a very short haircut. Perfect.

The scripts have kind of been learnt, I had no idea how to do it other than by saying the lines over and over again. I've got better over time and don't now feel the need to learn the whole thing in one like a play. That's what I tried to do at first. It expends so much energy. Now I learn a week at a time with a general 'loose' knowledge of the thing as a whole, it's so much easier.

I begin to receive paperwork, a shooting schedule comes through, money has been agreed upon, hands have been shaken, contracts signed and countersigned. A moment of clarity flashed into my pumpkin, a bean of truth that makes me heave. This shit was about to happen. *Spaced* was actually going to happen. The great Channel 4 swindle had been a success and I now have to walk the walk. Balls.

The night before the first day on set I spend puking my ring up. All night, no sleep, just being sick, such is the level of my nerves. As an aside, this feeling stays with me for years. There's hardly a job I do where I don't spend the night before being sick with nerves. I hate it. Now though, like line learning, it's better, I know the feeling and I've come to like it. Over the years, with knowledge and the odd technique and a lot more faith in myself that I've earned my place here at the table, the feeling has gone away.

On Monday morning, very early, the doorbell rings to Coogan's place and it's our driver. We get a bloody driver! Me and Simon get into the car. We drive and arrive at the studio in silence. The only time I now feel like this is before red carpets for one of my films. Not all of them, a *Paul* or a *World's End* or a *Cuban Fury*. You get the gist. The drive from the hotel to the cinema is one that I dread. I do the film for free, you pay me for the red carpets. It's not fun and it's not glamorous. That's the real work for me. The car pulls up through crowds of people craning to look at you, slightly disappointed you're not someone a little more famous. The car stops, a lovely grey-haired man called Paul opens the door. I breathe and BOOM . . . It's on. Nerves go, game face on. Let's smile and sign stuff and pose for selfies!

If Edgar had been unsure whether or not I could do it, meeting me that morning probably made him feel a lot worse. I was a fucking wreck. Seriously. I try and keep it subdued by not opening my mouth but sometimes there's so much of it, whatever *it* is, it kind of bursts out. Panic.

My eyes feel sweaty. I immediately meet loads of new people. Everyone's job title seems to be contracted down into letters, ADs HODs, DOPs. The studio was busy. Studios are always busy the first day of a shoot.

I barely touch my full English breakfast except for the sausages, eggs, fried-slices, bacons and mushrooms. I barely manage to wash it down with two strong coffees. I sit in my dressing room, dressed far too early in combat fatigues waiting for my execution to begin. Time passes quickly. I don't want it to. I want it to stop. I want to be back at Chiquito, flirting, laughing, not having a TV licence.

There's a knock at my door. A girl sticks her head in.

'Ready on set to line up, Nick.'

'Thanks.'

What the fuck does that mean? I stand and look. I'm in fatigues, I have a beret on. I've grown a big ginger moustache. What had I become? A charlatan moments from being found out.

A line-up is usually the first thing you do on any given shoot day. You get on the set and you walk the scene through. I didn't know that then. My credo at this point was say nothing and listen, don't fuck up. The first thing I ever shot on *Spaced* was the party scene where I supply security. I stand behind the door and appear shaking my side-arm happily.

All the guys are there. Lovely, weird, funny Mark Heap, lovely Katy, bloody lovely Julia Deakin, lovely Jess, smashing Edgar '8-ball' Wright and my darling home boy Simon 'Simon' Pegg. I relaxed slightly. It was only us. We talked a bit about how shit would go down and then we do a crew rehearsal. It's no longer just us. The crew streams in. My cold fear pops my top bulb and I panic. Simon stays me. We do the rehearsal and my little comedy pop-out makes the crew laugh. I think I suggest I'm found with the barrel in my mouth, as if Mike had been thinking about what it would feel like to end it all there and then.

It was a thing I did at home to make Simon and Smiley laugh, Edgar loved it too. It was essentially a charade I did for the guys where I'd load and discharge lots of different kinds of guns, shotguns, assault rifles, pistols and machine guns. Essentially a spree killer. (Grim.) It always ends with me doing a weird smile and offing myself. The guys would laugh at the dark dénouement. Sometimes imaginary gunfights would break out as locals fought to contain me. A lot of my darker comedy ends with me killing myself. Help . . .

The tension builds and for a moment I wish this gun was real. What must Simon have been thinking? This was his gamble. If I scream and run off, never coming back and they have to go on hiatus for two weeks while they recast my role at considerable fiscal cost to the production, which means a knock-on effect where no one gets wrap gifts, it would be his fault. It would also I imagine put a ding into our friendship. Or would it?

Back then I bailed on shit. I started things, I got all the gear and then I stopped. I couldn't be bothered. A couple of years before all this began – my new career – I decided I wanted to do an A-Level at night college. So I did. I was pretty skint at the time so a guy I knew, another Simon, who was my GM at the Mexican place, gave me the money for the course and off I went. Twice a week I'd take the tube to Old Street and attend a course to get me an English A-Level. I'd done so shit at school in terms of grades I felt like I needed an actual qualification. This is the first inkling in me that I couldn't be a waiter for ever.

I didn't know then, obviously, how things would turn out. I enjoyed the course and stayed for quite a while but as the exam drew nearer I got nervous and I stopped going. Classic me. I did the A-Level but never took the exam. That was me all over. Until *Spaced*.

The first AD says the words I will hear many times over the years to come but this first time dread punches me in the spleen.

'Final looks please, shooting this time.'

A burst of activity as every cast member is checked over and preened, brushes on faces, collars turned down. A lady puts what feels like Rizlas on my face and leaves them there for a while.

'What are these? They feel like Rizlas.'

'They are Rizlas. We use them to soak up the sweat.'

'Oh. Am I sweating that much?'

'Yeah.' She bustles off leaving three Rizlas glued onto my drippy five-head.

The AD then shouts something else.

'And turnover.' The floor is cleared. My Rizlas are ripped off. I'm powdered briefly. Other voices from other departments pipe up.

'Sound is at speed.'

'Rolling.'

'Mark it!'

Someone rushes in with a clapper board, hooray, finally, something I recognise! I love having a laugh with the clapper peeps, generally they don't answer you back or talk at the point of the clap. This is their big moment. That doesn't mean you can't talk to them though. Simon does it too, you give them a brief pep talk and then rate the board. Sometimes you do it really quietly.

SNAP – 'what a lovely board'. Or 'what a terrible board'. It makes the camera teams laugh, one of the main actors gently ragging on a young clapper loader.

There's none of that today though. My blood pumps into my hearts and for a moment I feel really weak.

'And . . . Action.'

From my vantage point, hidden behind the door, I can hear the scene unfolding but sadly any memory of my cue line is long dead. Oh fuckballs. When do I come out? Did we ascertain that? I'll just stay here. Maybe they won't notice. That's what I'll do, just stay here. A minute or so passes and I hear a line I feel I remember. It's the beginning of the cue, of my cue! This is it. Do it. Do actings now!

I pop out and wave my little gun. Say my line. I blush inside, then outside, and I retract back behind the door and wait for the scene to be done.

'And . . . cut!' Edgar sounds chipper. People emerge from their hiding places off the set and tweaks begin. Little lighting issues are dealt with, costume bits, make-up brushes are deployed. Edgar hops around giving notes if notes need to be given. He comes to me, excited.

'That was great! Let's do another one.'

'Okay!' So we do another one. And another.

You can always tell what Edgar thinks of a take by the way he says 'cut'. If it's bright and chipper then he likes it. If it's slightly elongated and unsure you know he has reservations about something.

We finished the first set-up. A wide. It's usually always a wide, or 'Master', then the camera pushes in for tighter coverage. It works great this way, it's economical usually, and sets the continuity for the rest of the scene. I felt good, in fact I felt great. I'd done it. I hadn't burst into flames causing a terrible fire, I hadn't turned to dust or melted. I did it. We crowded around the monitors to watch the take back. It was good. People laughed as I popped out. All I needed to do was know my lines and be funny. That was it.

* * *

As time passes Simon and I find our little routine. We like having a little routine. We'd shoot all day and then get dropped off at the pub at the end of our street. We'd have a couple of beers, debrief a bit, laugh at things that made us laugh during the day, then we'd look at tomorrow's work. I liked the rigidity of that. It gave me purpose. Something to focus on. I liked that.

I keep this kind of routine now when I shoot. It takes a lot of work and a partner who knows and accepts that this is the most important thing in your life for the next four months or so, longer in some cases. It takes its toll – sadly, when your partner sees you give your best on a set and then not much in your home life, it takes its toll.

For a big film all I do, literally, is work. I'll get up and do ninety minutes' line learning, then I'll shoot all day, come home, bit of food, then bed. I'll lie in bed reading the next day's work. I want to know everything. Everyone's role. Everyone's lines. I then read the call sheet from front to back. Every word. Who's working? What scenes are we doing? How many extras? What time is lunch called for? What props are needed? What's the weather going to be like? Everything. I want and need to know it all. If there's a unit list on the back, read it. Learn everyone's name. Bill Nighy taught me how important this is. It's really important. Why shouldn't an actor know everyone's name? It's just good manners. I started this method twelve years ago and I still do it today. I served and continue to serve an apprenticeship in this business that I hope will last for my whole lifetime. I hope it never ends.

Spaced continued. I got my head down and concentrated. I loved it. I loved the crew most of all I think. The crews thrill me and continue to thrill me. Day in day out they bust their humps making film and television. I only have to come in to do the shooting bit. Eight weeks, twelve weeks, a bit more, a lot more actually if I'm writing or producing something. Then I'm done. Crews maybe get to take the weekend off and then they start all over again. Actors, even successful actors, rarely go from job to job to job without a nice big sunny holiday in between. These brave boys and girls do it week in week out. The 5 a.m. calls. The weeks of nightshoots, being away from home and family in shit hotels that cast would never dream of staying in, and all because they have decided to follow a career in film and television. I've literally never seen any crew member fuck up on anything I've ever done then or since. They're amazing people.

With a fantastic crew, great cast and lovely script, the atmosphere on set was smashing. I fed off it. I grew, I got bigger, more confident. People couldn't believe I'd never done it before. What helped me was my friendship and chemistry with Simon. Apparently you couldn't then and can't now 'buy that shit'. People loved us together on screen. I loved us together anywhere.

* * *

The weeks bled into one another. My focus intensified. I saw bits of Callie but not much. My issues seemed to ebb away for a while, I still smoked the 'erb and drank a bit but I was happy working. I didn't need anything else.

Coming back to Steve's place was an absolute treat every night. It was a lovely open-plan, factory-style mews house and was done up beautifully. On the top of the house was a little roof garden. It was here Simon and I perfected a thing we loved called the 'bloodclart assassination'. It was simple but made us laugh. We'd fill a big champagne bottle with water. (Don't judge.) Then load a fake 9mm with a small steel ball bearing and conceal the weapon behind our backs. The game was then to pretend to be a fearsome Yardie gangster: you'd casually stroll up to the champagne bottle, say something in Jamaican-style patois, and then you'd pull the nine out and drill a ball bearing into the bottle.

'BLOODCLART!!!' we'd shout.

God, we laughed. The first time we did it we were amazed that the steel sphere penetrated the bottle leaving a perfect hole behind. No cracking, just a perfect hole. Little things please little minds I guess.

People often ask if me and Simon ever fight. The answer is very rarely. Of course we've had tiffs and barneys, we've been together for twenty-two years, it'd be strange if we hadn't.

Real big fights though are pretty rare. I can honestly only remember one face to face. There was another on the phone once during my honeymoon and one or two spats, I guess you'd call them, but that's about it. It hasn't been all sweetness and light though. I remember a time when we were living together in Kentish Town when we really didn't like one another. Seriously. It was serious. I think if we'd actually been boyfriend and girlfriend we'd be thinking about going on a break or moving out altogether. What was that all about?

I didn't think about this at all back then. Not when it was happening; I've thought about it since and I suppose the thing I put it down to was jealousy, plain and simple. What a terrible thing. I'm ashamed to say I wanted what he had. Hanging around with all these new people, seeing how happy he was, how success was starting to tickle his lovely plums, how popular he was, I thought it was as easy as that. I forgot how much work he'd put into it. Forgot how much he'd suffered for it. What he'd sacrificed. He earned everything that came his way. Shame on me. I worked my hole off too but for what? To what ends? Where was I heading? What was my fucking future? I was funny, people liked me, so why wasn't I earning big dollar? What a horrible chip to have. For days and then weeks and then months everything he said to me, everything he did, annoyed me. I know the same was true for Simon.

The money thing was an issue for me. I was pretty skint half the time and I didn't want him to have to lend me money so I could go out with him and his lovely, cool new friends. Even though I was desperate to go. I think that meant I spent a lot of time indoors being a weed hermit.

My delight at potions and smokeables I suspect played their part in our blip, our unmeshing. Things came to a head, we knew we had to sort things out but neither wanted to take the first step. This is how things never get better, when people refuse to take the first step, refuse to apologise. God, it was so close to being so very different.

We went out clubbing one night, me, Simon, Tony, Dion, the gang, South African shitheads and scumbags. Lovely. I went hard, got hammered, pissed, you know the deal. The club finished and, for whatever reason, missed rides and taxis meant me and Simon found ourselves together outside. We started to walk. It was a long way. I think we walked from Covent Garden all the way back to our place in Kentish Town.

It was silent and, as the sun rose, the day revealed itself to be grey and weatherless. We walked in silence. I love the early mornings in big cities. A place where a few hours from now millions of people will emerge from pots of steel and holes in the ground to earn a living and try to justify their place in the food chain. We were in that third shift. Just us, ravers, aliens and big-bummed African cleaners chatting and laughing on their phones. These are the people of the third shift.

As we walked something lovely happened, our hearts waved white flags and we started to talk. During that stroll we cried and shouted, laughed and held hands and by the time we pushed our heavy front door open we were back!

We were friends again after that. All the tension was gone and we moved forward, thick as thieves. We've continued to evolve with each new incarnation of our friendship, whether it be girlfriends, moving out, marriage or kids, we evolve and we work.

We did have one other row, I'd say it was Jeremy Kyle-like in its intensity. Drink played a part. And weakness, mine. I'd decided to stop smoking fags. I found it really hard. Simon was keen that I give up. I fancied giving it a go and I stopped. I'm not sure how long for. I want to say days but realistically it was more like hours.

It was the early afternoon and I think I'd had a couple of Night Nurse margaritas. We had people over, I know that much. Something happens, Simon says something, something about my weakness for giving in and having a ciggie. He calls me weak. Oh no. Oh god no. David Banner walks into his bedroom and shuts the door. His eyes pulse and throb. He loosens his tie in savage expectation. Oh fuck. Weak. Fuck. I get up and steam into his room. There are people there, who I don't know, don't remember or can't see. I explode. (Close up on green mushroom cloud expanding in eyeball.)

Right there and then we have a massive screaming match. Huge. The drink and Night Nurse combined means it's all pretty nonsensical. I have to hold onto a door frame with two hands because I'm afraid if I have a hand free I may grab at his throat meat. I have a vague notion of people standing around open-mouthed, some kind of intervention, and then it blows itself out. I wake up some time later. All is forgotten. Simon says sorry for calling me weak. He feels bad.

All the rest were just little bullshits. We had a barney once during *Hot Fuzz*. We're sat in a car, watching Martin Blower and Eve Draper speed past us. It was awkward because we were miked up and all the crew could hear us rowing. We sat in silence for three hours in that car while the crew eggshelled their way around us. What a pair of dicks.

One night years before when we were still living at Ivy Road, sleeping together on this shitty futon I owned, I got up to grab something from the end of the bed and Simon thought it would be funny to kick me off. It wasn't very high but it hurt and Simon's hysterical laughter as I floundered on the floor made it hurt a bit more. I fumed as we lay in bed in the dark in silence. Eventually it broke. I turned to him in the dark.

'I've got a job interview at Trebor tomorrow.'

We both laughed like idiots and it was over.

Simon's hurt me a lot over the years. The futon thing hurt; he's also slashed at me with a knife while we were fucking about on set one day, I still have the scar to prove it. The worst injury though was not all his fault. We'd had mates round and the day had got to the point where me and Simon were swigging Harvey's Bristol Cream out of the bottle. I suspect it wasn't our first either. Me and Simon find ourselves in my bedroom wrestling topless on the bed. (I promise you we've never had sex.) We had people round for fucksakes, why we were wrestling in my room seems weird now, and from a hosting point of view downright rude.

Anyhoo, at one point Simon flies at me, foolish, very foolish, my immense strength means I'm great up close. I do most of my best work up close. He's now in my arms in a perfect position for me to deploy an Atomic Power Bomb. I hesitate a second, fuck this, deploy! From a standing position I slam him onto and then through my bed with terrific force. The sound of smashing and cracking is frightening but the power bomb has been utilised with such force and elan we're both pretty fucking proud. We're also laughing like drains. The bed is completely destroyed. All the legs have fallen off and the mattress struts have shattered into splinters. A moment to get our breath back and we rise, surveying the damage.

It's at this point Simon notices the thumb on my right hand is hanging off. It's dangling loose. Just flapping there like a windsock. Oh. There's no pain so I pick it up and jam it back in. Hooray, I'm cured. It lolls off again, swinging like a catflap. Balls. Being a keen home doctor I prescribe for myself gaffer tape, and lots of it. As we've already seen, it's a technique that has served me well although one the British Medical Council tends to foolishly ignore. Imagine the savings the already creaking NHS could make with my self-care proposals.

While I'm securing the thumb into position our guests, upon hearing the Atomic Power Bomb and the smashing of a bed, come to investigate. There's the usual mix of horror and laughter. Andrew Maxwell is here and some girls including Chris, my future wife. Maxwell's attention immediately turns to my shattered bed. He talks ten to the dozen. There's a large group gathered in my room, and the girls fuss over my loose thumb while the hunky men work out how to fix my bed.

I hear Maxwell holler a command: 'Let's put the bed up on its side so we can see how fucked it is.'

It's only at this point that I realise what's going to happen in about one second. In about one second, these people, these fine Samaritans, friends, lovely comedy fun-girls, are going to see about five hundred hardcore porno mags under my bed. They're barely contained by two massive Ikea bags. Some of my Wank Du Jour are loose on the floor, close to hand. I panic – something I tend not to do any more, my embarrassment gland seems to have withered and died the older I've got. Back then, though, I panic. I start to flap about and fluster.

'Leave it, guys, I'm fine. I'll just sleep on it like it is, please, yeah? Leave it, leave it, please, put it down, I'll sleep on the debris, seriously, it's not . . .'

WANK MAGS!

The room actually goes silent for a moment. I laugh a bit. Mortified. It's only porn at the end of the day, no one was bothered. I think the boys were impressed and the girls were worried that I wasn't getting laid enough, which at this point was probably true.

Years later I do a show called *Danger! 50,000 Volts!* (which I'll cover in book 2). There's a lovely young lad working as a production assistant; I'm not sure how it came up but we start talking about porn one day. I'd moved in with Chris who was my gf at the time. She nudged me, and rightly so, into maybe getting rid of these mags. I didn't want to at first, and it was only after meeting this little Welsh fella who literally fell off his stool in his eagerness to get hold of this nearly pristine catalogue that I gave in. That was the thing. I could've got rid of them bit by bit, wrapped in a carrier, under a bridge or in a derelict factory but I couldn't bear to split the collection. Too much spunk went into these things for me to just fuck them off near a river for kids to find. No way.

This Welsh production assistant was a breath of fresh air. Once I explained my conundrum he sprang up.

'I'll have 'em!' he said.

'I'm not splitting up the collection.'

'You don't have to. I'll have 'em all.'

And indeed, he had them all. One evening after work he came round in his little red Nissan Micra and we silently moved the two bags from my place into his boot. It felt like moving a gorilla's body. We nodded, then shook hands while never really making eye contact.

'Look after them.' I said.

'I will.' he smiled

He got in, started the car and was gone. They were gone. Ten years' work, gone. I often wonder what happened to those guys. Fuck. Happy days . . .

I wake up with a scream at 3 a.m. I was having a terrible nightmare that I'd broken my thumb and had gaffer-taped the thing back together. Oh. I struggle to turn the light on and when I do I wish I hadn't. I'm lying on a mattress supported by columns of porn. Splinters and shattered pieces of bed lie all around. My hand is throbbing. Bits of black hand meat throb out through the gaps in the gaffer. Oh shit. Hospital for me. I'd broken my thumb pretty badly. Why did Simon keep injuring me? If I was his wife I think I'd have him put on some kind of register.

* * *

The thing about working on a show that everyone loves is you know eventually it's going to end. This is what was happening to *Spaced* right now. It was ending. It'd been my first job and the thought of it coming to an end made me feel very sad. I was also tremendously proud. I'd done something I'd never done before and I think I bloody nailed it.

I had no idea how popular *Spaced* would become. No idea if we'd do another one. No idea what to do with my newfound skill in front of the camera. Where next? I did think about these things briefly but I was still concentrating on getting this shit done. Not letting anyone down.

Making what I guess can be classed as cult TV and films is an odd thing. For the fans it's really important, it's their escape, the thing they set their Tivos for. It shouldn't be underestimated. Look at the massive convention circuit for godsakes. That tells you all you need to know. For me the geek, it was *Star Wars*, *Indiana Jones* and *X-Files* (to name but three!) but for me the actor, it's something you work on, love, have a hoot making, and then you move on. My brain tends to dump old content pretty much straight away so I can fit more dialogue in.

I think this is difficult for people to understand: why wouldn't you remember doing *Spaced*? Of course I do but that was the first thing I did and I've done countless TVs and fifteen or so films since then. That sounds like a boast, it's not meant to. Sorry.

* * *

During the shoot we were forced to move house yet again. Steve's dream mews was only ever a temporary measure, as much as it would've been nice to stay there living next door to Pepsi or was it Shirley? One day on the way back from a shoot Simon drives past an estate agent and notices a house to let in the window. He gets the car to stop so he can see it and then calls Smiley. Smiley goes up and looks and arranges a viewing. It's perfect.

Sometime later we move into Shepherds Hill in Highgate. It's amazing. I have, mostly, the nicest memories of that house. We had the whole bottom floor of a large Victorian mansion. It had a massive garden, which, as I've said many times before, was a real hotspot for European Jays. It felt like a big boys' house, new carpets throughout and its own fridge. It was really lovely.

The rent was split three ways at this place. It would be the first time I could properly pay my way. I spend a few hundred quid getting the bed me and Simon would later kill, some shelves, a simple table, a lamp. I felt so grown up. I had my money from *Spaced* and I thought the salad days would never end.

We finished shooting the show and it was a fabulous experience. It was the first time in my life I realised what I wanted to do. What I wanted to be. Thank heaven, I'd left it so late. All those years I'd lain in bed at night listening to my Jiminy Cricket tell me everything would be okay were finally justified.

For the first time ever in my life I had money in my bank. Not a lot but . . . I think people assume if you do a TV show or a film you're immediately a millionaire. I think I got paid a high four-figure sum for *Spaced*. It was more than I'd ever been paid before in one lump! I was earning £1.92 p/h at Mexican Restaurant Inc. It's all relative. One would be forgiven for thinking I'd been paid 600k the way I was living though. I was in a nice house with my best mates, money in the bank, just finished a TV show that everyone said I did great in. What could possibly go wrong?

I have no idea what I thought I'd do immediately after *Spaced*. I guess I imagined the work would just roll in. Right? Well maybe after the thing gets aired, but that wouldn't be for another year at least. I paid this no mind however. I also, through complete ignorance and the misguided belief that I, Nick Frost, someone who was above all this kind of shit, thought I wouldn't have to pay tax on it. What was I thinking? I just spent. I raved and drank and fucked about and had a great time.

* * *

During this period I was invited by Adam and Joe to a fancy party. I was chuffed and began to feel included in the scene. I'm not sure what the occasion was but my party instinct tells me either wrap or Christmas. No matter. For some reason I'd spent two months regrowing a big Zapata moustache after shaving my *Spaced* one off when we wrapped. I gave it to Edgar in a matchbox as a gift. He still has it although now it looks like a red marble. Gross.

I'd left the party at around two o'clock to get home in time to watch the first Evander Holyfield/Lennox Lewis fight. I was pretty pissed up as I walked around Farringdon looking for a taxi. I was outside a BP garage on the outskirts of an estate when I turned to see five youths bowling up towards me. Fuck!

As a man I had always been terrified of this happening – one on one fine, fair game, but this was different. This was the thing where, despite your best intentions of a noble fightback, through sheer weight of their numbers you would be completely emasculated and there was nothing you could do to prevent this. Nothing.

Many times as a younger man I'd mulled over the eternal question. Stabbed or slashed? For the record I'm all for the stabbing. Here's my logic: for someone who is terrified of having stitches the thought of having two or three hundred in a gaping chest or back slash is unthinkable. But the thought of being stuck and having an operation under a general anaes- thetic was complete bliss. How did we get here? Oh yeah, the guys surrounding me. The great stab or slash question now flickered through my processor. It was rudely interrupted by this . . .

'What are you fucking looking at, you fat cunt?'

As an opening remark it leaves little or no confusion as to what their intention is; as direct approaches go it's actually quite refreshing.

I'm fucked. I quickly formulate a strategy, this buys me the precious seconds I need to figure out a Jack Reacher-style plan to get me out of the pickle that's come to be known as 'The incident of the wrong moustache in danger town'.

Here's what happens next . . . With a powerful, fast-paced right hook I knock the main cunt out. Sparko, gone, jaw pops, eyes roll, he does the thing boxers do where their arms spasm into the sky, flapping at white ravens unseen. He might be dead. Gutted.

This completely throws a fox into the hen house. This has never happened to them before, their random victims never fight back. It's not the done thing. The toilet muffin behind me beeps and starts to panic. Whatevs. I spin, laying a pointy elbow into his soft human temple. He vomits and groans like a grieving widow. He collapses into a puddle of his own council estate honk. Three left.

A handsome, long-limbed simpleton swings one of his rangy paws at me. Christ he was slow. I step left and one step forward quickly rotating. I flick out a shattering back fist. Poor lad, he'd have to undergo four hours of painful NHS dental surgery.

I pull one of his oversized incisors from the back of my hand, I toss it to the floor and giggle like a wet Geisha, I close my eyes, and let the man chemicals flood through my brain. I cum.

The last two combatants are completely horrified. I get the feeling they've never seen a man involuntarily ejaculate during a Fatty Bash before. I see them think twice. Seeing me on all fours tasting my own seed they decide to fuck off. I survey the pile of human shit around me, and pulling Willy out I take a post-fight piss on them. I notice one of them has a Cadbury's Double Decker in his pocket. I reach in, open it and feed. Fuck, it tastes good. A black cab pulls up and I jump in.

'Where to, Guvnor?'

'Highgate please, Driver.'

'Good night?'

'Excellent.'

Job done . . .

My fantasy ends and to my horror I find I'm still surrounded. Skins, geezers, faceless, mirthless, dead behind the eyes. I mutter a cowardly retort to his original quesion:

'Nothing, mate.' My eyes cast down at the pavement.

The tension builds to a point where I think my femurs might snap and to my utter amazement they just saunter off. The ringleader gobs on the floor as a goodbye and they bowl off into the garage. Deep breath, big boy. Important decisions are now made quickly, decisions that could save my life. Don't run, this will trigger their chase response and you'll be killed, pray for a taxi.

A taxi doesn't come and I'm still there when they stalk out, all bogging me down. I should've run, they didn't need to see me still there. It's some kind of diss. They wander off. I breathe easy. I may have even smiled a bit. I'm free, you lucky twat.

From behind my right shoulder I hear a powerful haymaker whizzing past my ear. It catches me square on the button. Right on the chin. Flat footed. Pop. Lights out. Gone. Down like a sack of shit. No defence, no chance, knocked the fuck out.

I'm asleep for quite a while. Fortunately I come to just as they're changing shifts. Punches have now been replaced by penalty kicks to my head and its face that lives around the front. A refreshing change in martial techniques. Through all the violence and punch-guffing I can sense them tiring. I recall a weird calm descend on me, I'm either dying or I've just wet myself. After years of being terrified of this kind of thing happening I actually remember thinking that it wasn't too bad. This block of abstract thought lasts two seconds, no, one. Then I remember thinking that I'd quite like to go to sleep. One last giant boot to my face granted me my wish. I'd finally tired them out.

As I lay on the street in a puddle of my own claret, blind – they'd kicked my contact lenses out of my head – I remember a maroon car pulling up, screeching up, two men jump out, and chase these fuckheads off. What a brave and noble thing to do. I never got a chance to thank those men. I truly feel if it wasn't for them I would've died that night.

I miss the Lennox Lewis fight. Simon arrives to pick me up. He puts me to bed and soaks my once-beige now-claret jacket in a bath of cold water. What a sweet sweet man. He really looked after me.

I didn't feel afraid after that, didn't feel like I couldn't leave the house. On the contrary, I felt like statistically I'd had mine. I think I was relieved that the person who got the fuck kicked out of him was me and not some frail old lady. Like my brother Marc, I could take it. Just.

* * *

I begin to realise my massive *Spaced* pay cheque had all but disappeared. I'd pissed it up the wall. It was all gone. I don't even remember what I did. I wish now I could see that as a good thing. I don't. I think now, looking back, it fills me with shame. A little bit of shame.

I try and eke things out for as long as I can. It's not long. I have no money, no job, a girl who wished I looked more like David Beckham. What am I going to do? I know what I have to do but I deny it, deny myself, pride punching me in the tool at the very notion of what I was thinking.

I'd found a great little pub just round the corner called The Shepherds. Me and Simon walked past it a few times but it looked old and piss-soaked, so we avoided it for quite some time.

Being an unemployed actor now, I had most of my days free. Walking past one day with an *Evening Standard* under my arm I thought, 'Fuckit, go in.' And I did. If I ever write another one of these I'll go into it more, but that pub was massive. It became a massive part of my life. Of Simon's life. But back then it was a place to eat a lasagne and chips (lashings of white pepper), drink a pint of Stella, and look at the job vacancies in the back of the paper.

A few days later, it's a Saturday night, about half-past twelve, and I awake with a start from my wonderful dream of being an actor. I'm wearing a tight red polo shirt and I have a mop in my hand. I may or may not be wearing a corporate baseball cap. A single tear falls into my grubby mop bucket as I clean a floor covered in puddles of spilt cocktail and pieces of fractured bottle. I've just done my first return shift on the bar of Old Orleans, Finchley Road. (A taste of the Deep South.) I was right back where I started.

Can I tell you that things picked up for me? Professionally yes, of course they did. I got to write my autobiography – they just let anyone write autobiographies, you know. Shame, some real smart waiters and bartenders are out there with amazing lives. Not just bartenders, people, normal people with amazing stories to tell. Stories that'll be forgotten once they're gone. What a shame.

My professional success (relatively speaking) comes at a price though. I want to tell you that things got better for me emotionally but I can't, they didn't. Seemingly every time I did a film another member of my family died. Was this the price I had to pay for success? (Relatively speaking.)

Back then when I was in the midst of all that shit with friends and family, drink and other unmentionables, I never thought I'd be here. There were times, long, horrible, black times, when I just didn't want to exist. I would never kill myself but the thought of just, bing, disappearing was really attractive to me. What changed? I think one thing was I learnt to forgive. I forgave my mum. I was too angry. What is the point of being angry with an amazing woman who loved me more than anything but had a terrible disease she had no control over. Why be angry at that? It's too destructive.

One day about six years ago on a whim and with the crazy notion that by doing this I may free myself of something bleak, I took my car and drove the four hours to the small windy cemetery overlooking Withybush hospital where my mum's buried. I wasn't sure what I hoped to achieve but I knew what I wanted to do. I wanted to tell Mum that I had forgiven her. And that's what I did. I stood and sat and screamed and cried for ages. Me and Mum really hashed it out. An hour later, amazingly, I felt a million times lighter.

By and by shit goes down to fuck all this up again, but I'm not one to sit down and give up. Not any more. I think one could be forgiven for reading this book and shouting, 'You can't blame your mum, you hypocrite! You're just as bad!' I'd understand that. I'm not one for spoilers but I will say this, there have been lots of times since then when I feared I may tread the same path as Mum and Ian and Debbie, to trudge blindly into a genetic imperative, bound for a destruction I have no control over. I was afraid for a long time until something happened that changed me overnight, and I hope for ever. I say 'hope'. With the best will in the world none of us can tell the future.

After doing IVF a couple of times and being told potentially it'd be really difficult to conceive, me and Chris silently decide not to have kids. We justify this to ourselves by saying we can have eight holidays a year.

Then four years ago while I was shooting the BBC drama *Money*, Dad is diagnosed with terminal cancer. Nine months later my beautiful, soft, fragile, hero of a father is dead in my arms.

Everything I'd endured up to this point pales into insignificance compared to right then. An orphan at thirty-nine. It's not that young compared to some but very young compared to many. For months and months I grieve and drink and try to choose a suitable tree in Richmond Park that I can drive my powerful car into and obliterate this silent anger. What drama, poor Chris. Thankfully I never find my perfect Death Oak.

Some weeks after Dad dies, me and Chris are in her brother's house on a gorgeous island in the Baltic Sea. I have literally had a complete meltdown. This is it. If there's a god he will now intervene and take me away, if not for me then certainly for Chris. Enough is enough. I cry myself to sleep that night.

The next day I watch Chris come out of the toilet with a pregnancy test I had no idea she'd bought. Her hands tremble so much. My eyes widen. She is crying. I jump off the bed and leave my black duvet behind. I look at the test. Pregnant. Chris was pregnant. Instead of taking something away I was given something. I was going to be a daddy. My switch got flicked. This was now about someone and something much bigger than me. I promised that day that I'd do everything in my power to make sure Little Boy had a better time of it than me.

A lot goes on between the end of this book and my son popping out. Things change for me, to me, for the best and for the worst, but him popping out that day in June changed me for ever. I wrote this for him. So maybe he can one day read it – when he's much older, says Mum – and have the answers I've now sadly lost.

My family, my lovely, complicated, fun-packed, fucked-up, laughter-filled, tear-drenched, utterly devoted family, were now gone, replaced by one little boy, that gift. The past now had passed over, totally forgiven but never to be forgotten.

You have been watching...

The 70s! Me, Mum and Dad after my First Holy Communion at St Peter and St Paul's.

The Frost clan! From left to right. *Back Row*; Uncle Simon (Rosemarie's husband), Dad, Grandad Frost and Danny from Holland (Auntie Hazel's ex). *Middle*; Auntie Rosemarie, Mum, Auntie Francis, Helen (Grandad's wife), Cousin Simon. *Front row*; Auntie Hazel, Cousin Caroline, me, Cousin Paul and Uncle Brian.

Me and Mum outside
at 214 Raylodge Road.
This was when I came
back from Israel for
the first time.

My brother Ian.
What a little bruiser.

Me, Dad and my
sister Debbie outside
a pub called Corner
Piece. This was Uncle
Emmy and Grampie's
favourite pub.

Uncle Emmy with
Auntie Betty,
Auntie Marion and
Auntie Melanie.

Me, Mum and Dad
circa 1972. Look at
Dad's lovely dimple.
His lifelong beard meant
it was never seen that
much. Shame.

A goodnight kiss from
Papa Bear as Teddy
Edward looks on.

Auntie Sandra
and my Cousin
Matthew, (Fergs).

Me and Marc
on the beach at
Broadhaven.

First day of school
1976. Cute.

Marc, Ian and Debbie.

Grampie, Mum, me and Gran outside Millbrook.

Mum with a massive shotgun.

Me and Cousin Paul at his 4th birthday tea. Grandad offers some sage words of wartime advice.

Mum and her boys AKA Peggy and the Mitchell Triplets.

My beautiful sisters Deborah and Sarah.

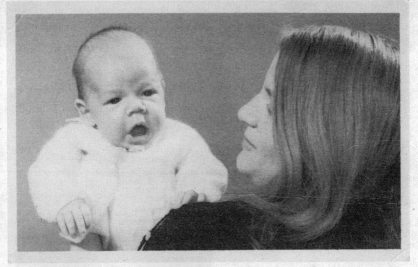

Me and Mum.

Grampie on the
beach. Kickin' it
1940s style.

Mum and Grandad Frost.
Wanstead, 1970s.

Me strangling
Mum. Christmas
in Highgate.
Circa 1999.

My lovely
Uncle Emmy.

Me and Pops.
Why's my hair
blonde. I look
demented.

Acknowledgements

Mum and Dad. I miss and love you more than you could ever know.

My boy and his fantastic mother Christina. Mark and Emma Lesbirel. Big Vern, a giant of a man in every way. Trudy, one of my surrogate mums, thank you.
Gill Pegg, my other surrogate mum, thank you!
Sarah and Gary and the boys.
Sweet Sheba.

Simon, Mo, Smiley, Bunny, Tony, Jax, Dion, Edgar, Danny Brown, Vicki, Fergie, James, Nira, Jeremy, Beevs, Hayley Stubbs, Kevin Eldon – I love you all. Bad Boys for life.

Hannah Black and the Hodder crew. Thank you.
Big Talk Productions.
Working Title.
Public Eye communications, Nate, Libby and the gorgeous Ciara Parkes.
Tom Drumm. Josh Katz. Christian Hodell and Mikey.
Conor and Sam and the Troika crew. Dr. Christina Romete.

People I knew well but now don't. Waiters and food service professionals all over the world.

Rugby. (The sport not the town)
Israel/Palestine.
Wales.
British Waterways.
Stella Artois. PG Tips.
Ciggies.
Coffee.
Sweet sweet Mary Jane, gone now but definitely not forgotten.

Hard House I love you.
Ravers I love you.
Jimi Hendrix. Hunter S Thompson. Jim Jarmusch. Woody Allen. Mulder and Scully. Steven Spielberg. John Williams. *The Simpsons*. George Lucas. Roy Neary. *Indiana Jones*. *The Young Ones*. Bill Nighy. Martin Amis. The Smiths. The Bluetones. Shit pubs. Sunny Side Up! Aleksander Solzhenitsyn. Alexander Shulgin. Timothy Leary. Milan Kundera. West Ham Utd.
Close Encounters of the Third Kind. Falafel. McDonalds. Meat Fruit. Good curries. Global knives. Non-stick pans and decent ovens. Onions. TV.

AHL forever!